HARROW

— HEDGE MAGIC —

COUNTY
™

HARROW

← HEDGE MAGIC →

COUNTY

Script
CULLEN BUNN

Art and Lettering
TYLER CROOK

DARK HORSE BOOKS

President and Publisher
MIKE RICHARDSON

Editor
DANIEL CHABON

Associate Editor
CARDNER CLARK

Designer
KEITH WOOD

Digital Art Technician
CHRISTIANNE GOUDREAU

NEIL HANKERSON Executive Vice President · TOM WEDDLE Chief Financial Officer · RANDY STRADLEY Vice President of Publishing

MATT PARKINSON Vice President of Marketing · DAVID SCROGGY Vice President of Product Development

DALE LaFOUNTAIN Vice President of Information Technology · CARA NIECE Vice President of Production and Scheduling

NICK McWHORTER Vice President of Media Licensing · MARK BERNARDI Vice President of Book Trade and Digital Sales

KEN LIZZI General Counsel · DAVE MARSHALL Editor in Chief · DAVEY ESTRADA Editorial Director · SCOTT ALLIE Executive Senior Editor

CHRIS WARNER Senior Books Editor · CARY GRAZZINI Director of Specialty Projects · LIA RIBACCHI Art Director

VANESSA TODD Director of Print Purchasing · MATT DRYER Director of Digital Art and Prepress

MICHAEL GOMBOS Director of International Publishing and Licensing

Published by Dark Horse Books
A division of Dark Horse Comics, Inc.
10956 SE Main Street
Milwaukie, OR 97222

First edition: October 2017
ISBN 978-1-50670-208-7

International Licensing: (503) 905-2377 · Comic Shop Locator Service: (888) 266-4226

Harrow County Volume 6: Hedge Magic

This volume collects Harrow County #21–#24.

10 9 8 7 6 5 4 3 2 1
Printed in China

DarkHorse.com

Library of Congress Cataloging-in-Publication Data

Names: Bunn, Cullen, author. | Crook, Tyler, artist, letterer.

Title: Hedge magic / script, Cullen Bunn ; art and lettering, Tyler Crook.

Description: First edition. | Milwaukie, OR : Dark Horse Books, 2017. |
  Series: Harrow County ; Volume 6 | "This volume collects Harrow County
  #21-#24"

Identifiers: LCCN 2017018581 | ISBN 9781506702087 (paperback)

Subjects: LCSH: Comic books, strips, etc. | BISAC: COMICS & GRAPHIC NOVELS /
  Horror. | COMICS & GRAPHIC NOVELS / Fantasy.

Classification: LCC PN6728.H369 B865 2017 | DDC 741.5/973--dc23

LC record available at https://lccn.loc.gov/2017018581

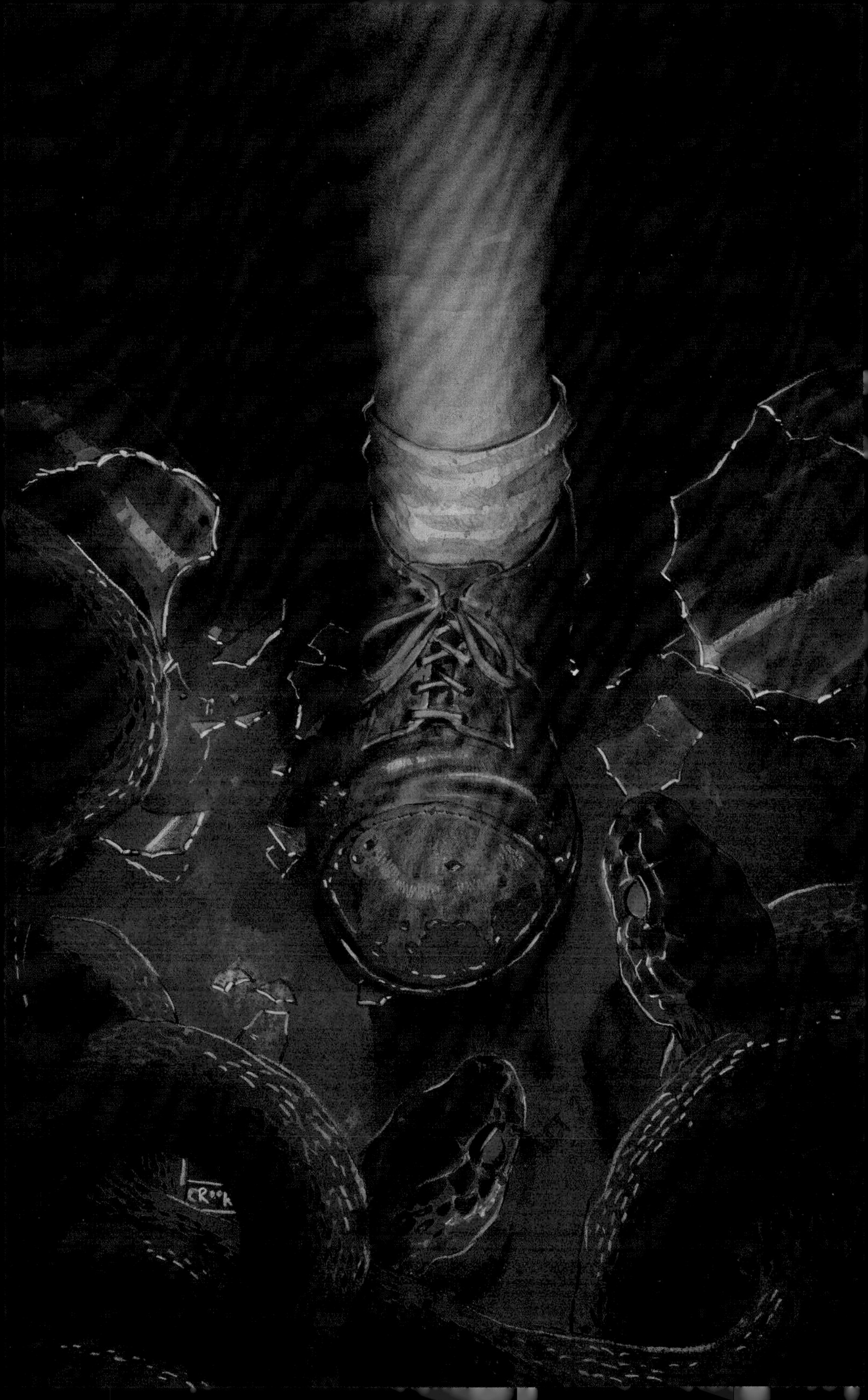
CROOK

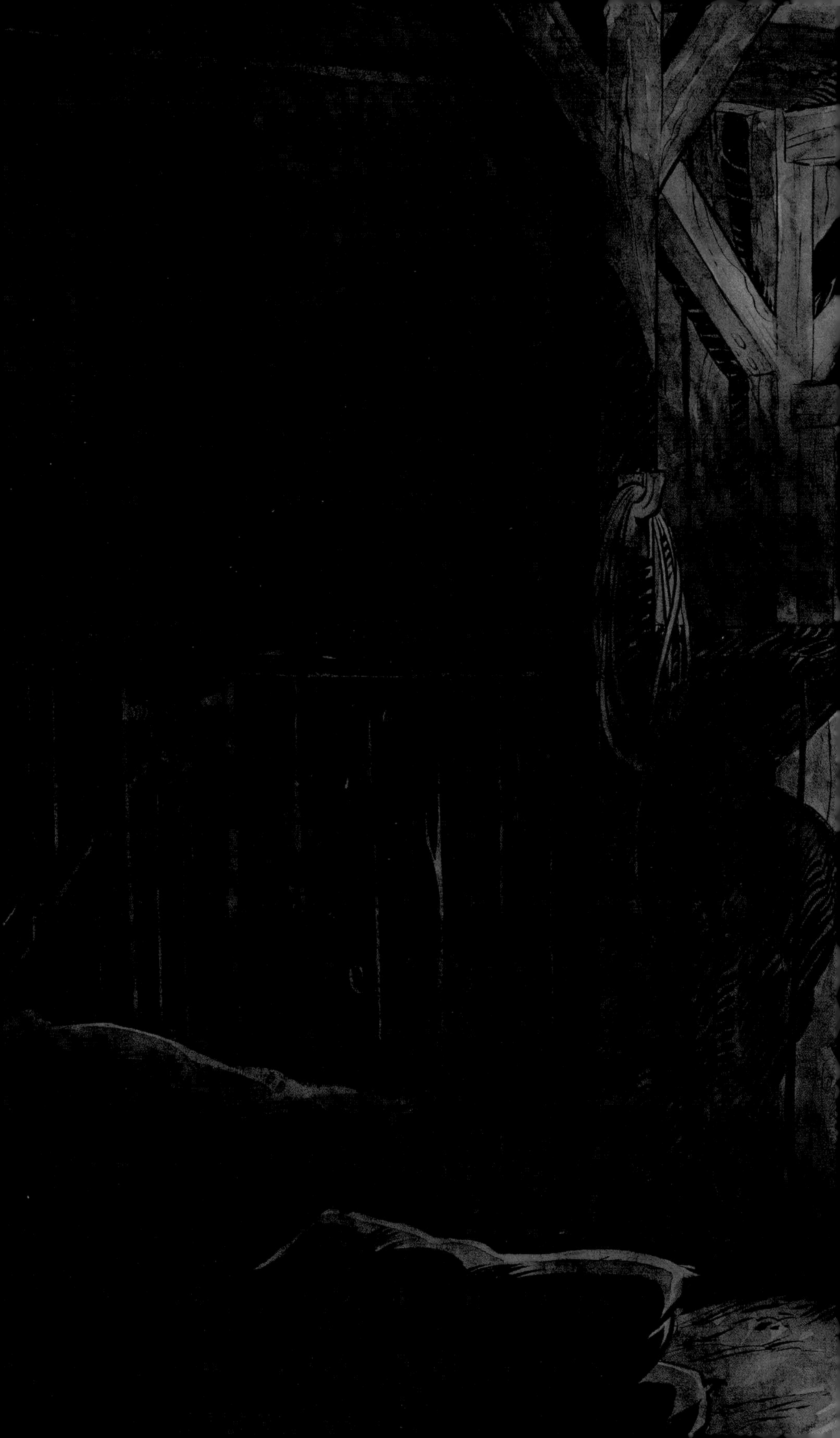

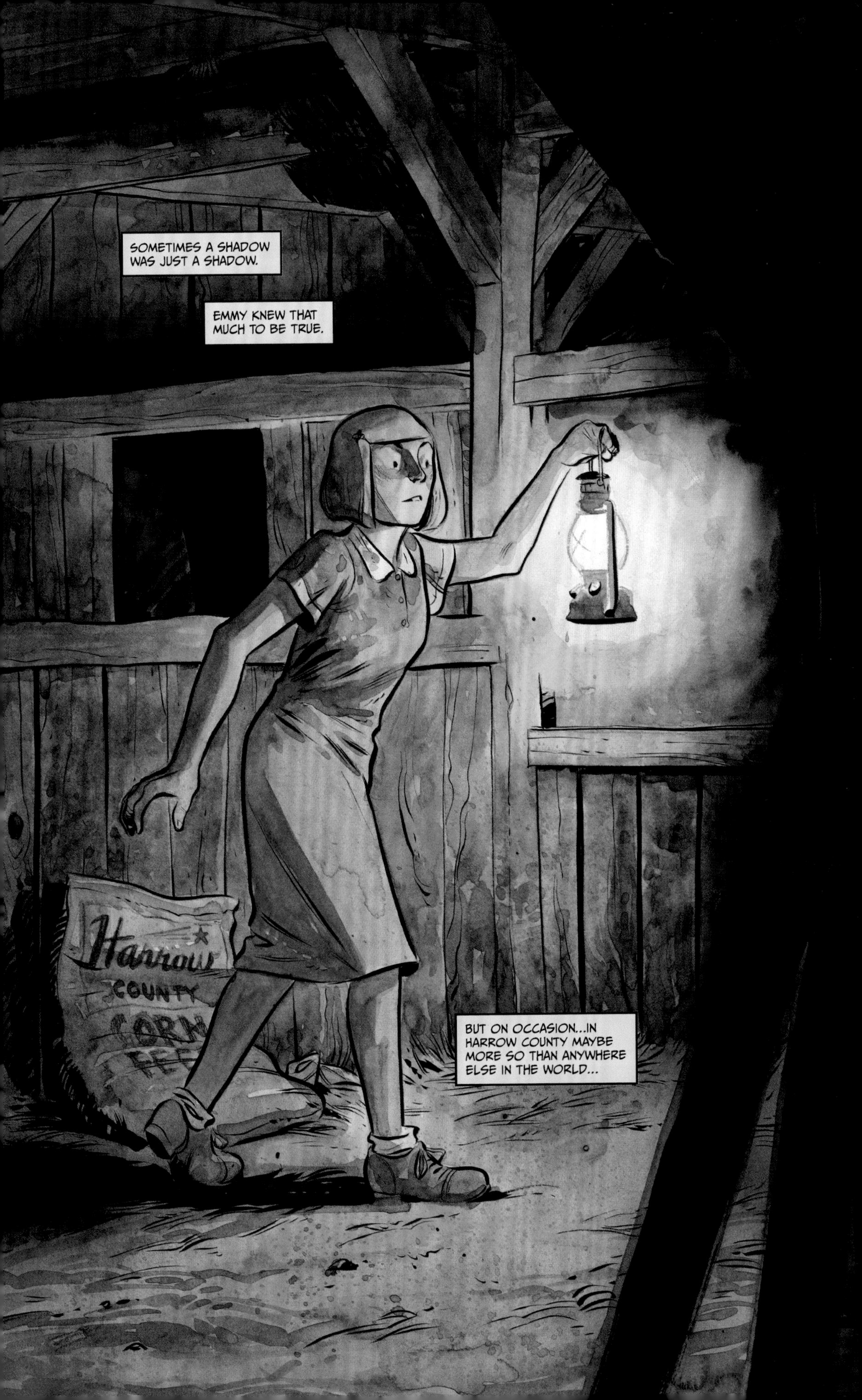
SOMETIMES A SHADOW WAS JUST A SHADOW.
EMMY KNEW THAT MUCH TO BE TRUE.
BUT ON OCCASION...IN HARROW COUNTY MAYBE MORE SO THAN ANYWHERE ELSE IN THE WORLD...

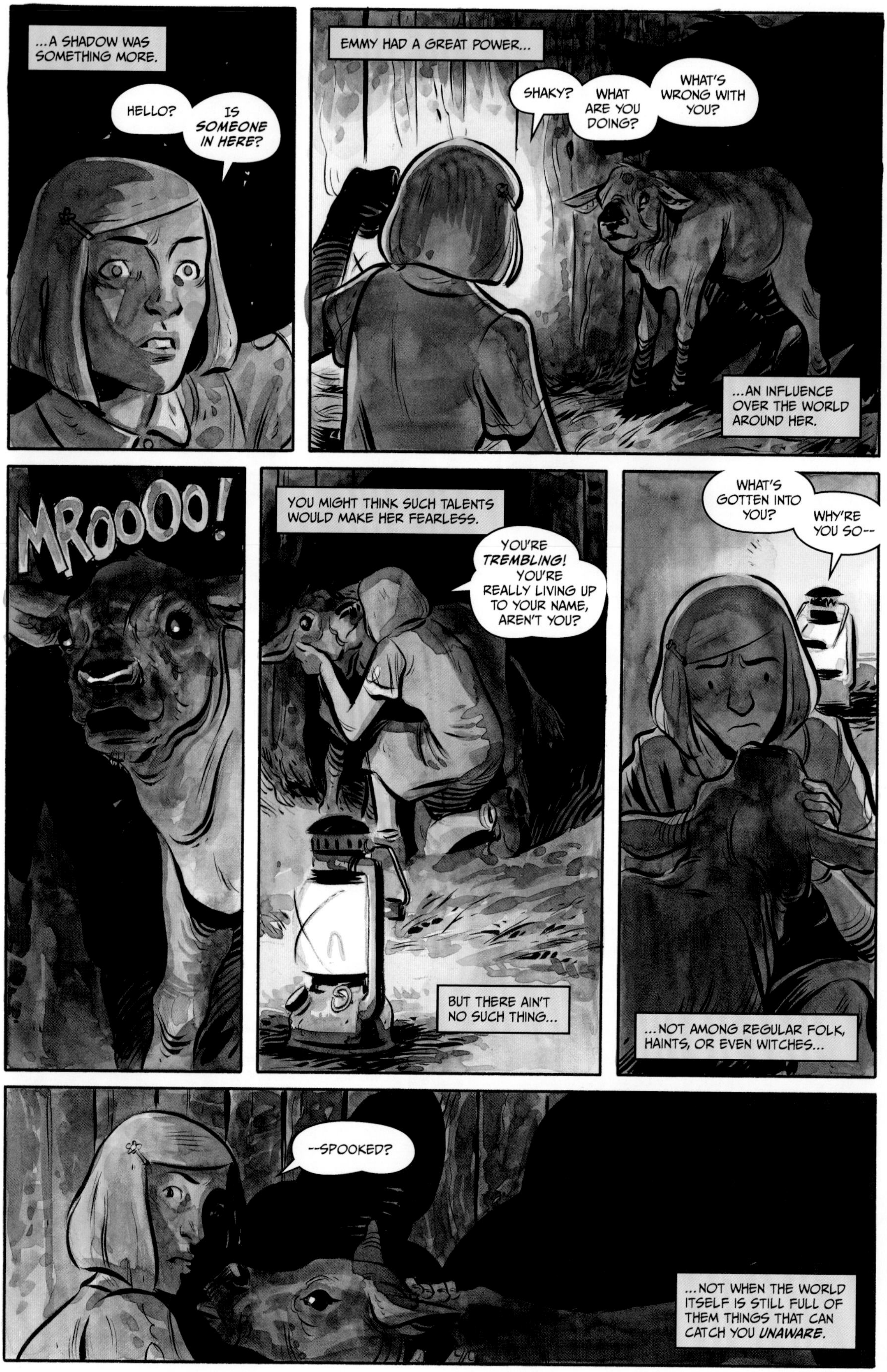
...A SHADOW WAS SOMETHING MORE.
HELLO?
IS *SOMEONE* IN HERE?
EMMY HAD A GREAT POWER...
SHAKY?
WHAT ARE YOU DOING?
WHAT'S WRONG WITH YOU?
...AN INFLUENCE OVER THE WORLD AROUND HER.
MROOOO!
YOU MIGHT THINK SUCH TALENTS WOULD MAKE HER FEARLESS.
YOU'RE *TREMBLING*! YOU'RE REALLY LIVING UP TO YOUR NAME, AREN'T YOU?
BUT THERE AIN'T NO SUCH THING...
WHAT'S GOTTEN INTO YOU?
WHY'RE YOU SO--
...NOT AMONG REGULAR FOLK, HAINTS, OR EVEN WITCHES...
--SPOOKED?
...NOT WHEN THE WORLD ITSELF IS STILL FULL OF THEM THINGS THAT CAN CATCH YOU *UNAWARE*.

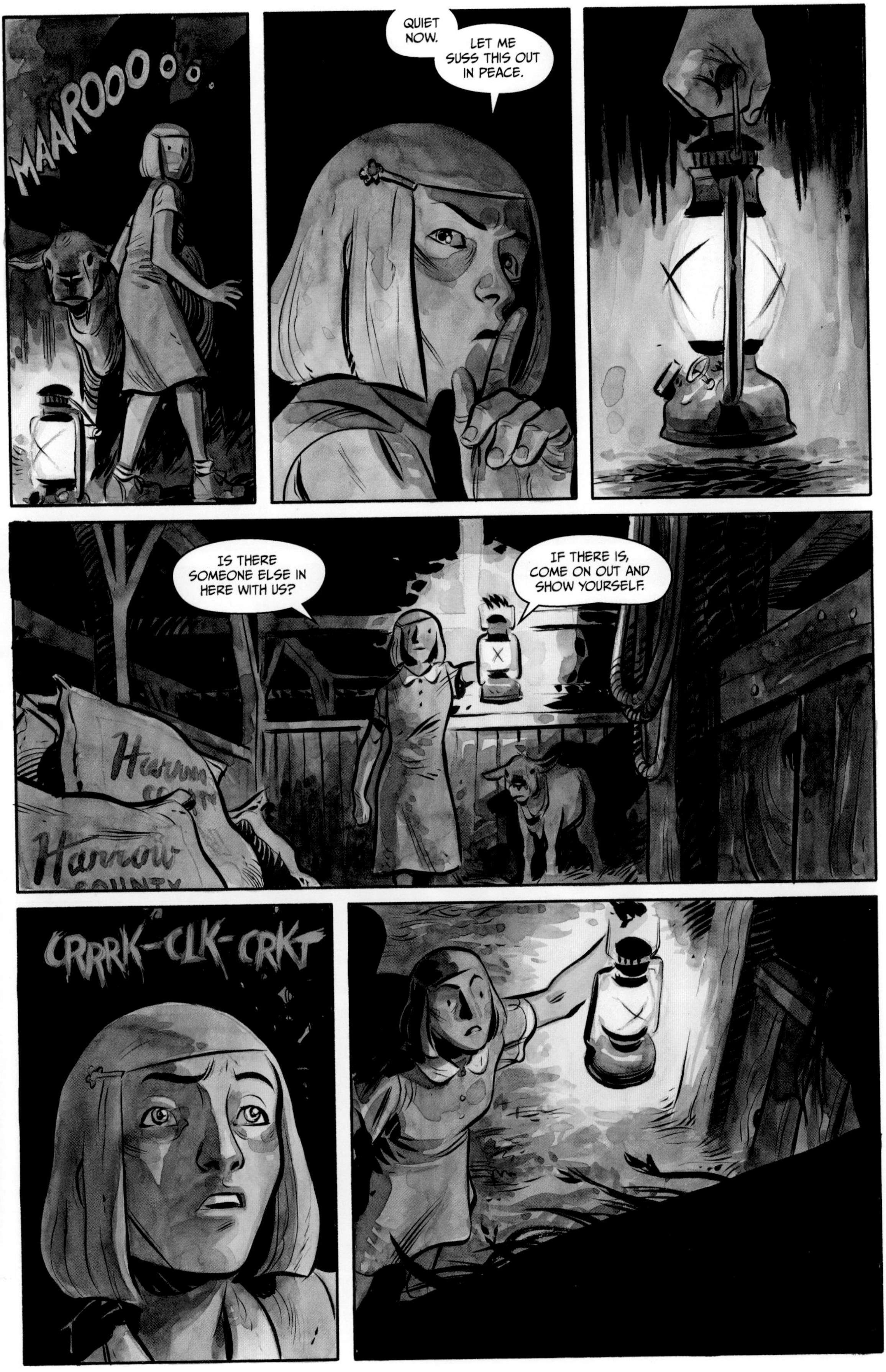
MAAROOOooo
QUIET NOW.
LET ME SUSS THIS OUT IN PEACE.
IS THERE SOMEONE ELSE IN HERE WITH US?
IF THERE IS, COME ON OUT AND SHOW YOURSELF.
Harrow County
CRRRK-CLK-CRKT

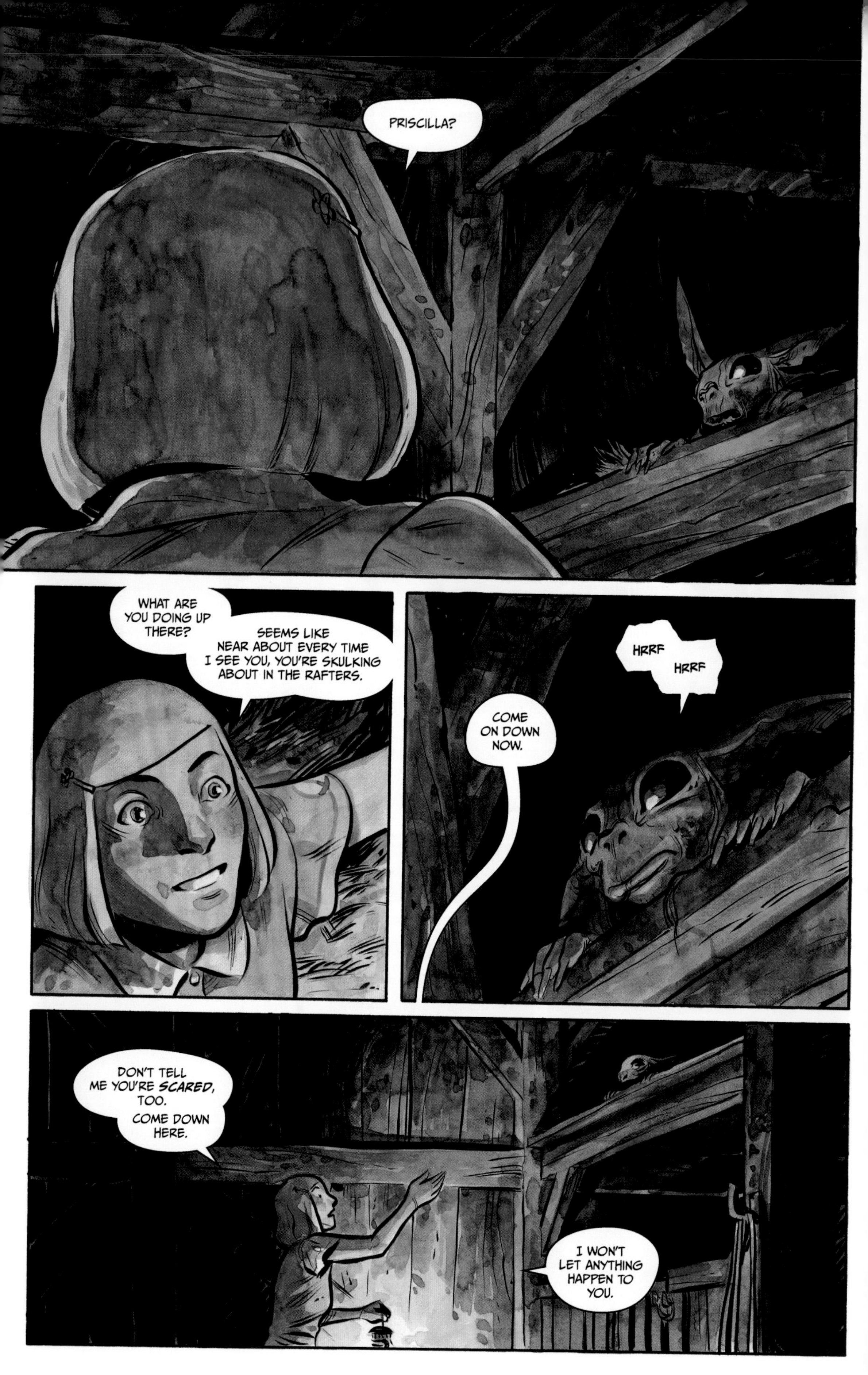
PRISCILLA?
WHAT ARE YOU DOING UP THERE?
SEEMS LIKE NEAR ABOUT EVERY TIME I SEE YOU, YOU'RE SKULKING ABOUT IN THE RAFTERS.
HRRF HRRF
COME ON DOWN NOW.
DON'T TELL ME YOU'RE *SCARED*, TOO.
COME DOWN HERE.
I WON'T LET ANYTHING HAPPEN TO YOU.

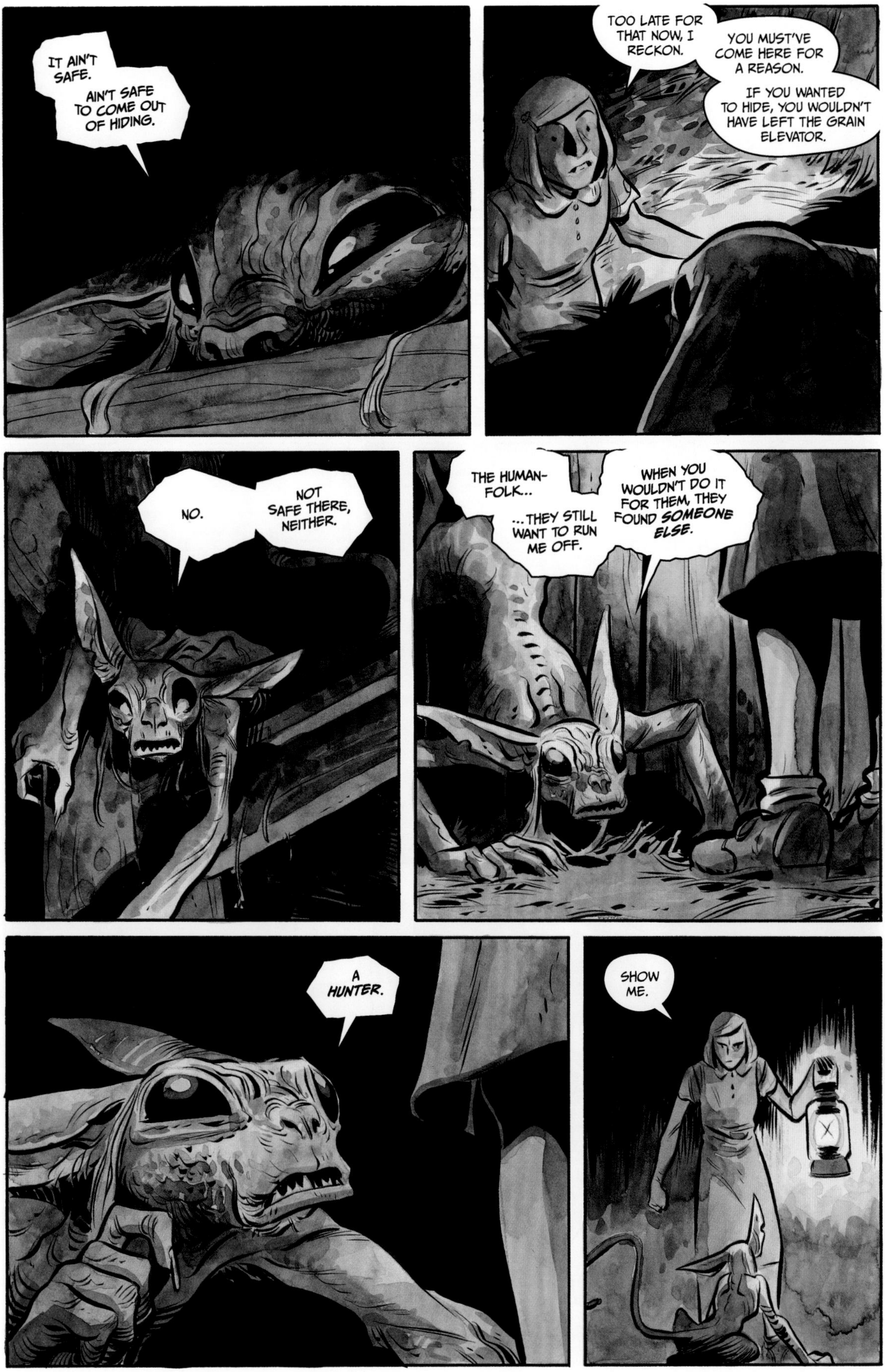
IT AIN'T SAFE.
AIN'T SAFE TO COME OUT OF HIDING.
TOO LATE FOR THAT NOW, I RECKON.
YOU MUST'VE COME HERE FOR A REASON.
IF YOU WANTED TO HIDE, YOU WOULDN'T HAVE LEFT THE GRAIN ELEVATOR.
NO.
NOT SAFE THERE, NEITHER.
THE HUMAN-FOLK...
...THEY STILL WANT TO RUN ME OFF.
WHEN YOU WOULDN'T DO IT FOR THEM, THEY FOUND SOMEONE ELSE.
A HUNTER.
SHOW ME.

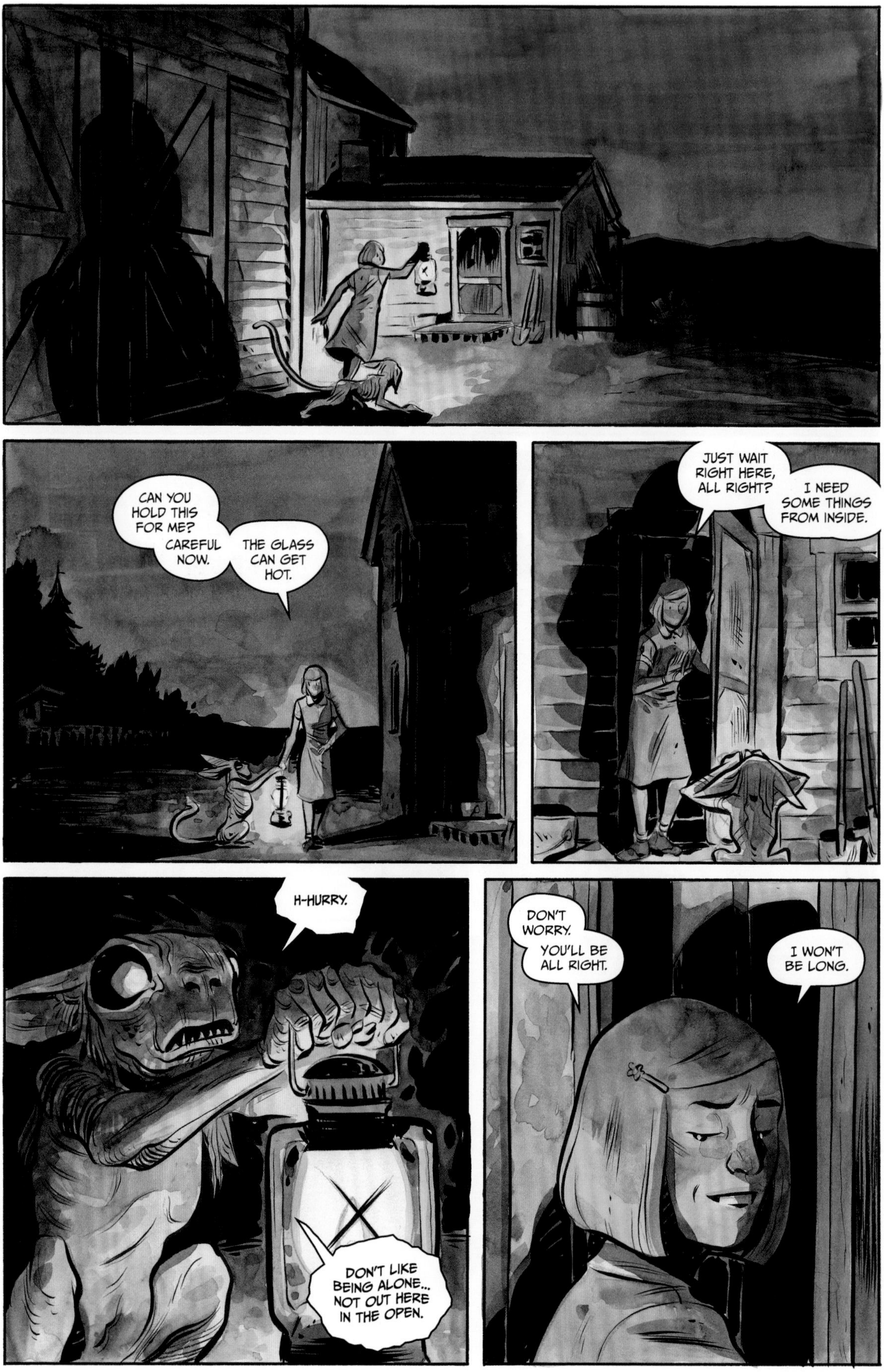
CAN YOU HOLD THIS FOR ME?
CAREFUL NOW.
THE GLASS CAN GET HOT.
JUST WAIT RIGHT HERE, ALL RIGHT?
I NEED SOME THINGS FROM INSIDE.
H-HURRY.
DON'T LIKE BEING ALONE... NOT OUT HERE IN THE OPEN.
DON'T WORRY.
YOU'LL BE ALL RIGHT.
I WON'T BE LONG.

H-HURRY.

LANTERNS COMFORT HUMAN-FOLKS.

BUT NOT HAINTS.

NO LANTERN CAN KEEP ME SAFE.

IF HUMAN-FOLKS ARE AFRAID OF THE *DARK*...

...THEN SHOULDN'T HAINTS BE AFRAID, TOO, OF WHAT THE *LIGHT* DRAWS OUT?

SNF- SNF-

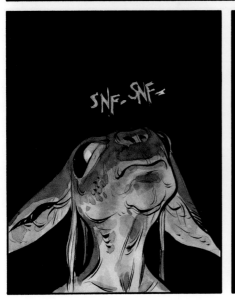

HUNTER'S OUT THERE...

...OUT THERE RIGHT NOW...

...AND I AIN'T THE ONLY ONE BEING HUNTED.

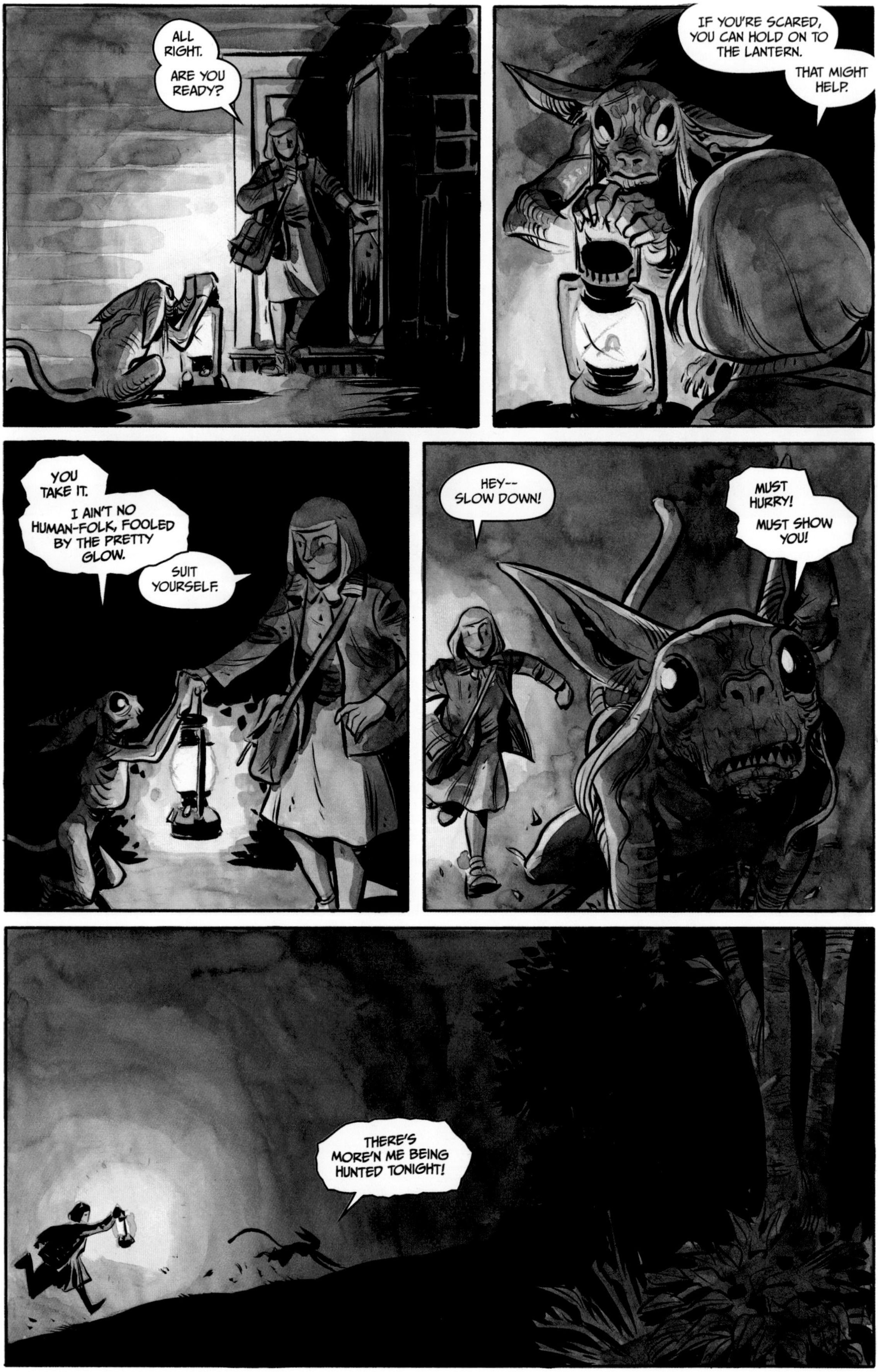
ALL RIGHT.
ARE YOU READY?
IF YOU'RE SCARED, YOU CAN HOLD ON TO THE LANTERN.
THAT MIGHT HELP.
YOU TAKE IT.
I AIN'T NO HUMAN-FOLK, FOOLED BY THE PRETTY GLOW.
SUIT YOURSELF.
HEY-- SLOW DOWN!
MUST HURRY!
MUST SHOW YOU!
THERE'S MORE'N ME BEING HUNTED TONIGHT!

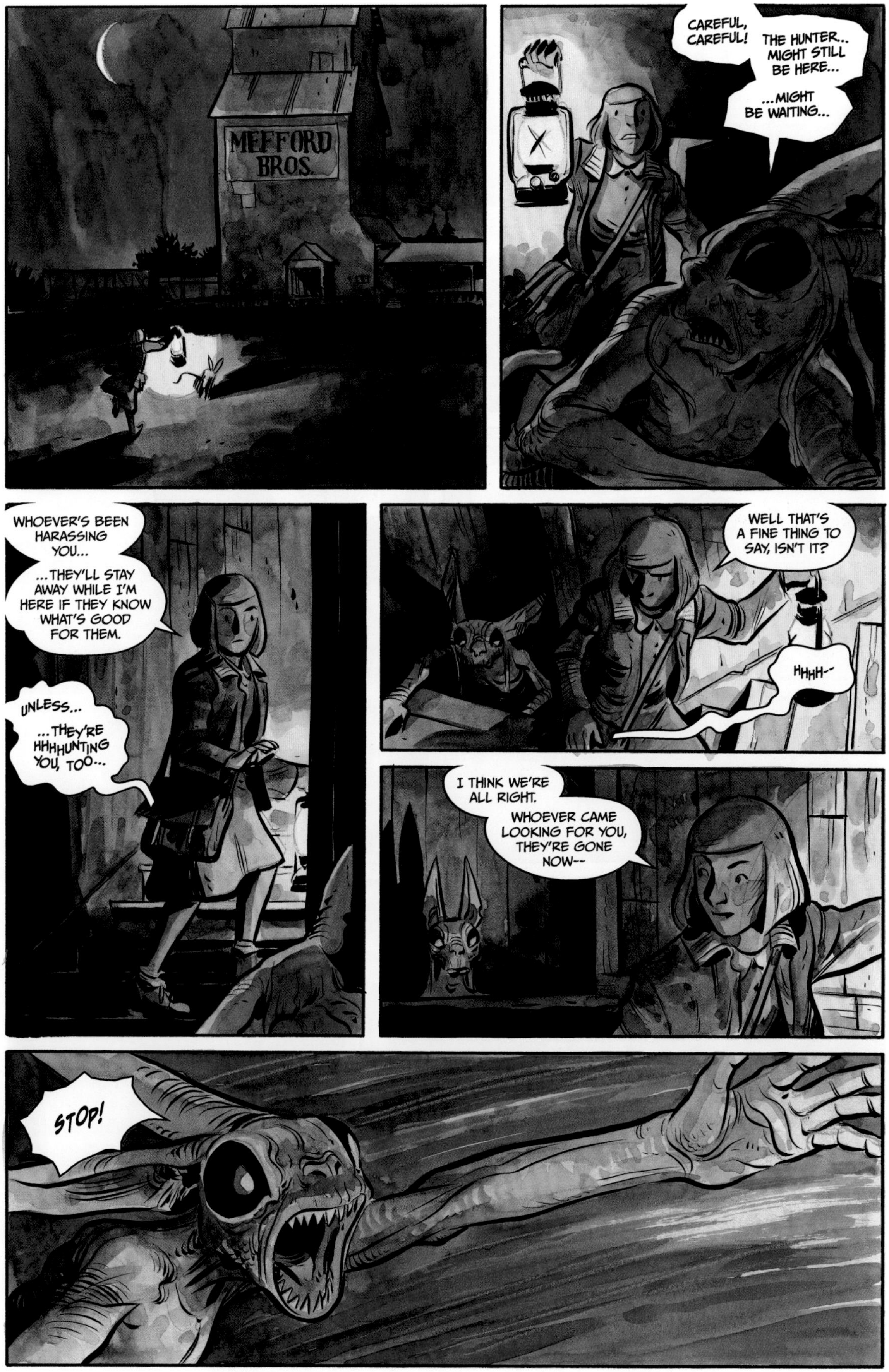
MEFFORD BROS.
CAREFUL, CAREFUL!
THE HUNTER.. MIGHT STILL BE HERE...
...MIGHT BE WAITING...
WHOEVER'S BEEN HARASSING YOU...
...THEY'LL STAY AWAY WHILE I'M HERE IF THEY KNOW WHAT'S GOOD FOR THEM.
UNLESS...
...THEY'RE HHHHUNTING YOU, TOO...
WELL THAT'S A FINE THING TO SAY, ISN'T IT?
HHHH--
I THINK WE'RE ALL RIGHT.
WHOEVER CAME LOOKING FOR YOU, THEY'RE GONE NOW--
STOP!

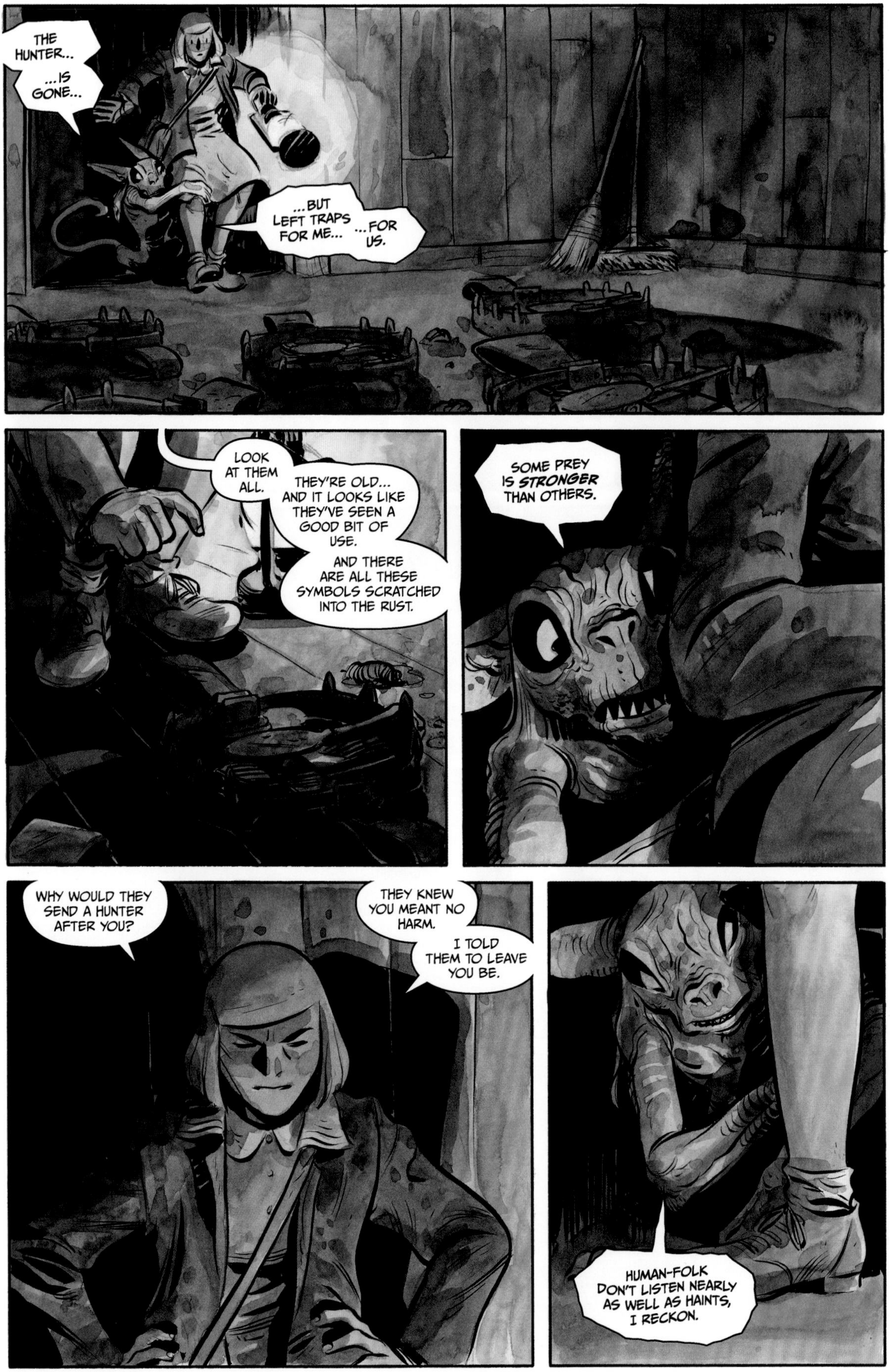
THE HUNTER...
...IS GONE...
...BUT LEFT TRAPS FOR ME...
...FOR US.
LOOK AT THEM ALL.
THEY'RE OLD... AND IT LOOKS LIKE THEY'VE SEEN A GOOD BIT OF USE.
AND THERE ARE ALL THESE SYMBOLS SCRATCHED INTO THE RUST.
SOME PREY IS STRONGER THAN OTHERS.
WHY WOULD THEY SEND A HUNTER AFTER YOU?
THEY KNEW YOU MEANT NO HARM.
I TOLD THEM TO LEAVE YOU BE.
HUMAN-FOLK DON'T LISTEN NEARLY AS WELL AS HAINTS, I RECKON.

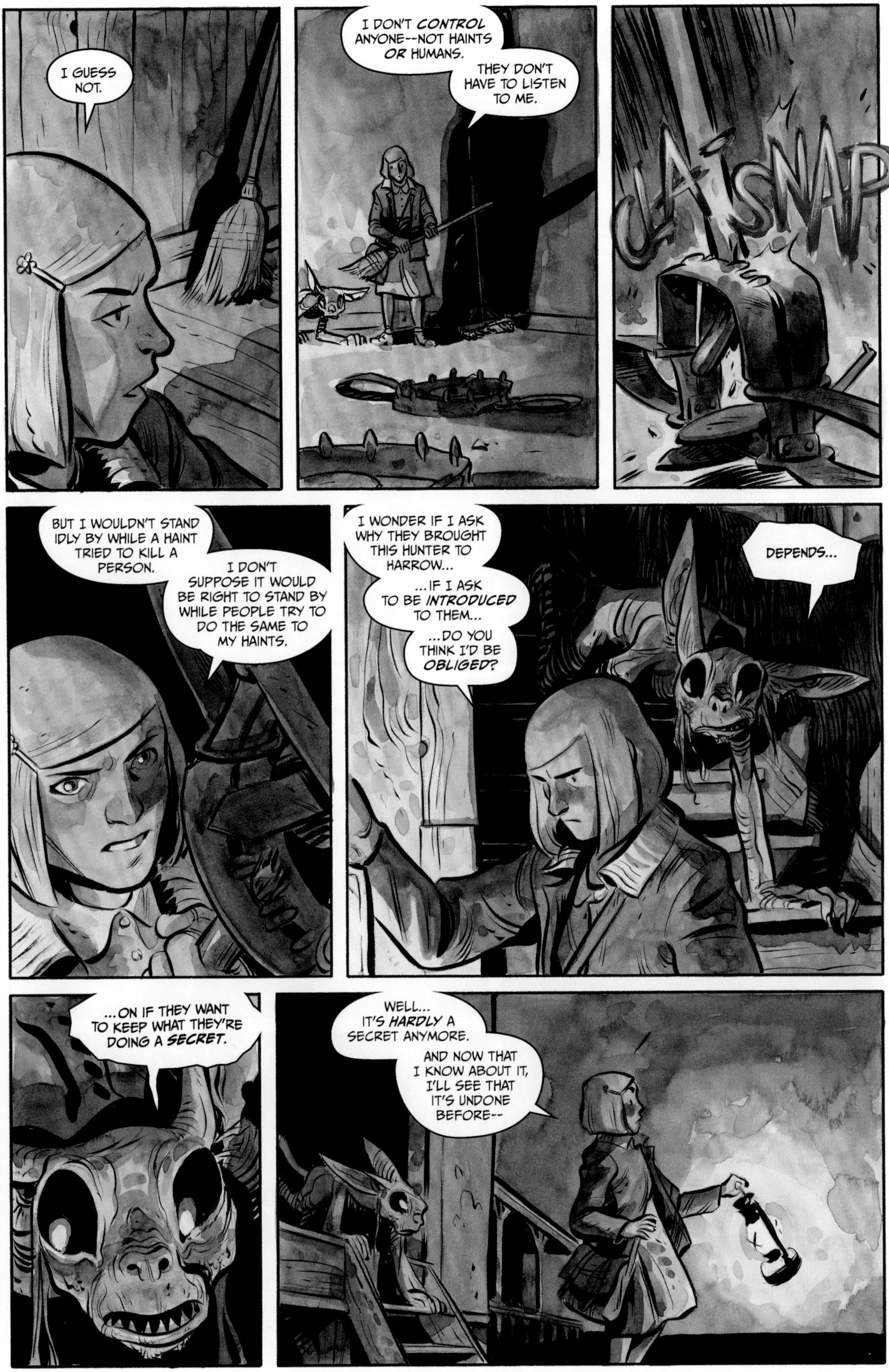
I GUESS NOT.
I DON'T *CONTROL* ANYONE--NOT HAINTS *OR* HUMANS.
THEY DON'T HAVE TO LISTEN TO ME.
CLA'SNAP
BUT I WOULDN'T STAND IDLY BY WHILE A HAINT TRIED TO KILL A PERSON.
I DON'T SUPPOSE IT WOULD BE RIGHT TO STAND BY WHILE PEOPLE TRY TO DO THE SAME TO MY HAINTS.
I WONDER IF I ASK WHY THEY BROUGHT THIS HUNTER TO HARROW...
...IF I ASK TO BE *INTRODUCED* TO THEM...
...DO YOU THINK I'D BE *OBLIGED?*
DEPENDS...
...ON IF THEY WANT TO KEEP WHAT THEY'RE DOING A *SECRET.*
WELL... IT'S *HARDLY* A SECRET ANYMORE.
AND NOW THAT I KNOW ABOUT IT, I'LL SEE THAT IT'S UNDONE BEFORE--

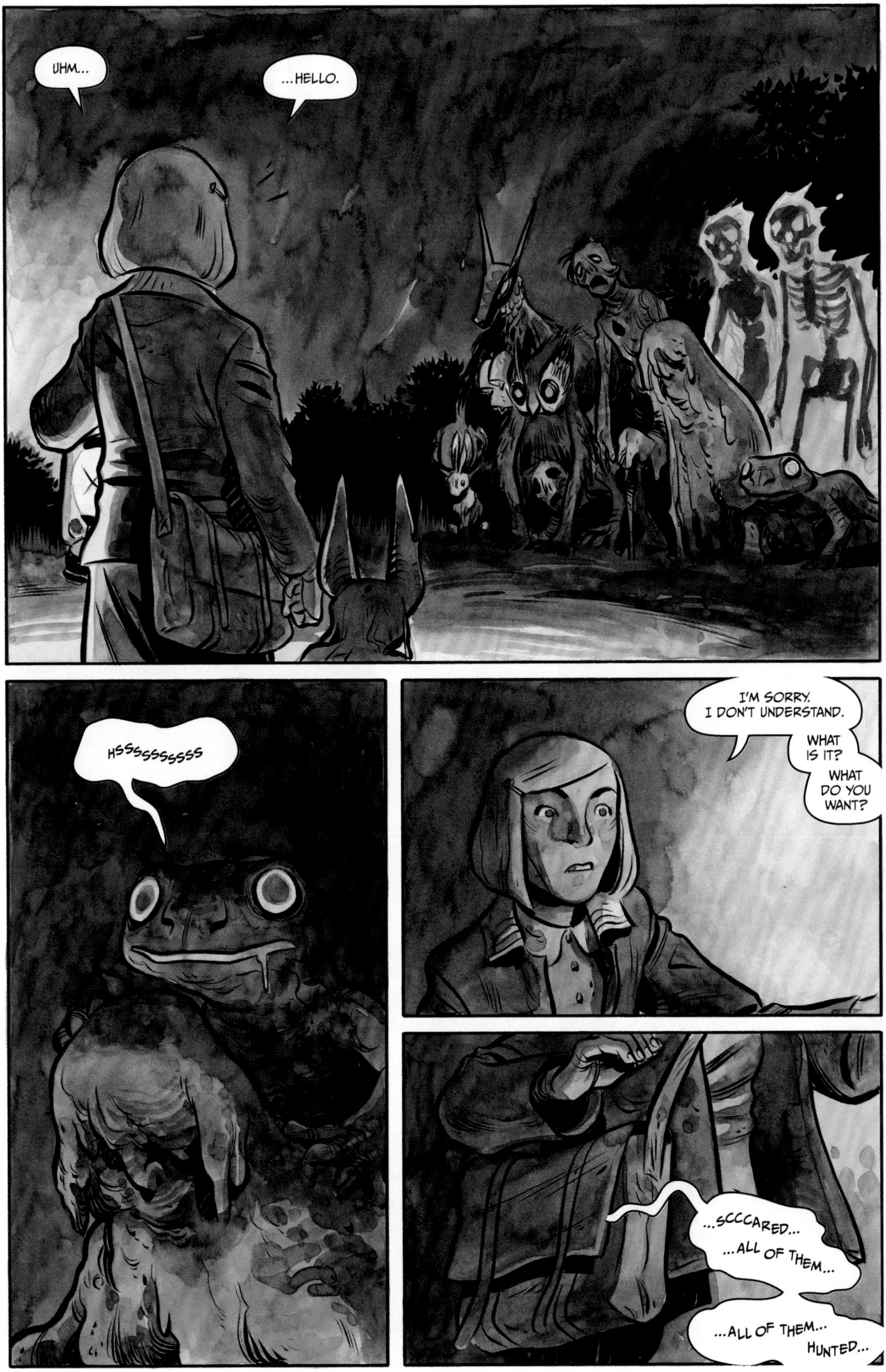
UHM...
...HELLO.
HSSSSSSSSSS
I'M SORRY. I DON'T UNDERSTAND.
WHAT IS IT?
WHAT DO YOU WANT?
...SCCCARED...
...ALL OF THEM...
...ALL OF THEM... HUNTED...

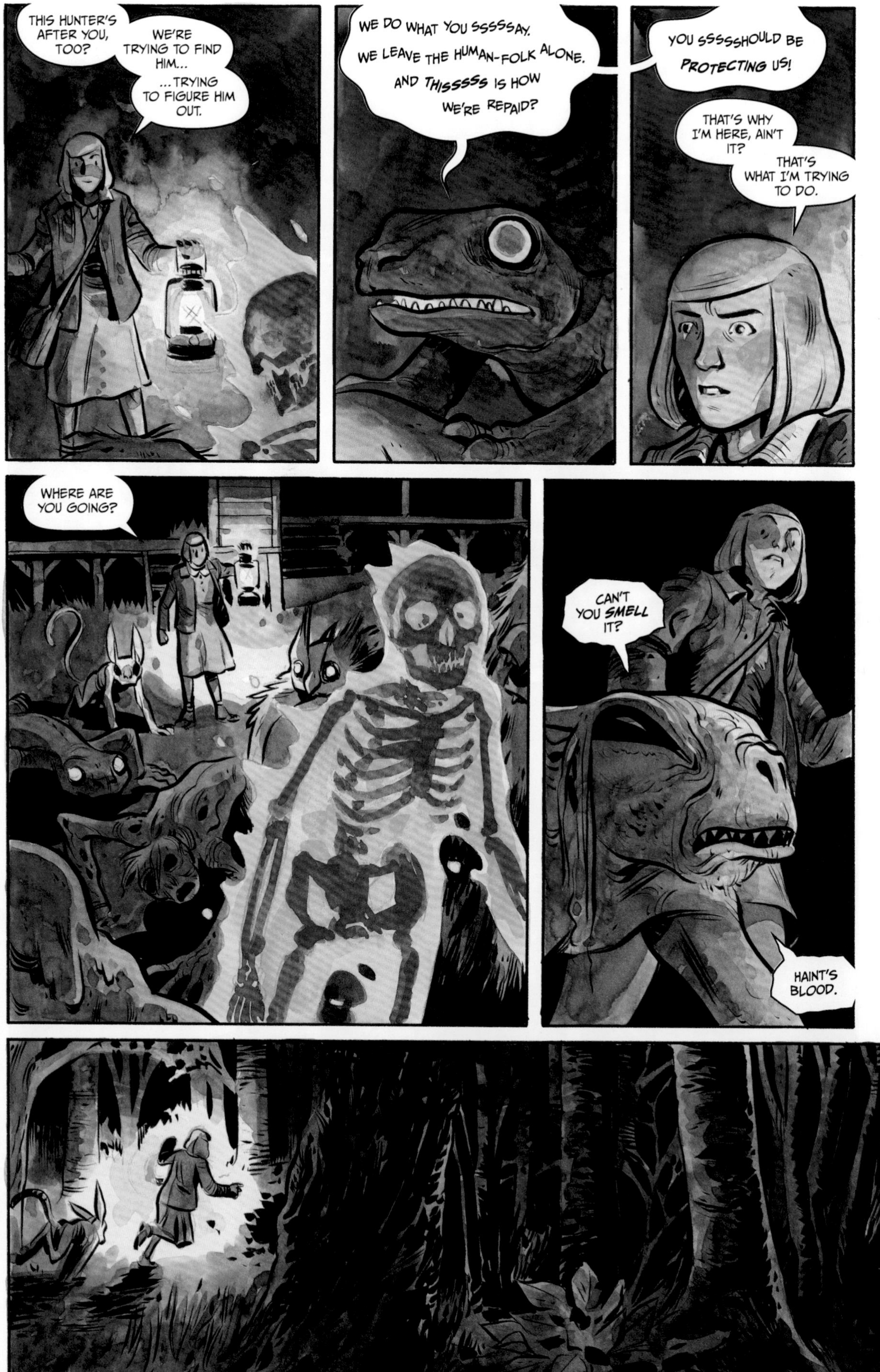
THIS HUNTER'S AFTER YOU, TOO?
WE'RE TRYING TO FIND HIM...
...TRYING TO FIGURE HIM OUT.
WE DO WHAT YOU SSSSSAY.
WE LEAVE THE HUMAN-FOLK ALONE.
AND THISSSSS IS HOW WE'RE REPAID?
YOU SSSSSHOULD BE PROTECTING US!
THAT'S WHY I'M HERE, AIN'T IT?
THAT'S WHAT I'M TRYING TO DO.
WHERE ARE YOU GOING?
CAN'T YOU SMELL IT?
HAINT'S BLOOD.

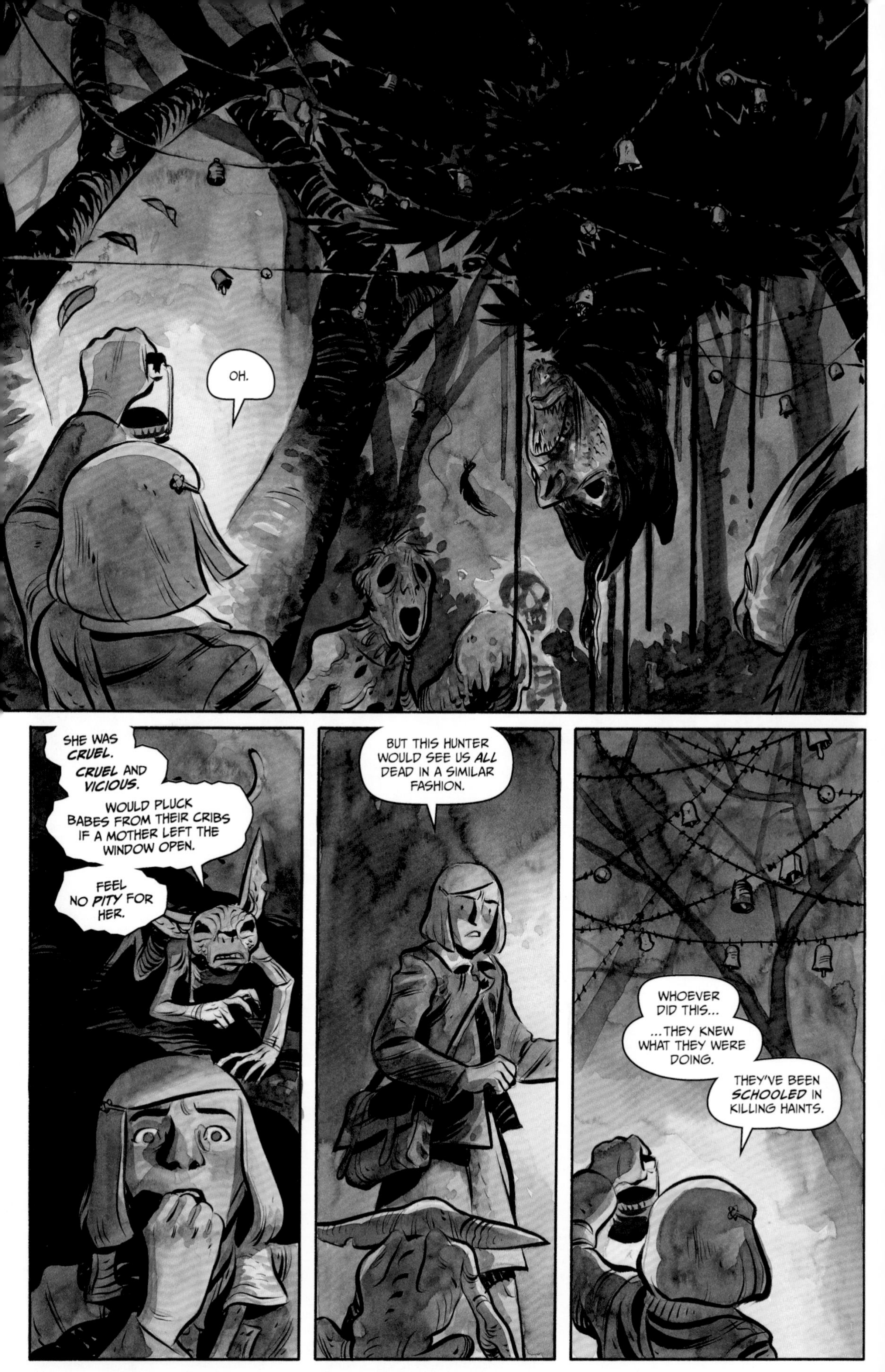
OH.
SHE WAS CRUEL.
CRUEL AND VICIOUS.
WOULD PLUCK BABES FROM THEIR CRIBS IF A MOTHER LEFT THE WINDOW OPEN.
FEEL NO PITY FOR HER.
BUT THIS HUNTER WOULD SEE US ALL DEAD IN A SIMILAR FASHION.
WHOEVER DID THIS...
...THEY KNEW WHAT THEY WERE DOING.
THEY'VE BEEN SCHOOLED IN KILLING HAINTS.

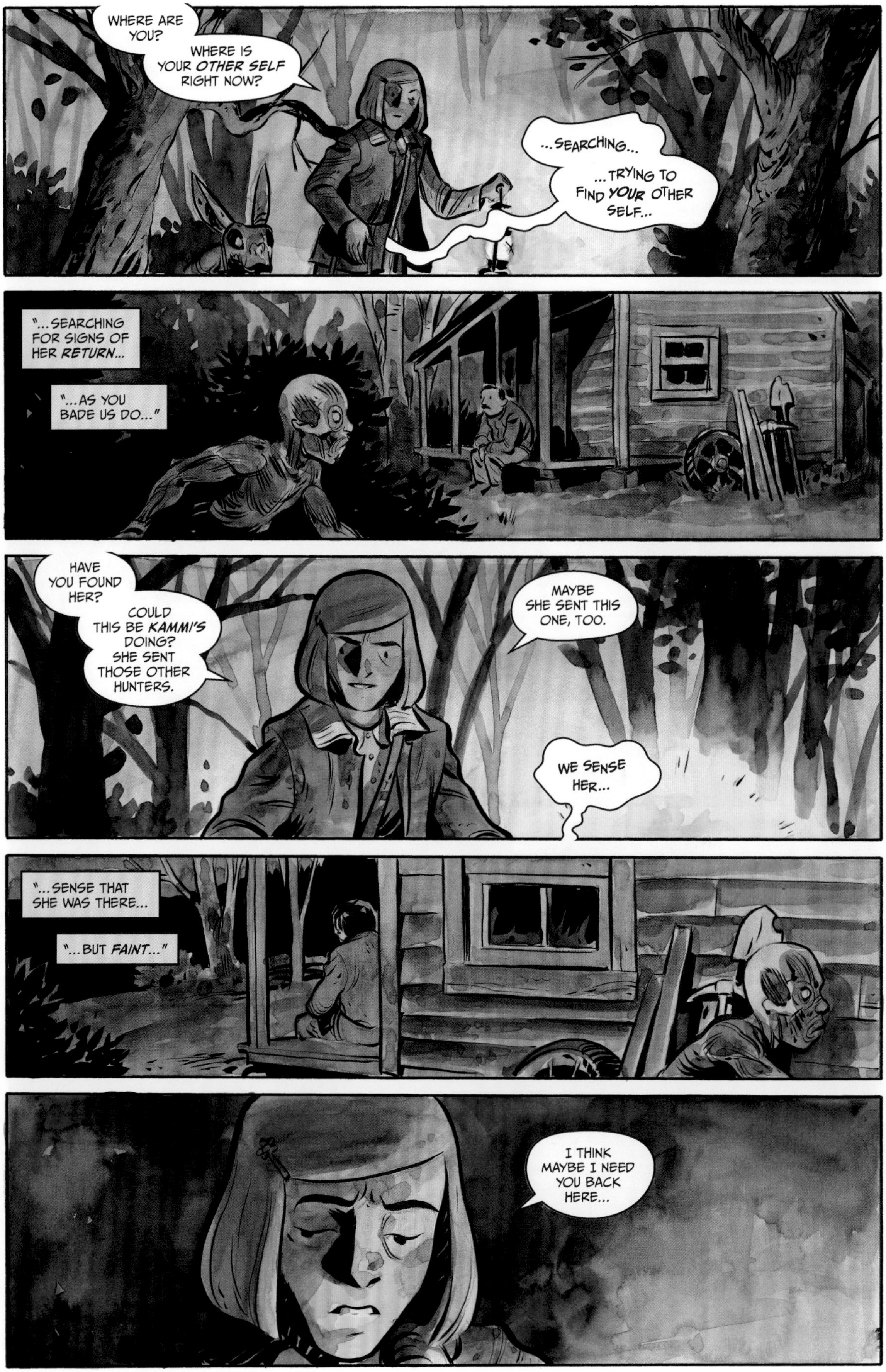
WHERE ARE YOU?
WHERE IS YOUR OTHER SELF RIGHT NOW?
...SEARCHING...
...TRYING TO FIND YOUR OTHER SELF...
"...SEARCHING FOR SIGNS OF HER RETURN...
"...AS YOU BADE US DO..."
HAVE YOU FOUND HER?
COULD THIS BE KAMMI'S DOING? SHE SENT THOSE OTHER HUNTERS.
MAYBE SHE SENT THIS ONE, TOO.
WE SENSE HER...
"...SENSE THAT SHE WAS THERE...
"...BUT FAINT..."
I THINK MAYBE I NEED YOU BACK HERE...

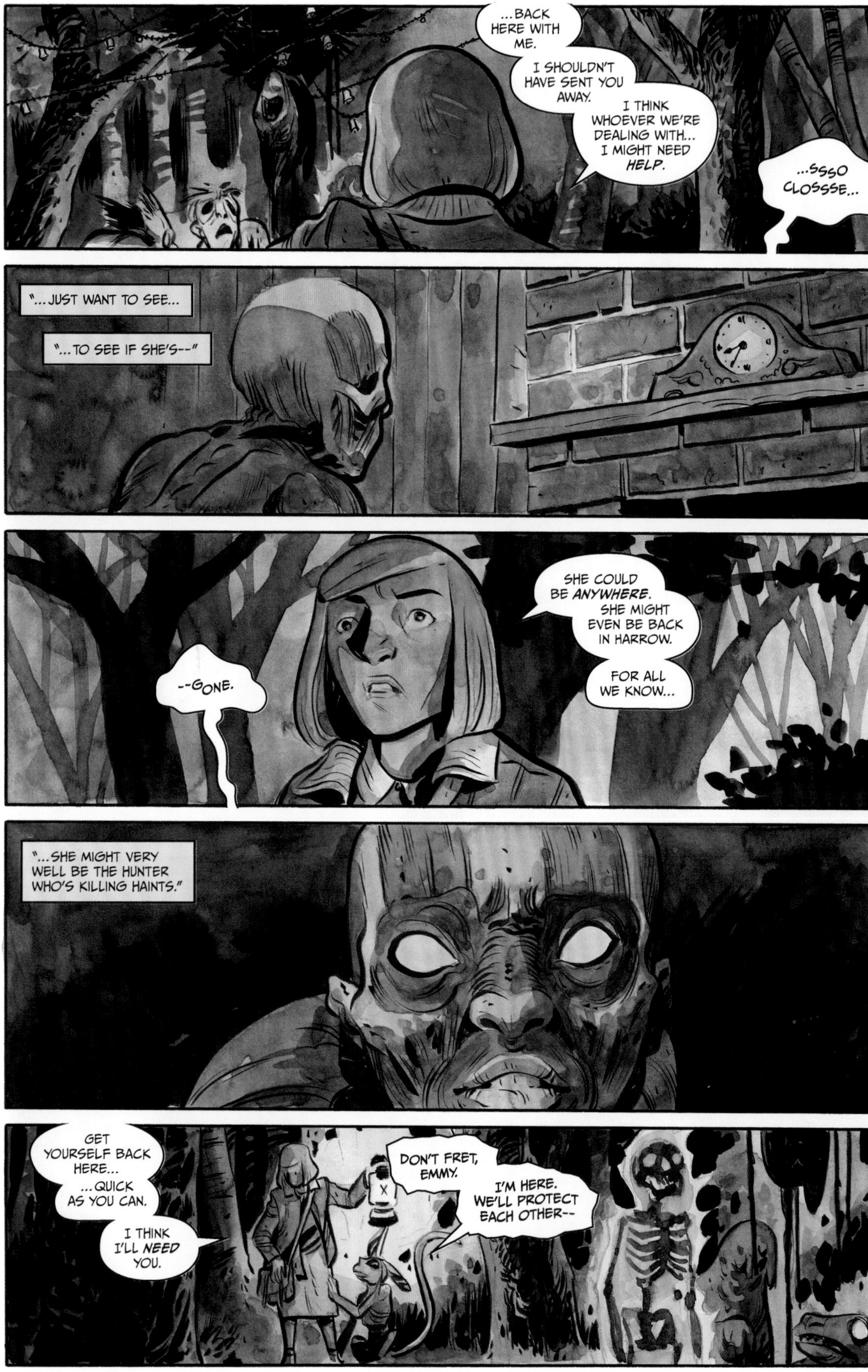
...BACK HERE WITH ME.
I SHOULDN'T HAVE SENT YOU AWAY.
I THINK WHOEVER WE'RE DEALING WITH... I MIGHT NEED HELP.
...SSSO CLOSSSE...
"...JUST WANT TO SEE...
"...TO SEE IF SHE'S--"
SHE COULD BE ANYWHERE. SHE MIGHT EVEN BE BACK IN HARROW.
FOR ALL WE KNOW...
--GONE.
"...SHE MIGHT VERY WELL BE THE HUNTER WHO'S KILLING HAINTS."
GET YOURSELF BACK HERE...
...QUICK AS YOU CAN.
I THINK I'LL NEED YOU.
DON'T FRET, EMMY.
I'M HERE. WE'LL PROTECT EACH OTHER--

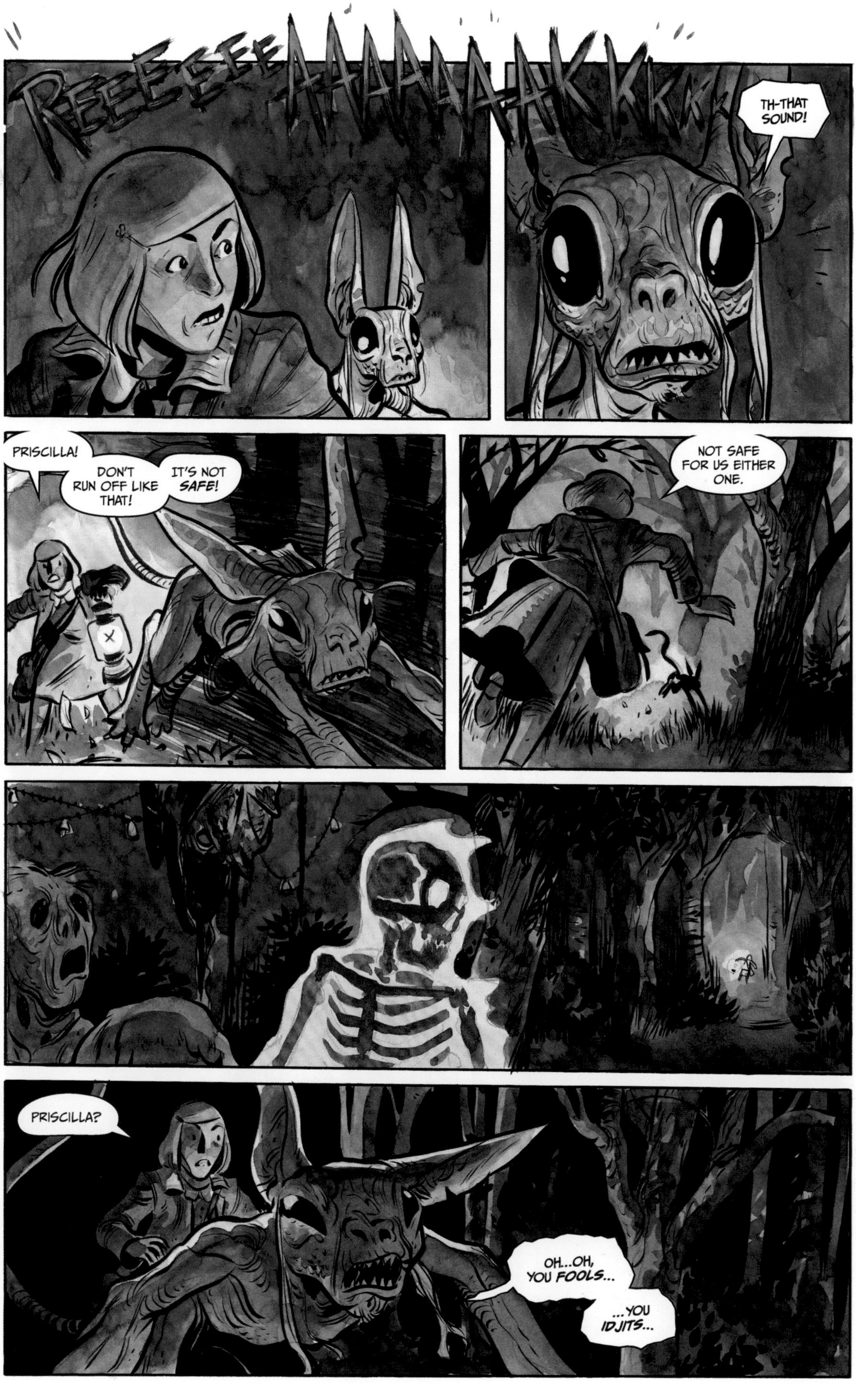
REEEEEEEAAAAAAAKKKK
TH-THAT SOUND!
PRISCILLA!
DON'T RUN OFF LIKE THAT!
IT'S NOT *SAFE!*
NOT SAFE FOR US EITHER ONE.
PRISCILLA?
OH...OH, YOU *FOOLS...*
...YOU *IDJITS...*

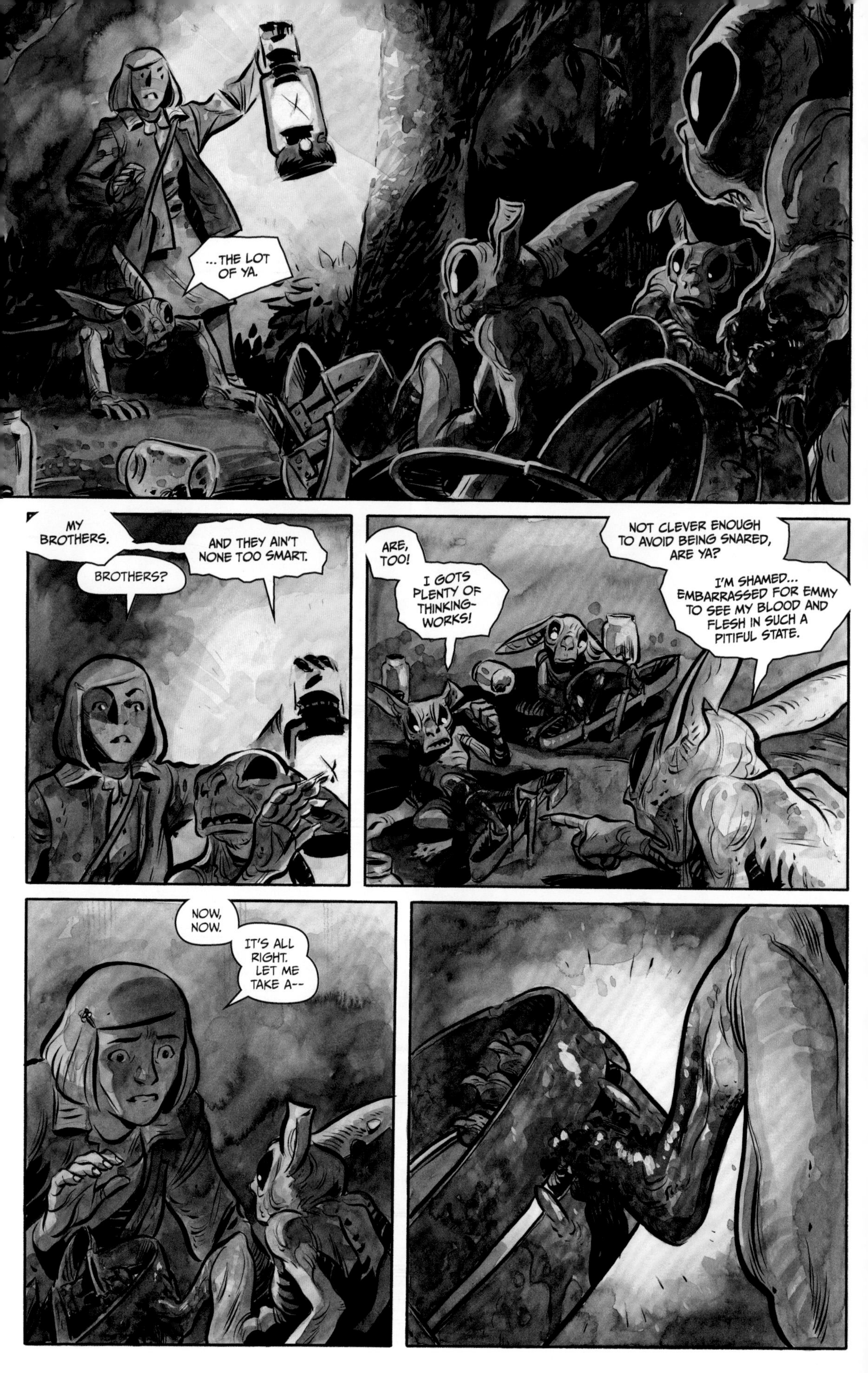
...THE LOT OF YA.
MY BROTHERS.
BROTHERS?
AND THEY AIN'T NONE TOO SMART.
ARE, TOO!
I GOTS PLENTY OF THINKING-WORKS!
NOT CLEVER ENOUGH TO AVOID BEING SNARED, ARE YA?
I'M SHAMED... EMBARRASSED FOR EMMY TO SEE MY BLOOD AND FLESH IN SUCH A PITIFUL STATE.
NOW, NOW.
IT'S ALL RIGHT. LET ME TAKE A--

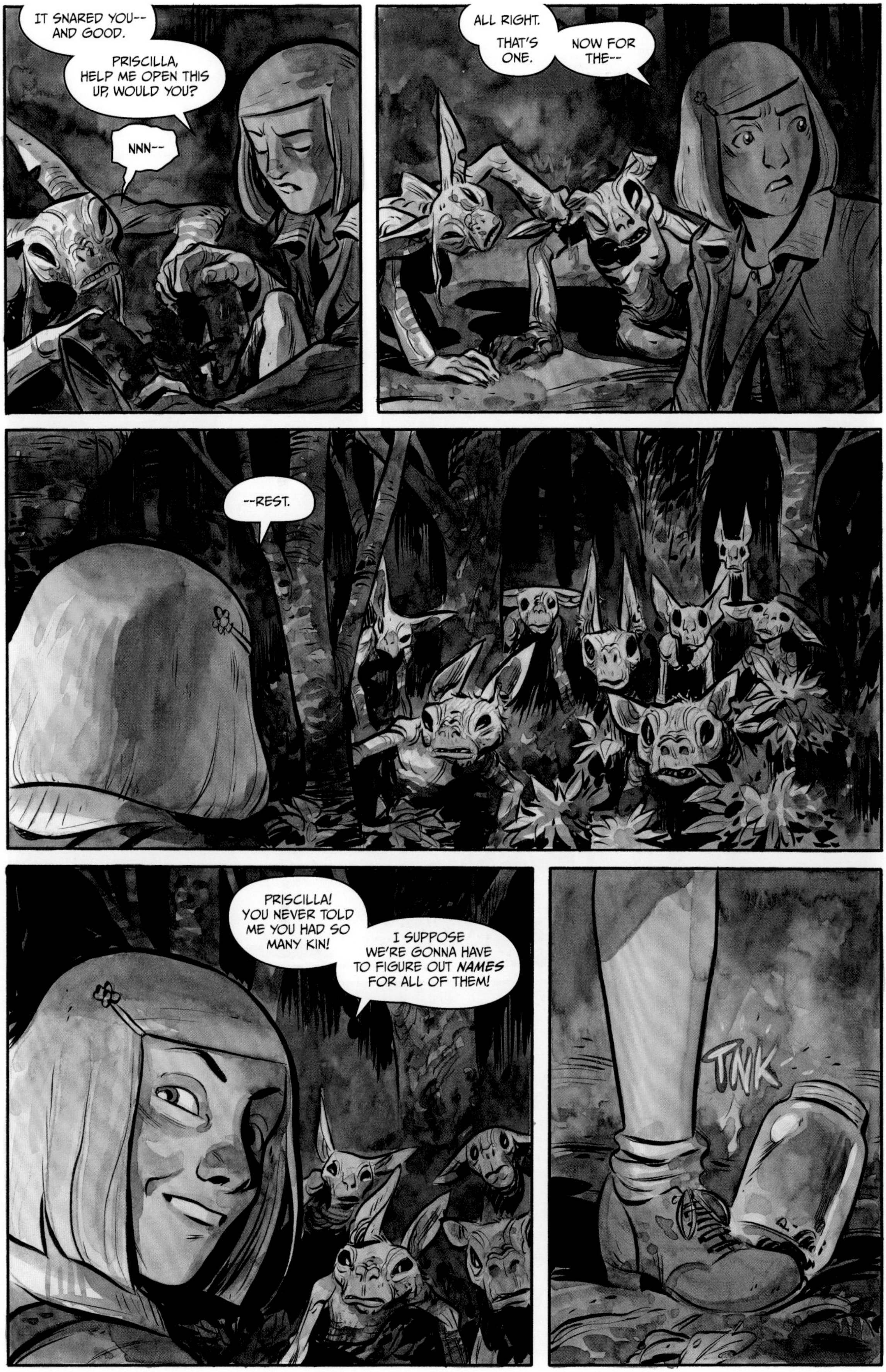
IT SNARED YOU-- AND GOOD.
PRISCILLA, HELP ME OPEN THIS UP, WOULD YOU?
NNN--
ALL RIGHT.
THAT'S ONE.
NOW FOR THE--
--REST.
PRISCILLA! YOU NEVER TOLD ME YOU HAD SO MANY KIN!
I SUPPOSE WE'RE GONNA HAVE TO FIGURE OUT NAMES FOR ALL OF THEM!
TNK

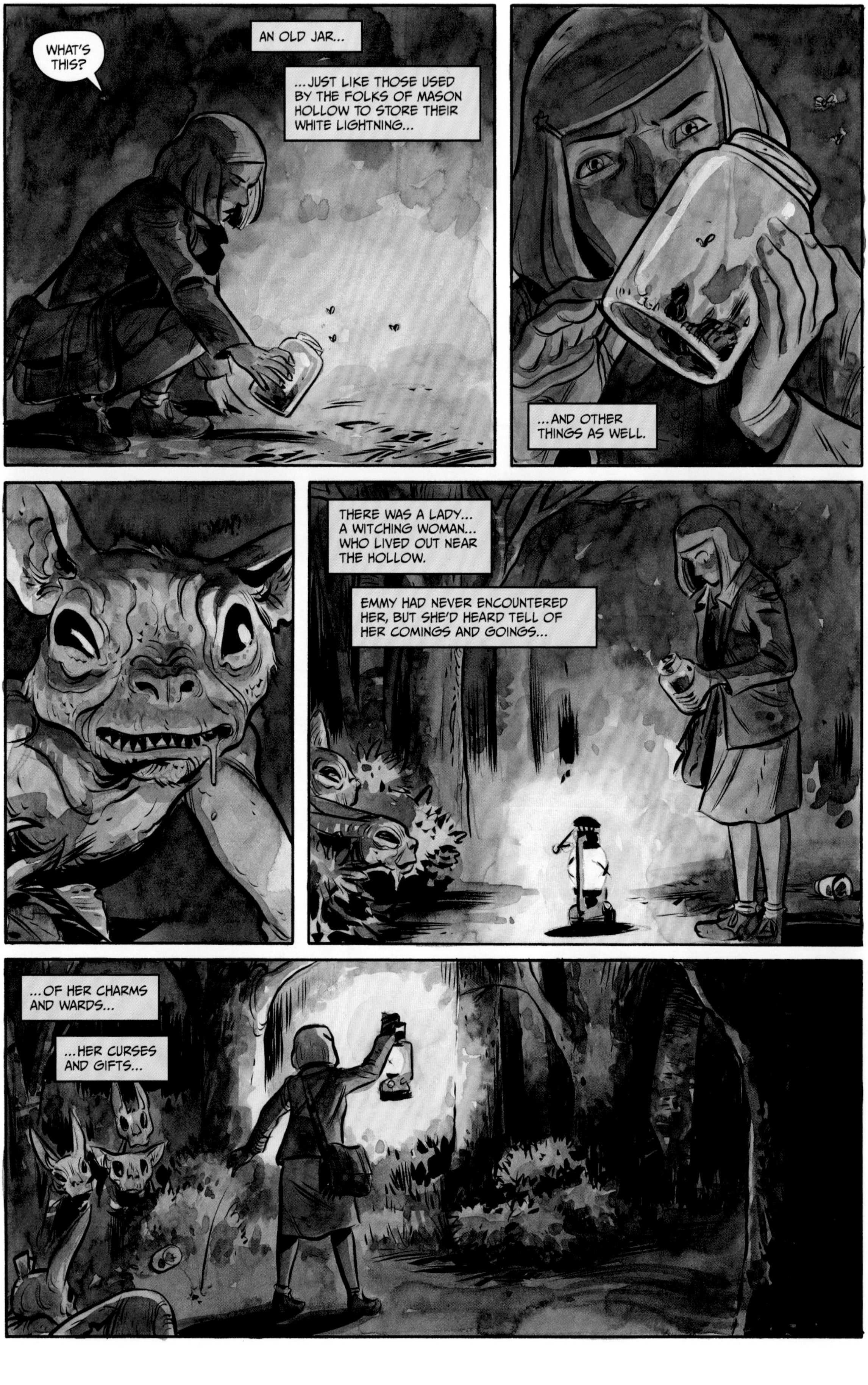
WHAT'S THIS?
AN OLD JAR...
...JUST LIKE THOSE USED BY THE FOLKS OF MASON HOLLOW TO STORE THEIR WHITE LIGHTNING...
...AND OTHER THINGS AS WELL.
THERE WAS A LADY... A WITCHING WOMAN... WHO LIVED OUT NEAR THE HOLLOW.
EMMY HAD NEVER ENCOUNTERED HER, BUT SHE'D HEARD TELL OF HER COMINGS AND GOINGS...
...OF HER CHARMS AND WARDS...
...HER CURSES AND GIFTS...

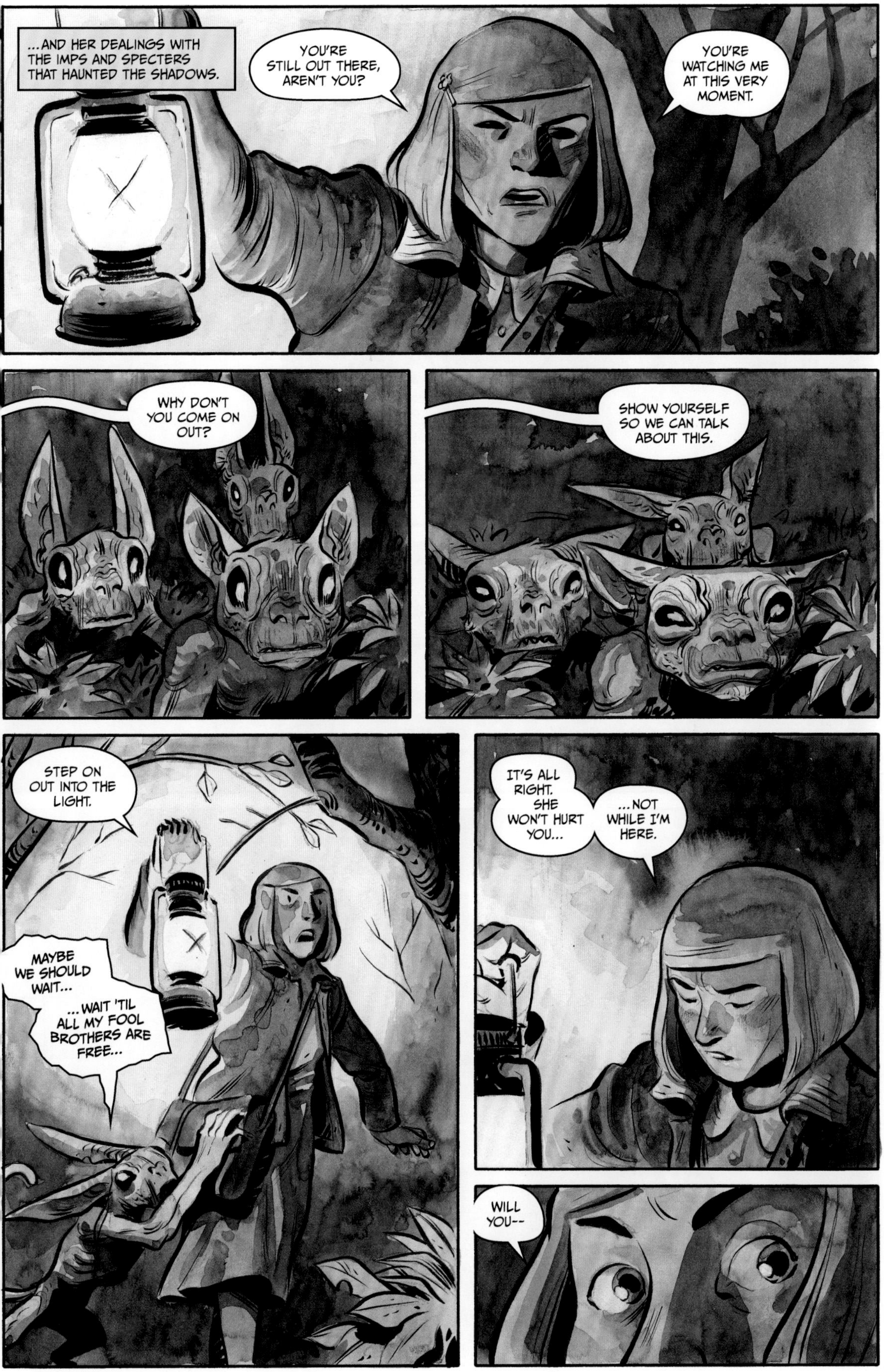
...AND HER DEALINGS WITH THE IMPS AND SPECTERS THAT HAUNTED THE SHADOWS.
YOU'RE STILL OUT THERE, AREN'T YOU?
YOU'RE WATCHING ME AT THIS VERY MOMENT.
WHY DON'T YOU COME ON OUT?
SHOW YOURSELF SO WE CAN TALK ABOUT THIS.
STEP ON OUT INTO THE LIGHT.
MAYBE WE SHOULD WAIT...
...WAIT 'TIL ALL MY FOOL BROTHERS ARE FREE...
IT'S ALL RIGHT. SHE WON'T HURT YOU...
...NOT WHILE I'M HERE.
WILL YOU--

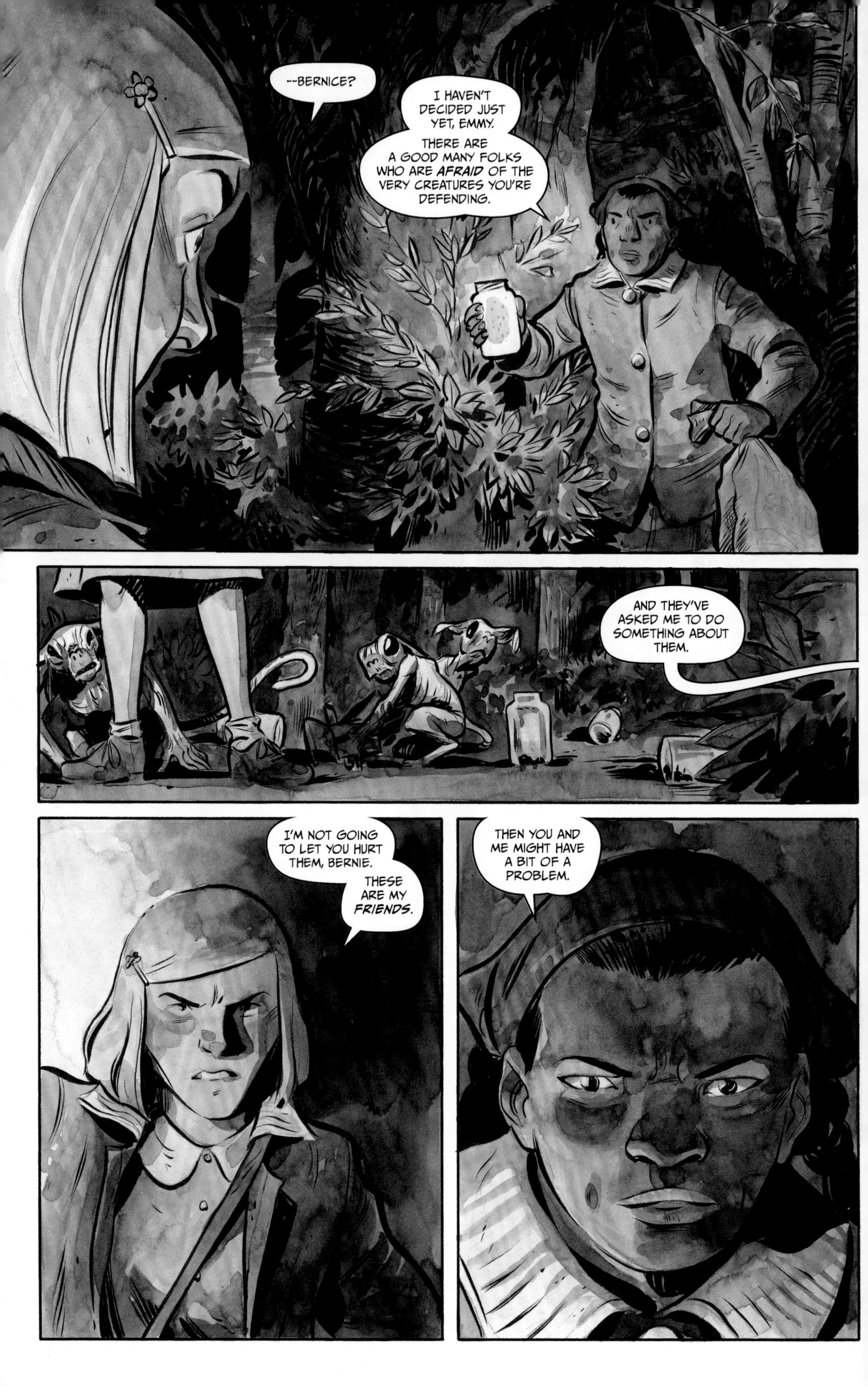
--BERNICE?
I HAVEN'T DECIDED JUST YET, EMMY.
THERE ARE A GOOD MANY FOLKS WHO ARE *AFRAID* OF THE VERY CREATURES YOU'RE DEFENDING.
AND THEY'VE ASKED ME TO DO SOMETHING ABOUT THEM.
I'M NOT GOING TO LET YOU HURT THEM, BERNIE.
THESE ARE MY *FRIENDS*.
THEN YOU AND ME MIGHT HAVE A BIT OF A PROBLEM.

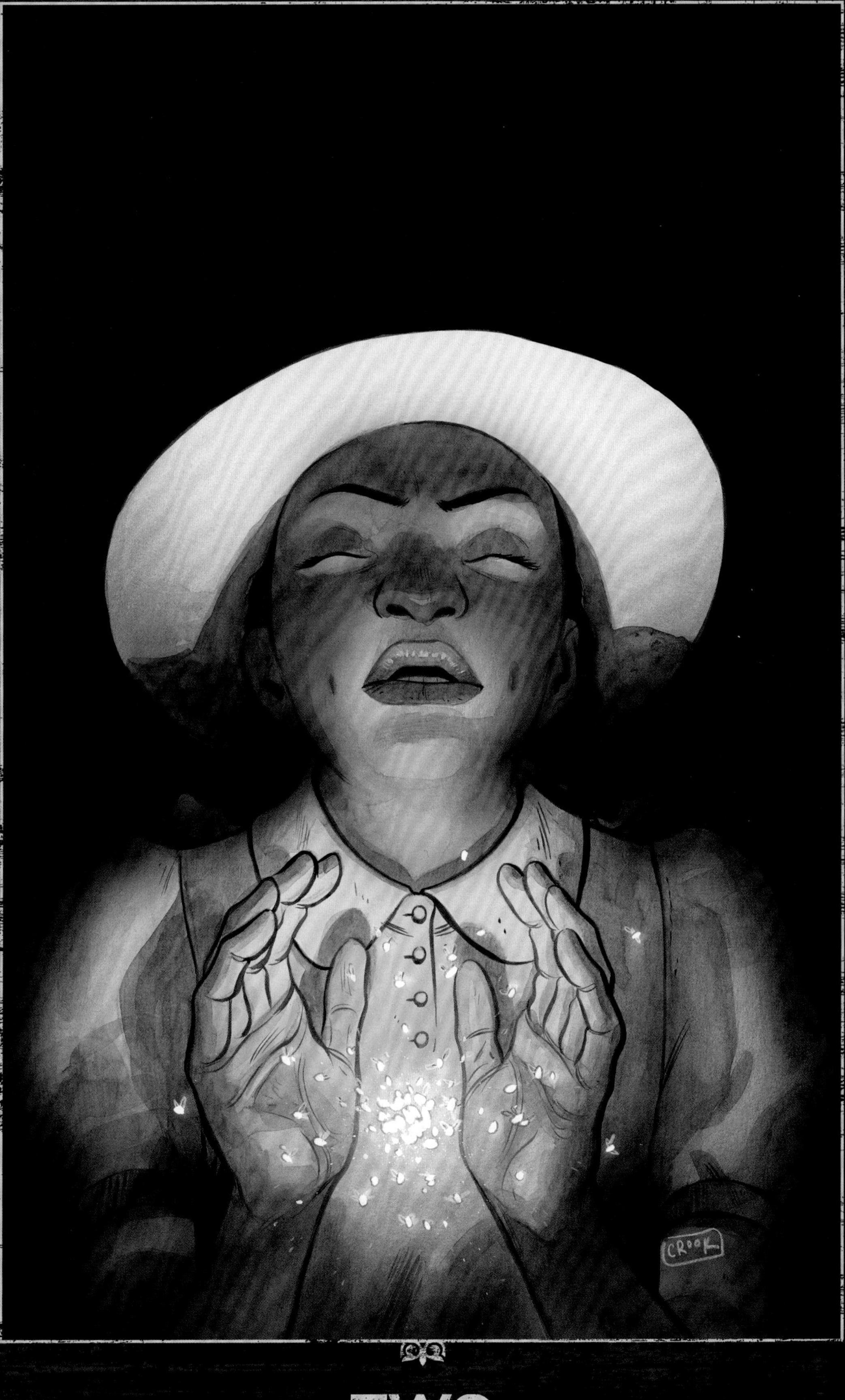
CROOK

TWO

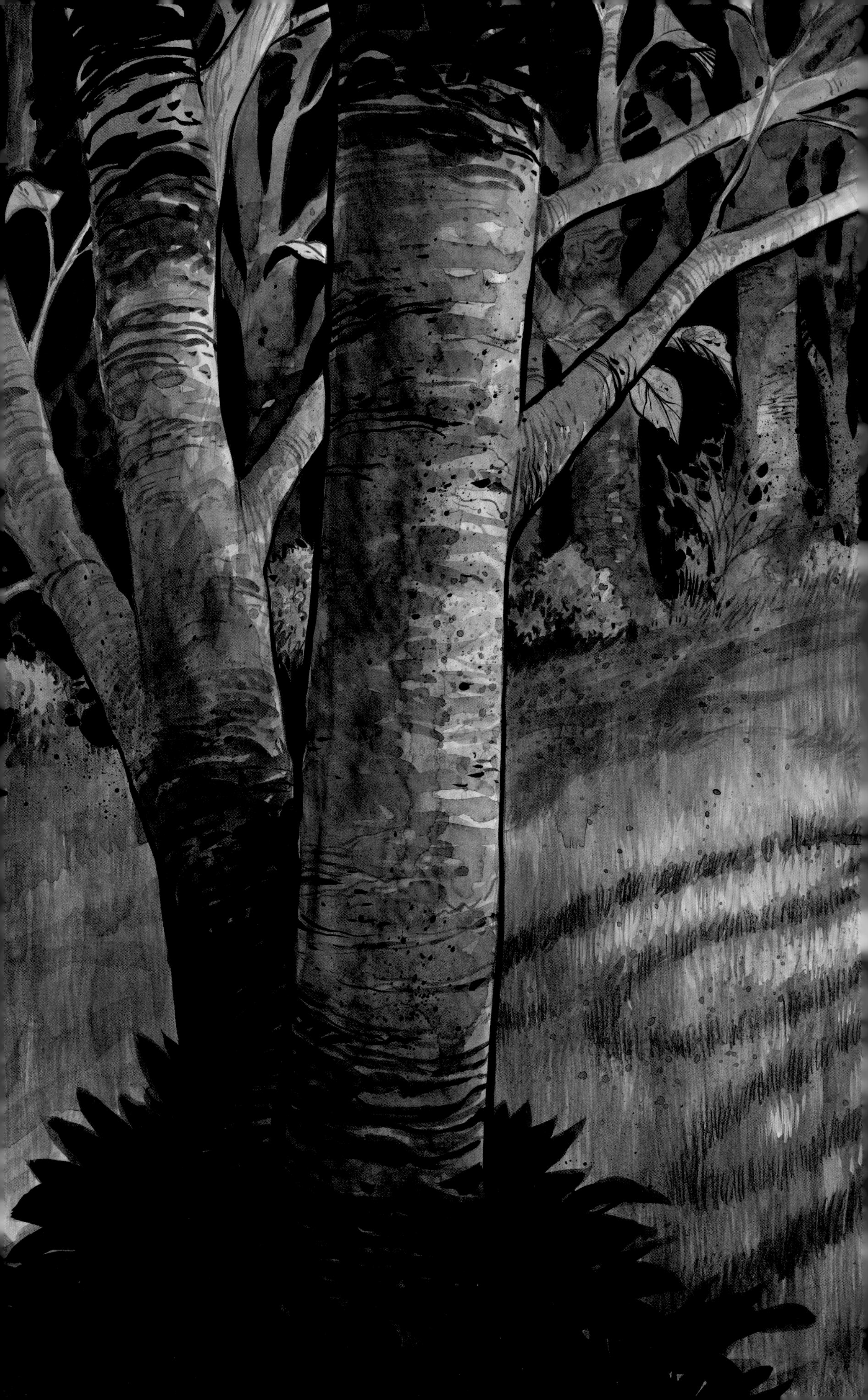

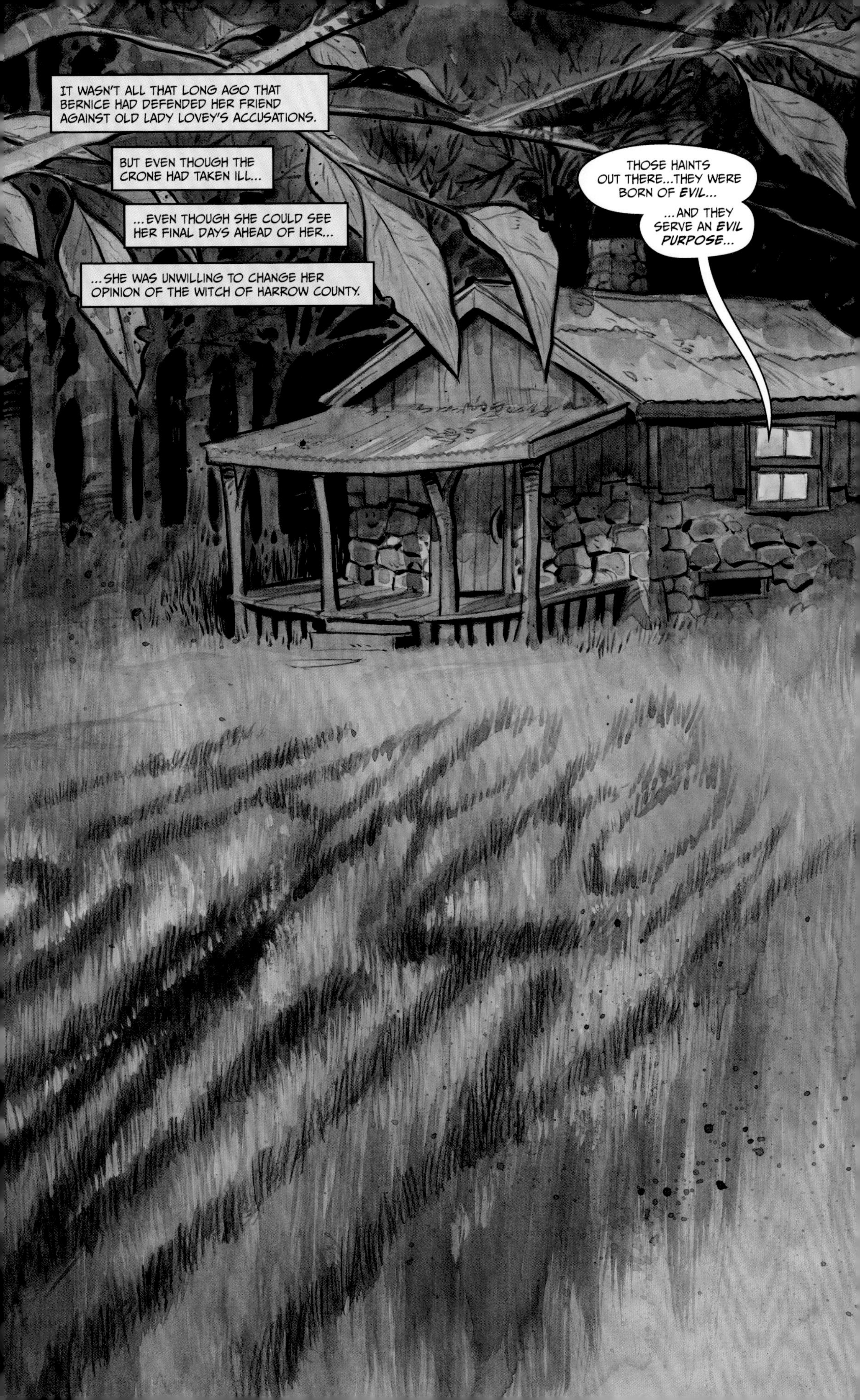
IT WASN'T ALL THAT LONG AGO THAT BERNICE HAD DEFENDED HER FRIEND AGAINST OLD LADY LOVEY'S ACCUSATIONS.
BUT EVEN THOUGH THE CRONE HAD TAKEN ILL...
...EVEN THOUGH SHE COULD SEE HER FINAL DAYS AHEAD OF HER...
...SHE WAS UNWILLING TO CHANGE HER OPINION OF THE WITCH OF HARROW COUNTY.
THOSE HAINTS OUT THERE...THEY WERE BORN OF *EVIL*...
...AND THEY SERVE AN *EVIL PURPOSE*...

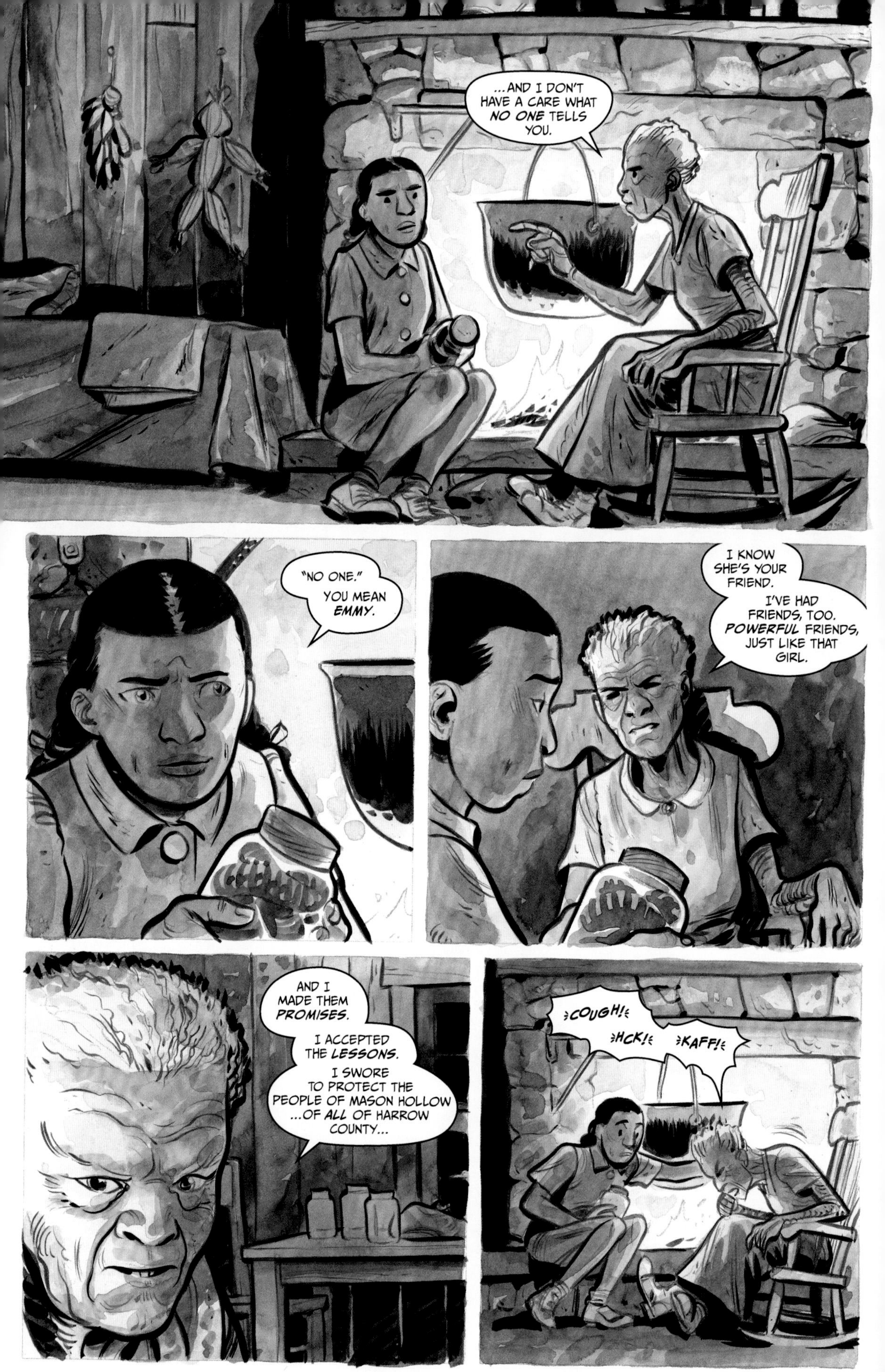
...AND I DON'T HAVE A CARE WHAT NO ONE TELLS YOU.
"NO ONE." YOU MEAN EMMY.
I KNOW SHE'S YOUR FRIEND.
I'VE HAD FRIENDS, TOO. POWERFUL FRIENDS, JUST LIKE THAT GIRL.
AND I MADE THEM PROMISES.
I ACCEPTED THE LESSONS.
I SWORE TO PROTECT THE PEOPLE OF MASON HOLLOW ...OF ALL OF HARROW COUNTY...
COUGH!
HCK!
KAFF!

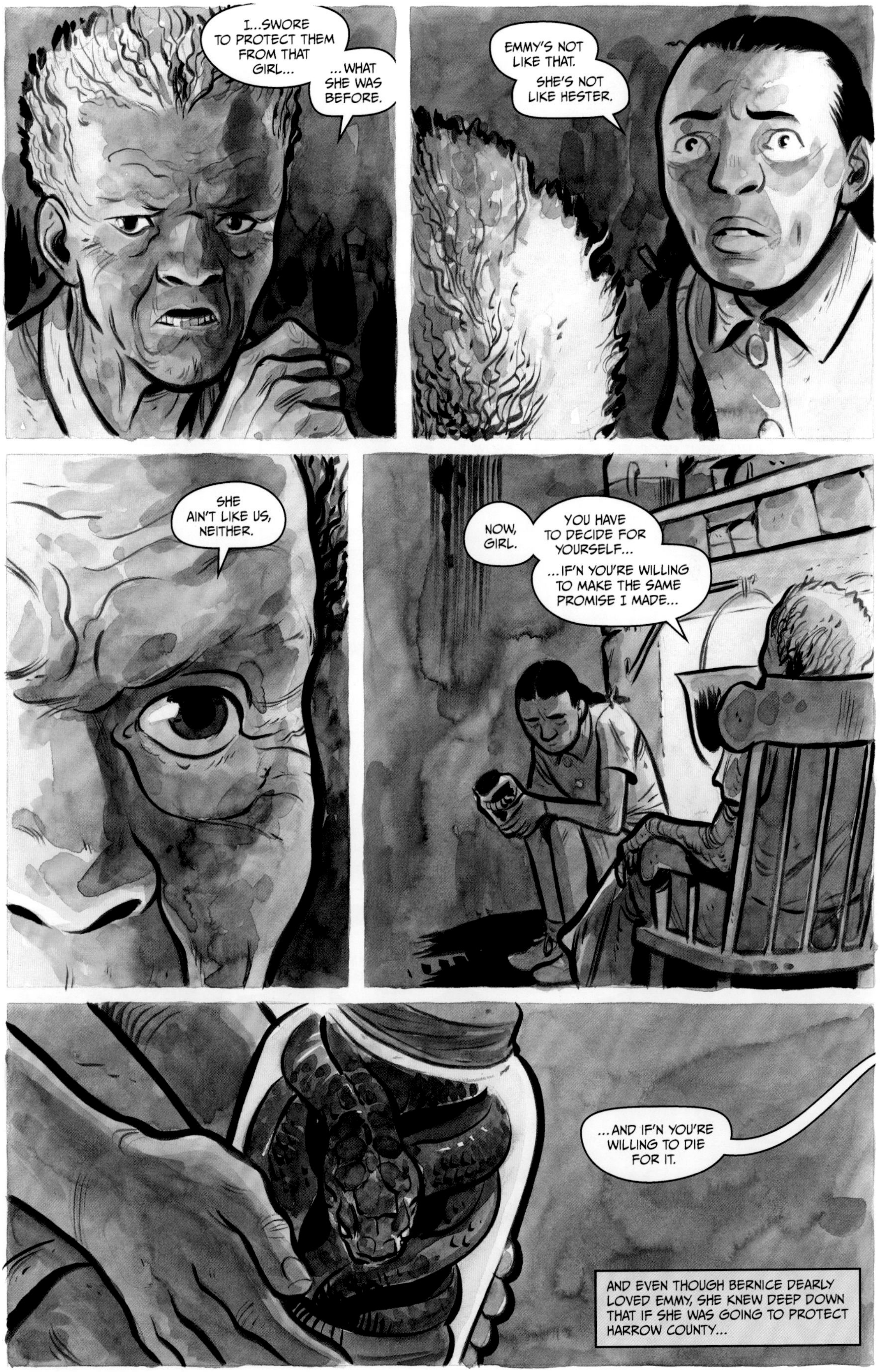
I...SWORE TO PROTECT THEM FROM THAT GIRL...
...WHAT SHE WAS BEFORE.
EMMY'S NOT LIKE THAT.
SHE'S NOT LIKE HESTER.
SHE AIN'T LIKE US, NEITHER.
NOW, GIRL.
YOU HAVE TO DECIDE FOR YOURSELF...
...IF'N YOU'RE WILLING TO MAKE THE SAME PROMISE I MADE...
...AND IF'N YOU'RE WILLING TO DIE FOR IT.
AND EVEN THOUGH BERNICE DEARLY LOVED EMMY, SHE KNEW DEEP DOWN THAT IF SHE WAS GOING TO PROTECT HARROW COUNTY...

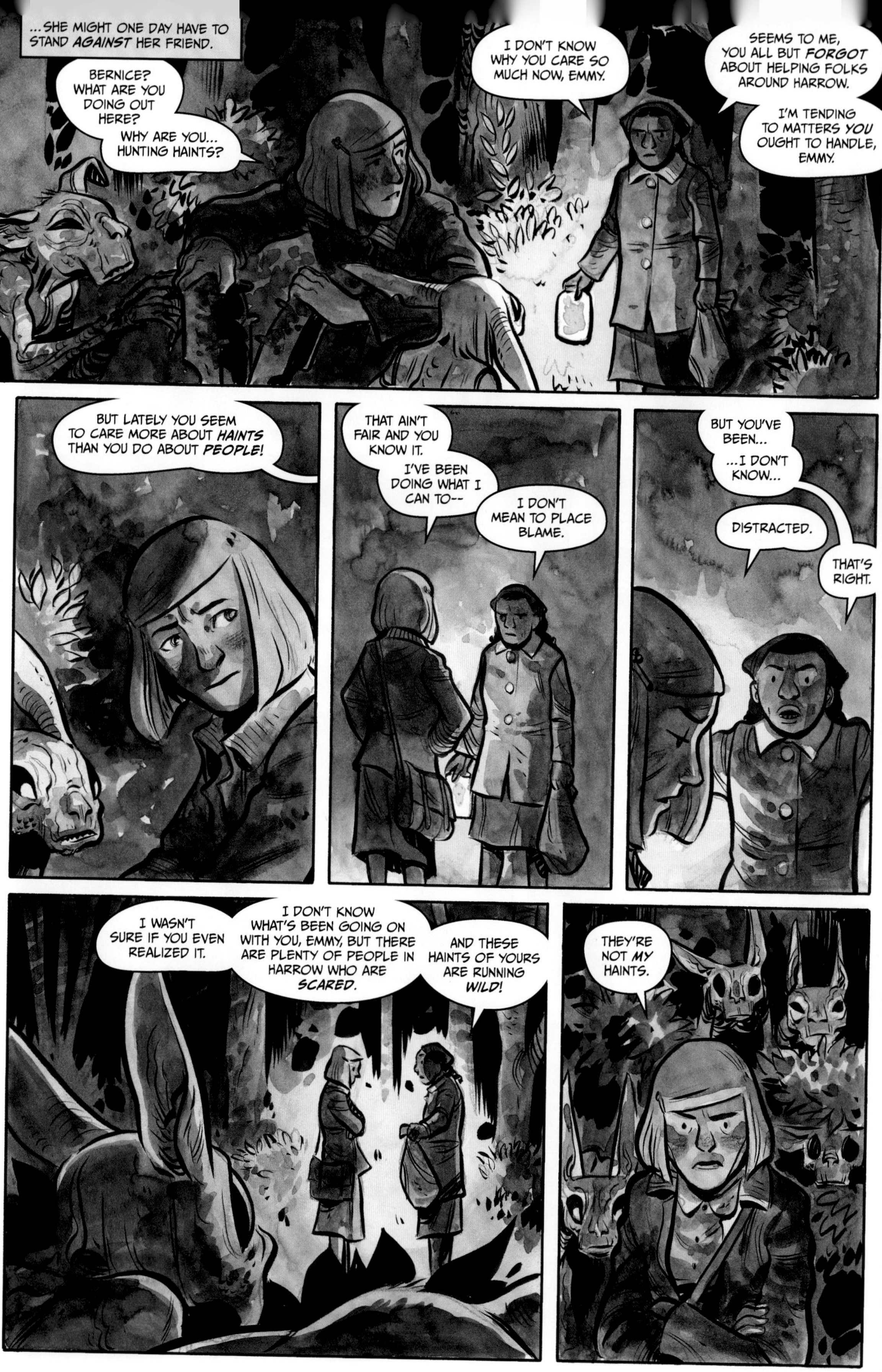
...SHE MIGHT ONE DAY HAVE TO STAND AGAINST HER FRIEND.
BERNICE? WHAT ARE YOU DOING OUT HERE?
WHY ARE YOU... HUNTING HAINTS?
I DON'T KNOW WHY YOU CARE SO MUCH NOW, EMMY.
SEEMS TO ME, YOU ALL BUT FORGOT ABOUT HELPING FOLKS AROUND HARROW.
I'M TENDING TO MATTERS YOU OUGHT TO HANDLE, EMMY.
BUT LATELY YOU SEEM TO CARE MORE ABOUT HAINTS THAN YOU DO ABOUT PEOPLE!
THAT AIN'T FAIR AND YOU KNOW IT.
I'VE BEEN DOING WHAT I CAN TO--
I DON'T MEAN TO PLACE BLAME.
BUT YOU'VE BEEN...
...I DON'T KNOW...
DISTRACTED.
THAT'S RIGHT.
I WASN'T SURE IF YOU EVEN REALIZED IT.
I DON'T KNOW WHAT'S BEEN GOING ON WITH YOU, EMMY, BUT THERE ARE PLENTY OF PEOPLE IN HARROW WHO ARE SCARED.
AND THESE HAINTS OF YOURS ARE RUNNING WILD!
THEY'RE NOT MY HAINTS.

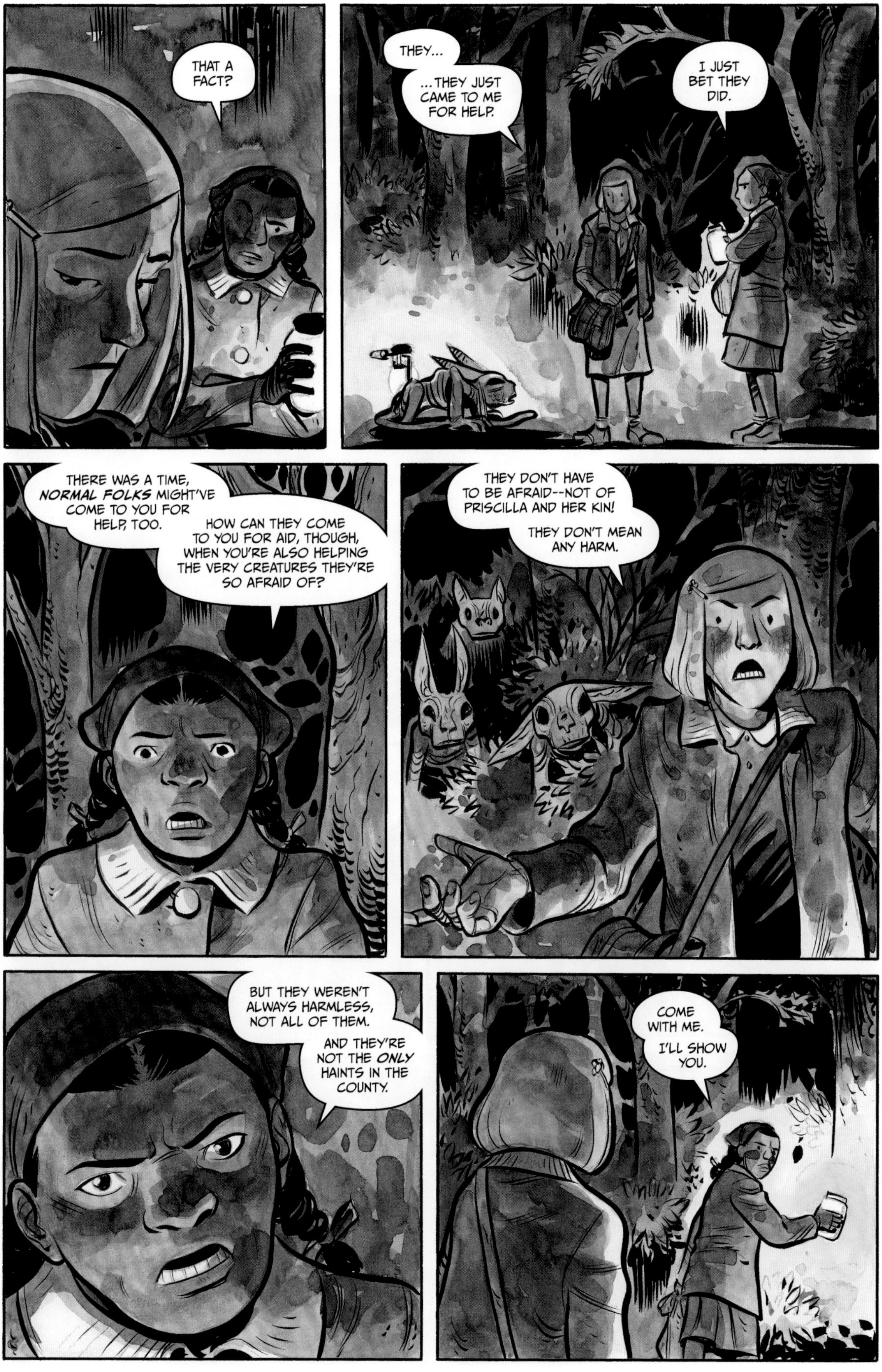
THAT A FACT?
THEY...
...THEY JUST CAME TO ME FOR HELP.
I JUST BET THEY DID.
THERE WAS A TIME, NORMAL FOLKS MIGHT'VE COME TO YOU FOR HELP, TOO.
HOW CAN THEY COME TO YOU FOR AID, THOUGH, WHEN YOU'RE ALSO HELPING THE VERY CREATURES THEY'RE SO AFRAID OF?
THEY DON'T HAVE TO BE AFRAID--NOT OF PRISCILLA AND HER KIN!
THEY DON'T MEAN ANY HARM.
BUT THEY WEREN'T ALWAYS HARMLESS, NOT ALL OF THEM.
AND THEY'RE NOT THE ONLY HAINTS IN THE COUNTY.
COME WITH ME.
I'LL SHOW YOU.

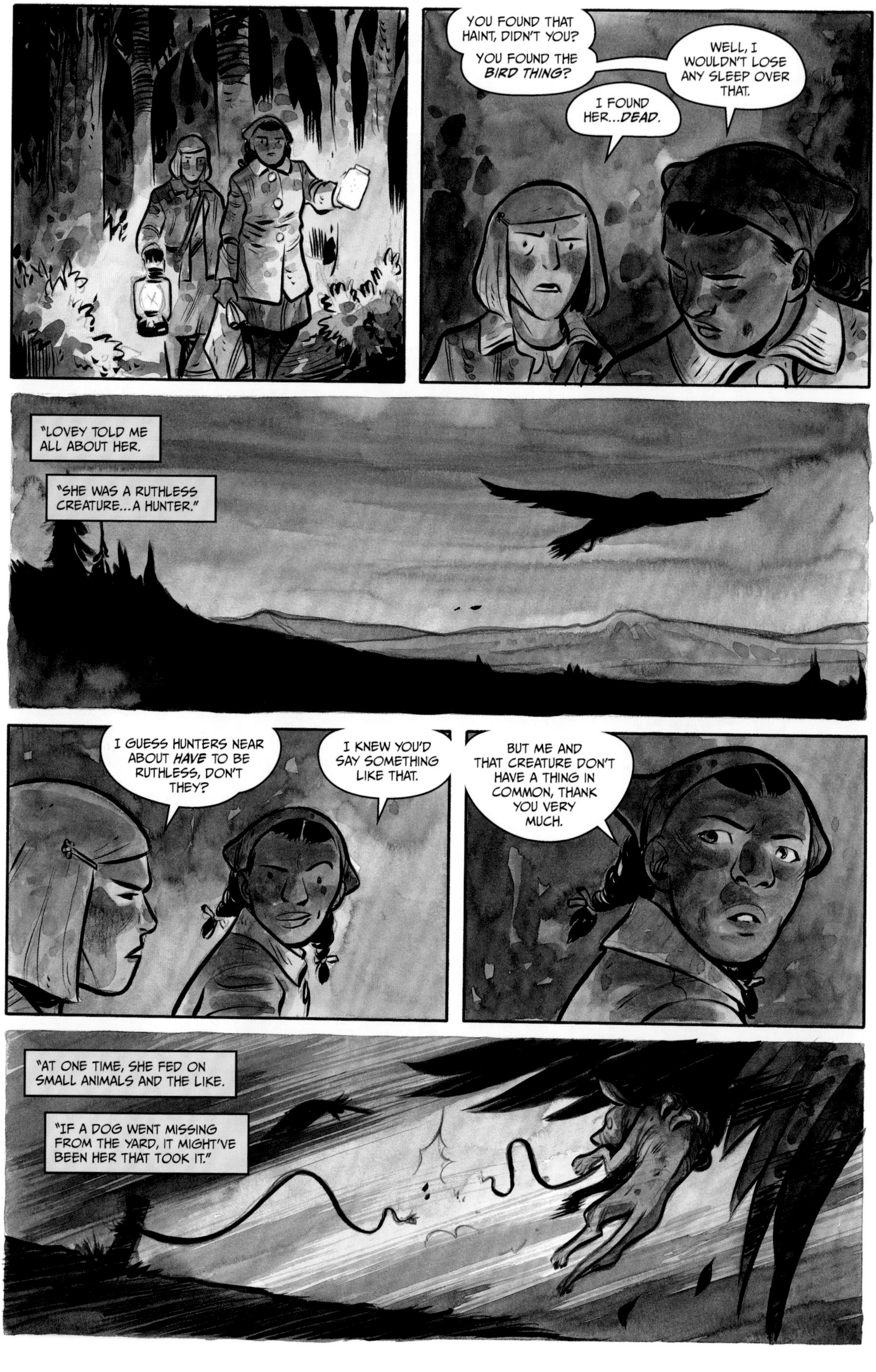
YOU FOUND THAT HAINT, DIDN'T YOU?
YOU FOUND THE *BIRD THING*?
I FOUND HER...*DEAD*.
WELL, I WOULDN'T LOSE ANY SLEEP OVER THAT.
"LOVEY TOLD ME ALL ABOUT HER.
"SHE WAS A RUTHLESS CREATURE...A HUNTER."
I GUESS HUNTERS NEAR ABOUT *HAVE* TO BE RUTHLESS, DON'T THEY?
I KNEW YOU'D SAY SOMETHING LIKE THAT.
BUT ME AND THAT CREATURE DON'T HAVE A THING IN COMMON, THANK YOU VERY MUCH.
"AT ONE TIME, SHE FED ON SMALL ANIMALS AND THE LIKE.
"IF A DOG WENT MISSING FROM THE YARD, IT MIGHT'VE BEEN HER THAT TOOK IT."

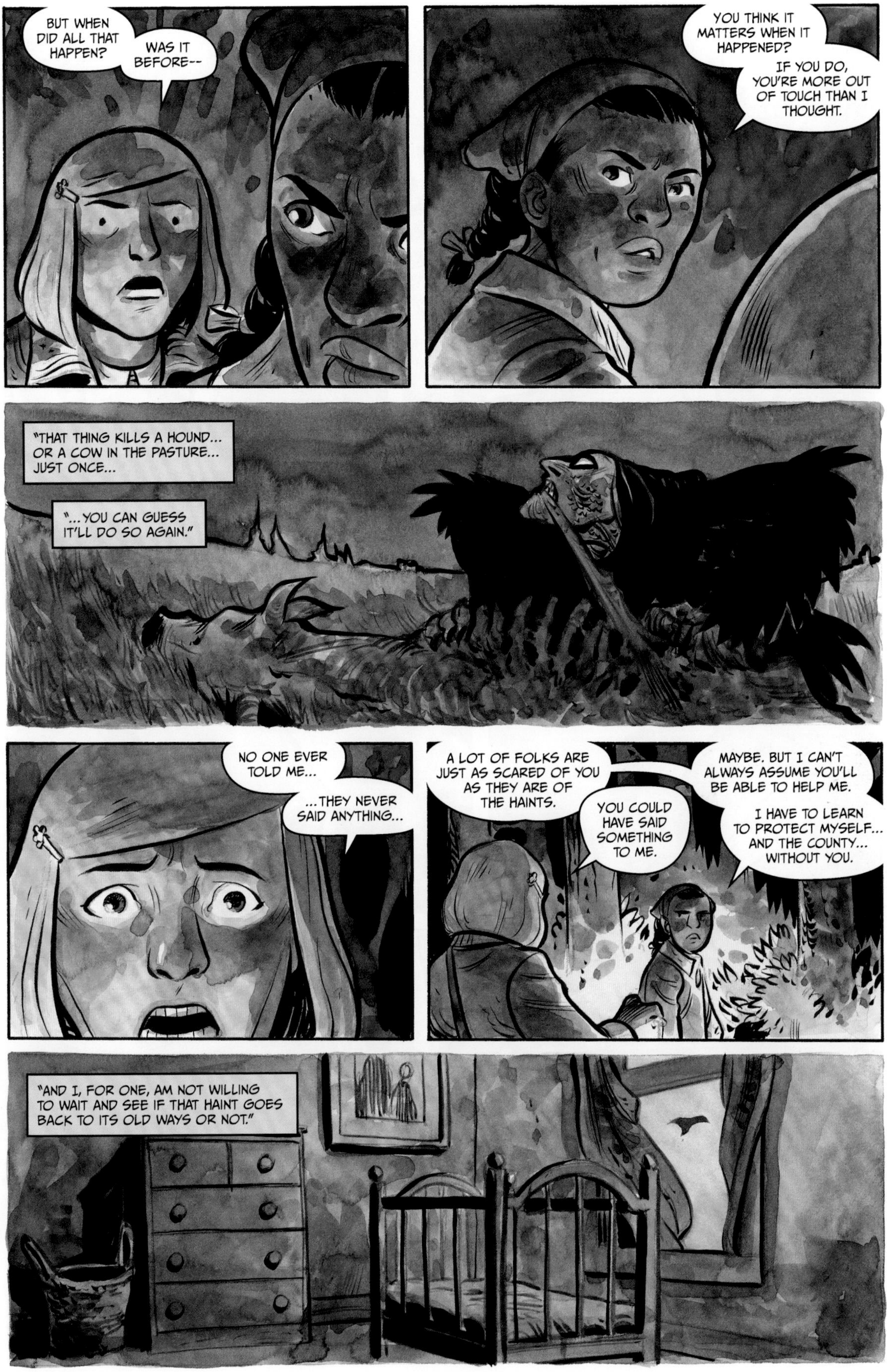
BUT WHEN DID ALL THAT HAPPEN?
WAS IT BEFORE--
YOU THINK IT MATTERS WHEN IT HAPPENED?
IF YOU DO, YOU'RE MORE OUT OF TOUCH THAN I THOUGHT.
"THAT THING KILLS A HOUND... OR A COW IN THE PASTURE... JUST ONCE...
"...YOU CAN GUESS IT'LL DO SO AGAIN."
NO ONE EVER TOLD ME...
...THEY NEVER SAID ANYTHING...
A LOT OF FOLKS ARE JUST AS SCARED OF YOU AS THEY ARE OF THE HAINTS.
YOU COULD HAVE SAID SOMETHING TO ME.
MAYBE. BUT I CAN'T ALWAYS ASSUME YOU'LL BE ABLE TO HELP ME.
I HAVE TO LEARN TO PROTECT MYSELF... AND THE COUNTY... WITHOUT YOU.
"AND I, FOR ONE, AM NOT WILLING TO WAIT AND SEE IF THAT HAINT GOES BACK TO ITS OLD WAYS OR NOT."

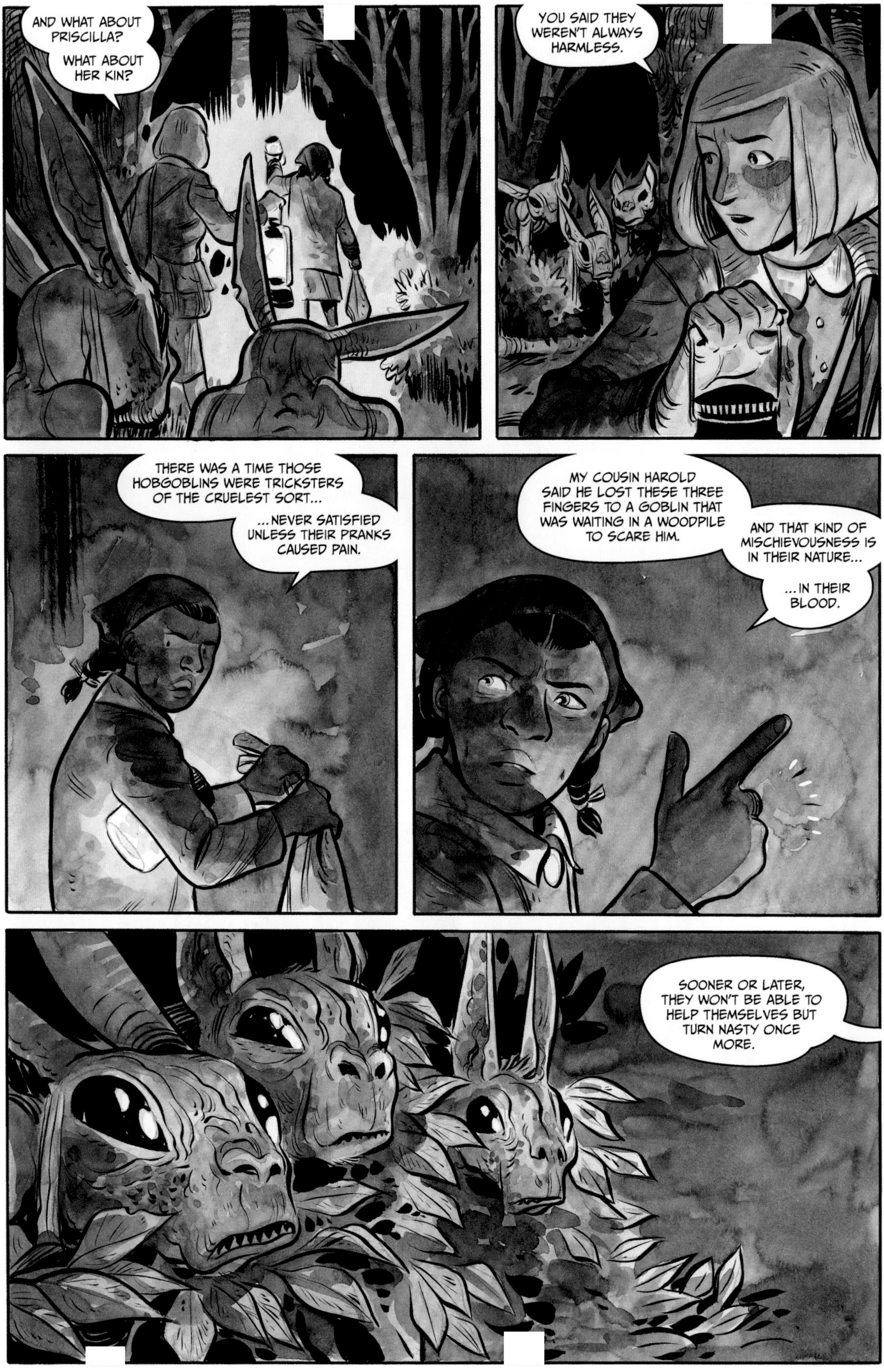
AND WHAT ABOUT PRISCILLA?
WHAT ABOUT HER KIN?
YOU SAID THEY WEREN'T ALWAYS HARMLESS.
THERE WAS A TIME THOSE HOBGOBLINS WERE TRICKSTERS OF THE CRUELEST SORT...
...NEVER SATISFIED UNLESS THEIR PRANKS CAUSED PAIN.
MY COUSIN HAROLD SAID HE LOST THESE THREE FINGERS TO A GOBLIN THAT WAS WAITING IN A WOODPILE TO SCARE HIM.
AND THAT KIND OF MISCHIEVOUSNESS IS IN THEIR NATURE...
...IN THEIR BLOOD.
SOONER OR LATER, THEY WON'T BE ABLE TO HELP THEMSELVES BUT TURN NASTY ONCE MORE.

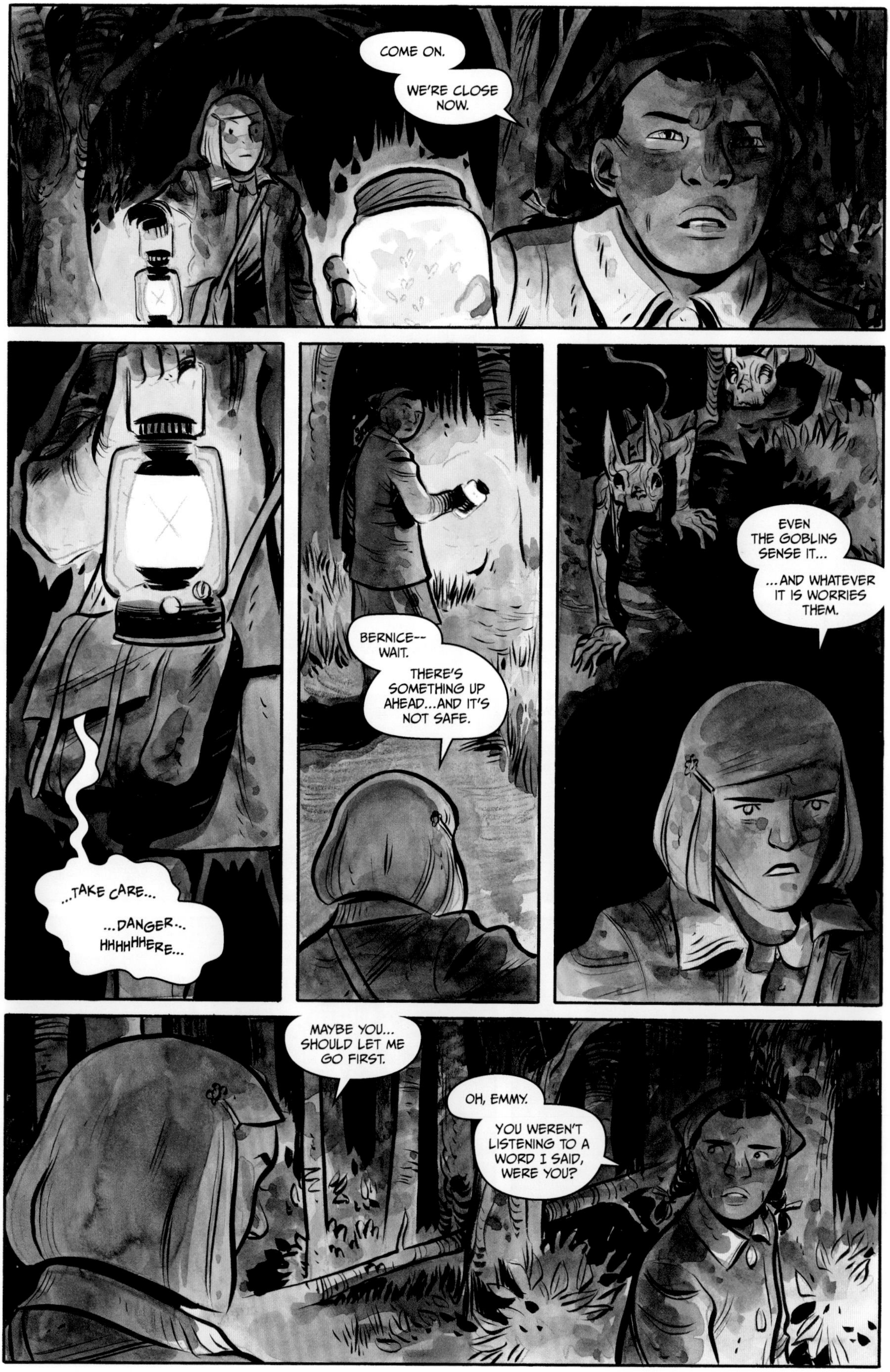
COME ON.
WE'RE CLOSE NOW.
...TAKE CARE... ...DANGER... HHHHHHERE...
BERNICE-- WAIT.
THERE'S SOMETHING UP AHEAD...AND IT'S NOT SAFE.
EVEN THE GOBLINS SENSE IT...
...AND WHATEVER IT IS WORRIES THEM.
MAYBE YOU... SHOULD LET ME GO FIRST.
OH, EMMY.
YOU WEREN'T LISTENING TO A WORD I SAID, WERE YOU?

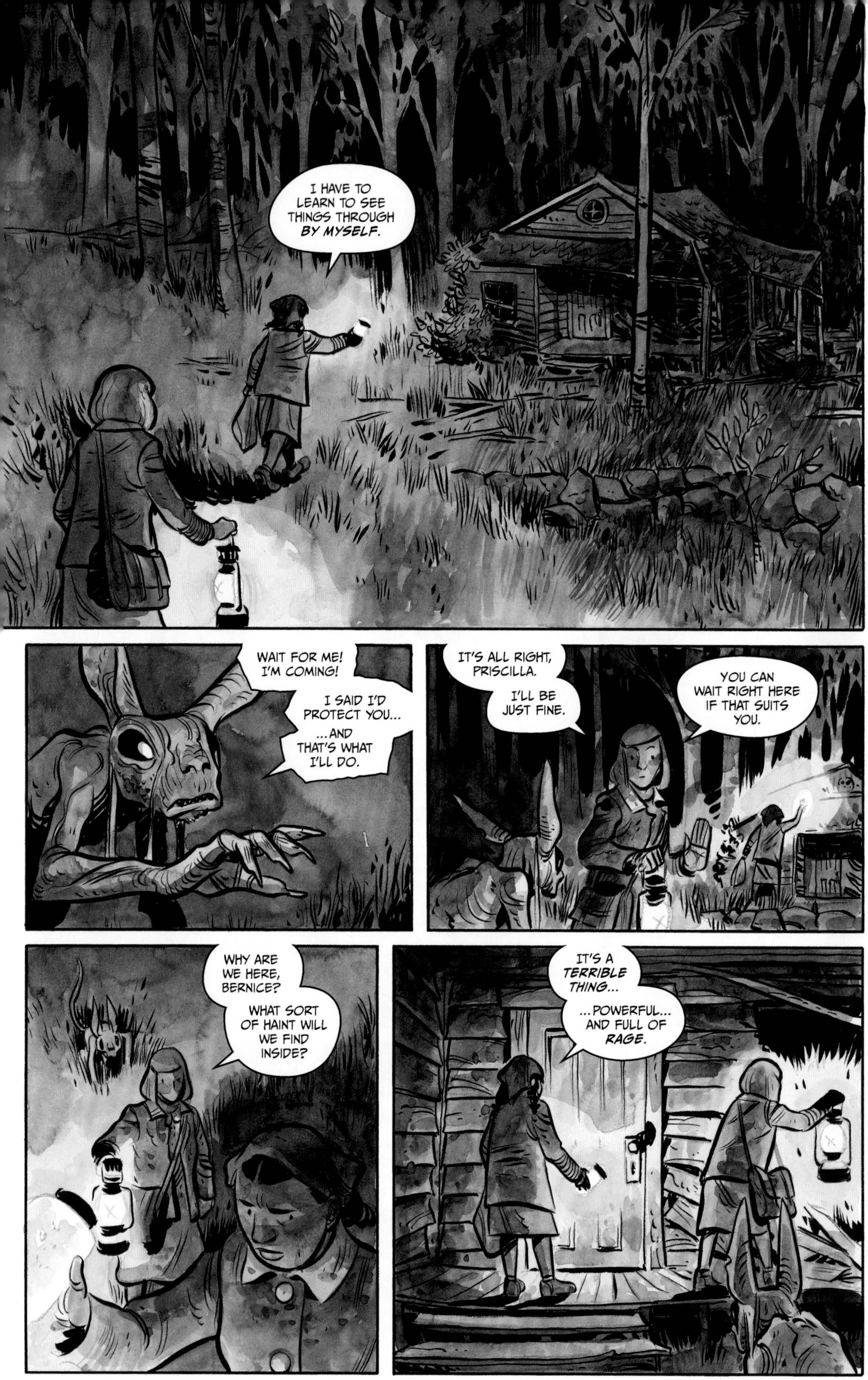
I HAVE TO LEARN TO SEE THINGS THROUGH *BY MYSELF*.
WAIT FOR ME! I'M COMING!
I SAID I'D PROTECT YOU...
...AND THAT'S WHAT I'LL DO.
IT'S ALL RIGHT, PRISCILLA.
I'LL BE JUST FINE.
YOU CAN WAIT RIGHT HERE IF THAT SUITS YOU.
WHY ARE WE HERE, BERNICE?
WHAT SORT OF HAINT WILL WE FIND INSIDE?
IT'S A *TERRIBLE THING*...
...POWERFUL... AND FULL OF *RAGE*.

IT'S TRAPPED INSIDE... BUT WHO KNOWS FOR HOW LONG?

THIS HOUSE IS CRUMBLING TO DUST, MORE AND MORE EVERY DAY...AND THEN IT WILL BE FREE.

I'M NOT SO SURE, BERNICE.

I DON'T SEE ANYTHING.

LOOK AGAIN.

LOOK THROUGH THIS KEYHOLE HERE.

TELL ME WHAT YOU SEE.

I SEE...

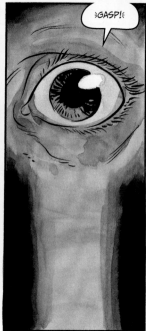

≒GASP!≒

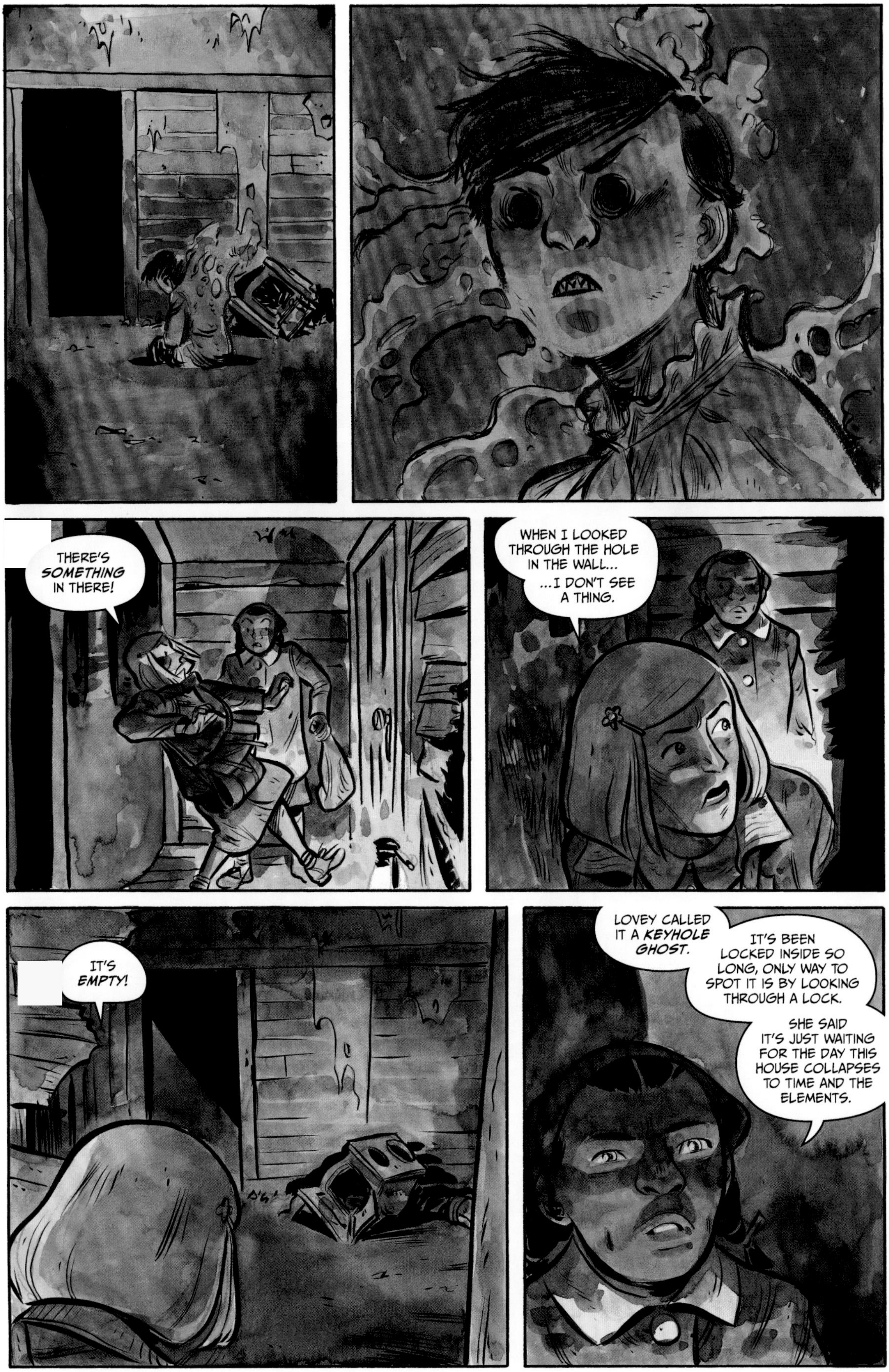
THERE'S SOMETHING IN THERE!
WHEN I LOOKED THROUGH THE HOLE IN THE WALL...
...I DON'T SEE A THING.
IT'S EMPTY!
LOVEY CALLED IT A KEYHOLE GHOST.
IT'S BEEN LOCKED INSIDE SO LONG, ONLY WAY TO SPOT IT IS BY LOOKING THROUGH A LOCK.
SHE SAID IT'S JUST WAITING FOR THE DAY THIS HOUSE COLLAPSES TO TIME AND THE ELEMENTS.

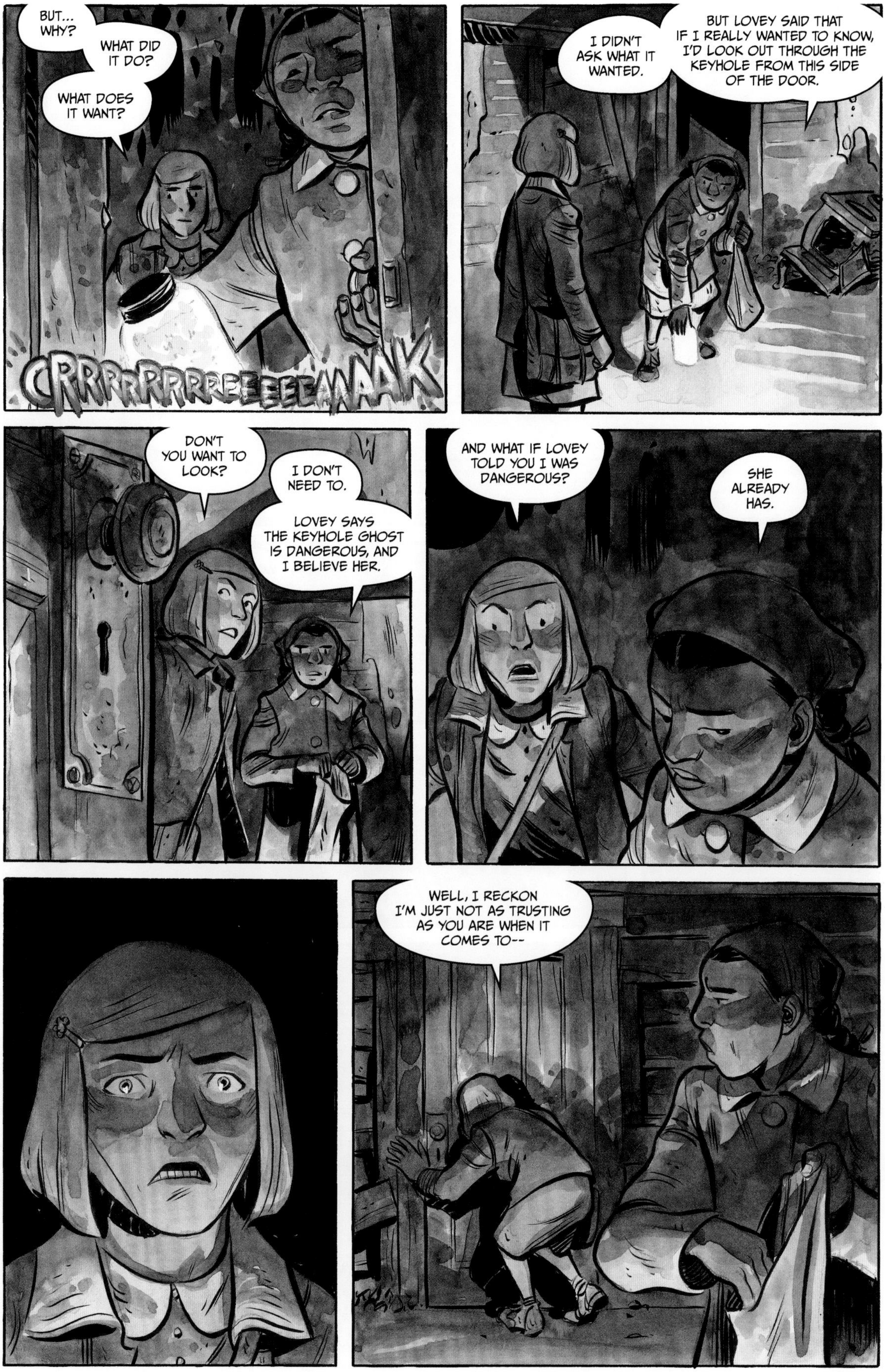
BUT... WHY?
WHAT DID IT DO?
WHAT DOES IT WANT?
CRRRRRRRRREEEEEEAAAAK
I DIDN'T ASK WHAT IT WANTED.
BUT LOVEY SAID THAT IF I REALLY WANTED TO KNOW, I'D LOOK OUT THROUGH THE KEYHOLE FROM THIS SIDE OF THE DOOR.
DON'T YOU WANT TO LOOK?
I DON'T NEED TO.
LOVEY SAYS THE KEYHOLE GHOST IS DANGEROUS, AND I BELIEVE HER.
AND WHAT IF LOVEY TOLD YOU I WAS DANGEROUS?
SHE ALREADY HAS.
WELL, I RECKON I'M JUST NOT AS TRUSTING AS YOU ARE WHEN IT COMES TO--

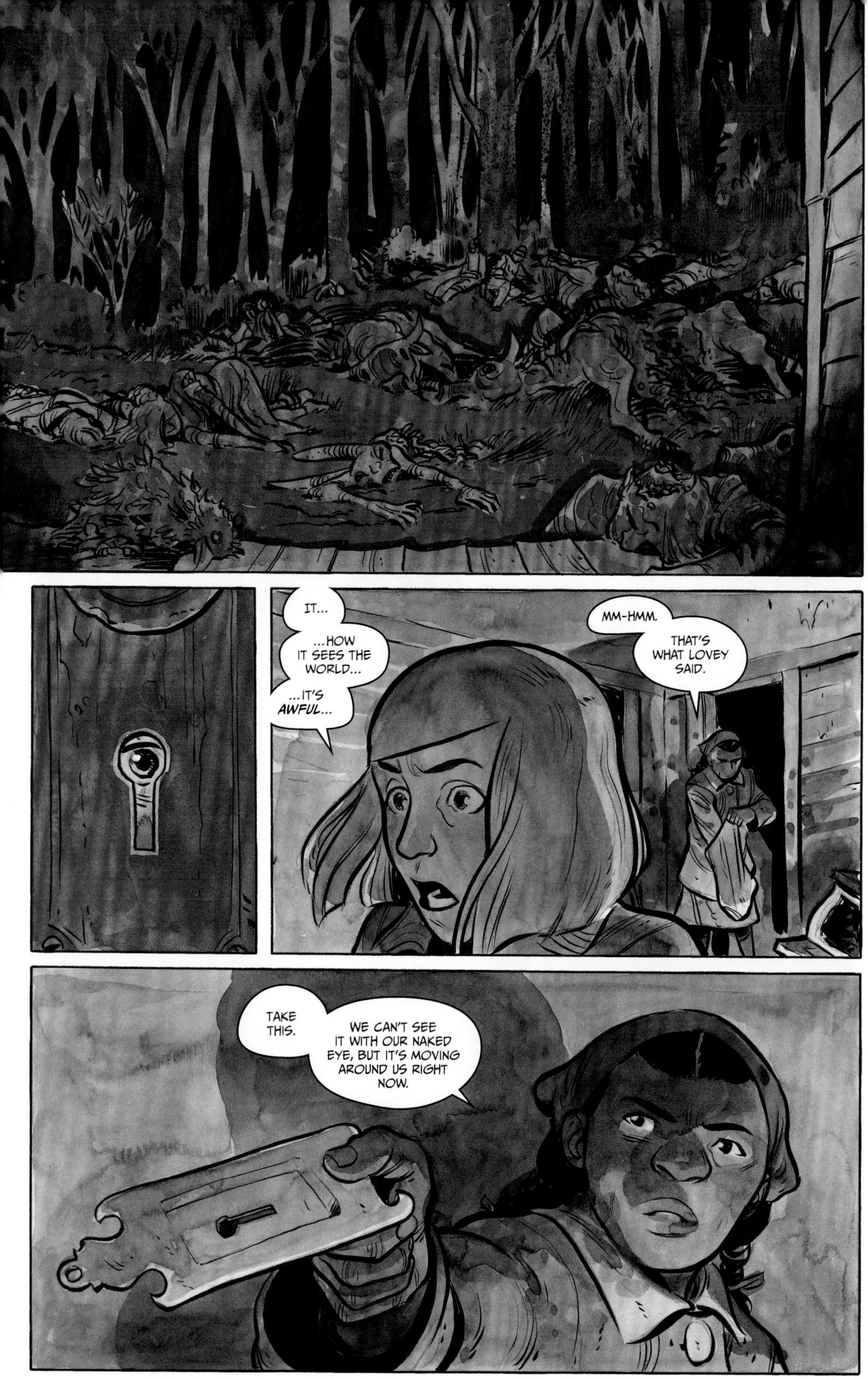
IT...
...HOW IT SEES THE WORLD...
...IT'S *AWFUL*...
MM-HMM.
THAT'S WHAT LOVEY SAID.
TAKE THIS.
WE CAN'T SEE IT WITH OUR NAKED EYE, BUT IT'S MOVING AROUND US RIGHT NOW.

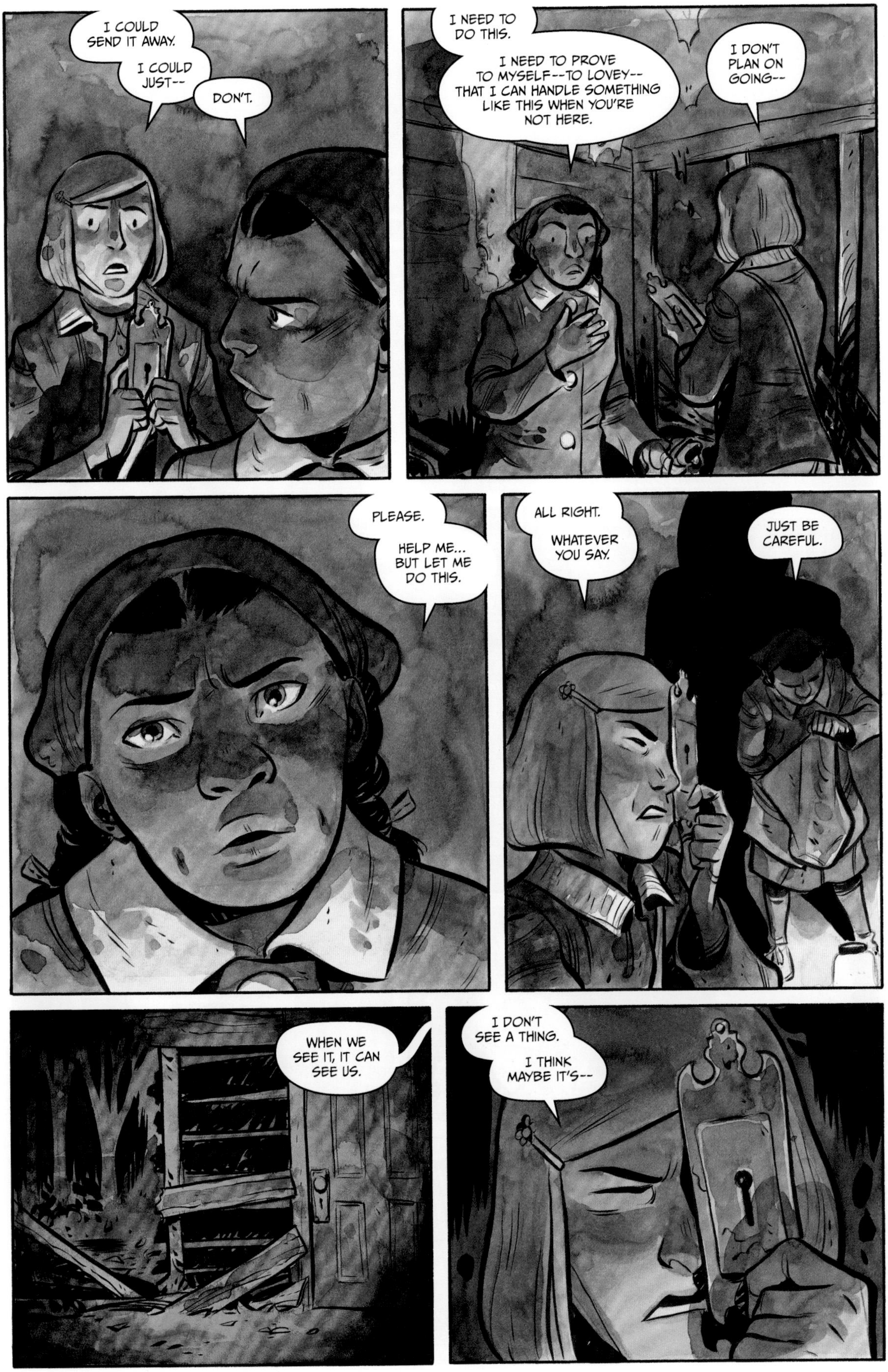
I COULD SEND IT AWAY.
I COULD JUST--
DON'T.
I NEED TO DO THIS.
I NEED TO PROVE TO MYSELF--TO LOVEY--THAT I CAN HANDLE SOMETHING LIKE THIS WHEN YOU'RE NOT HERE.
I DON'T PLAN ON GOING--
PLEASE.
HELP ME... BUT LET ME DO THIS.
ALL RIGHT.
WHATEVER YOU SAY.
JUST BE CAREFUL.
WHEN WE SEE IT, IT CAN SEE US.
I DON'T SEE A THING.
I THINK MAYBE IT'S--

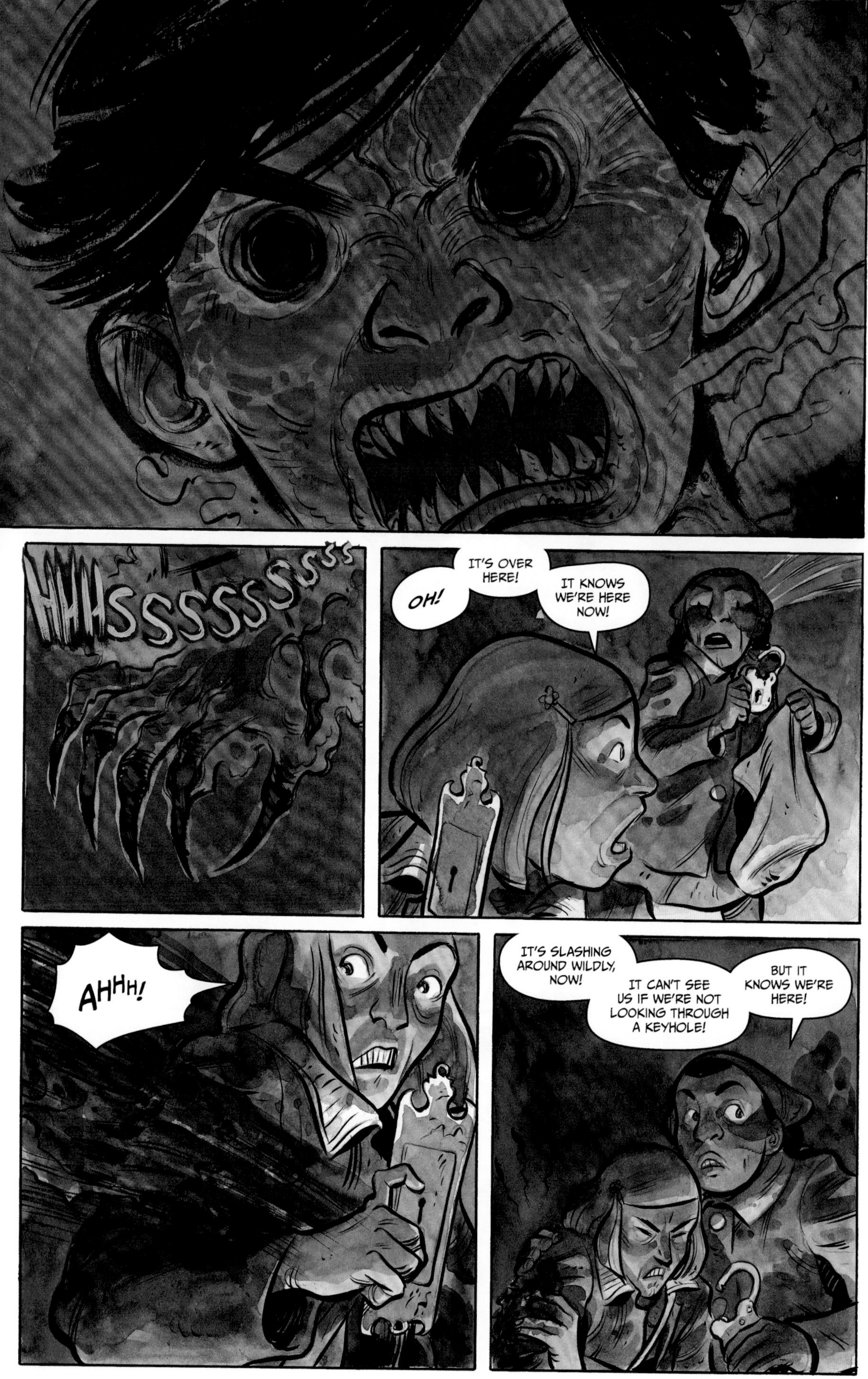
HHHSSSSSSSSSS
IT'S OVER HERE!
OH!
IT KNOWS WE'RE HERE NOW!
AHHH!
IT'S SLASHING AROUND WILDLY, NOW!
IT CAN'T SEE US IF WE'RE NOT LOOKING THROUGH A KEYHOLE!
BUT IT KNOWS WE'RE HERE!

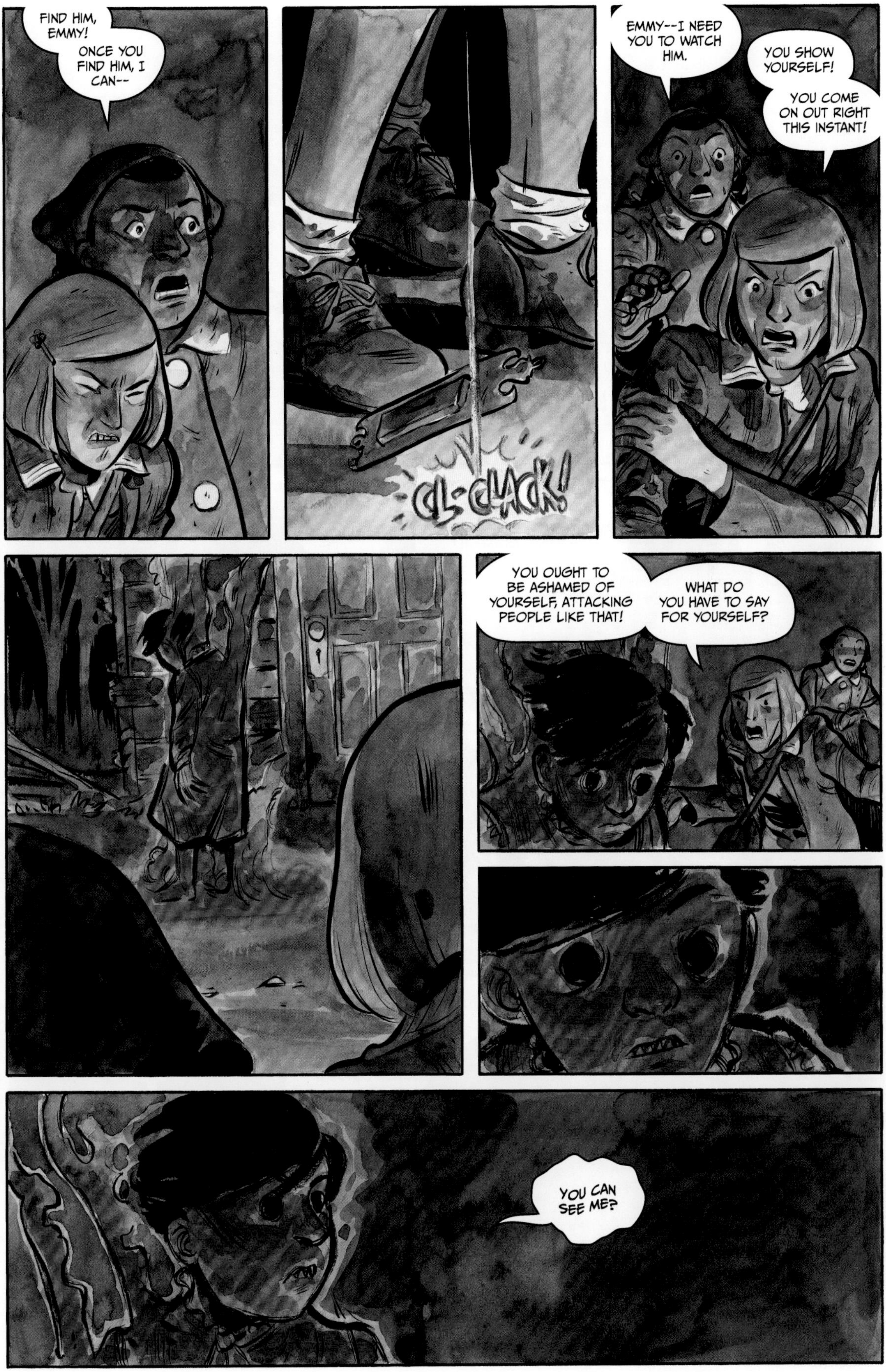
FIND HIM, EMMY!
ONCE YOU FIND HIM, I CAN--
CL-CLACK!
EMMY--I NEED YOU TO WATCH HIM.
YOU SHOW YOURSELF!
YOU COME ON OUT RIGHT THIS INSTANT!
YOU OUGHT TO BE ASHAMED OF YOURSELF, ATTACKING PEOPLE LIKE THAT!
WHAT DO YOU HAVE TO SAY FOR YOURSELF?
YOU CAN SEE ME?

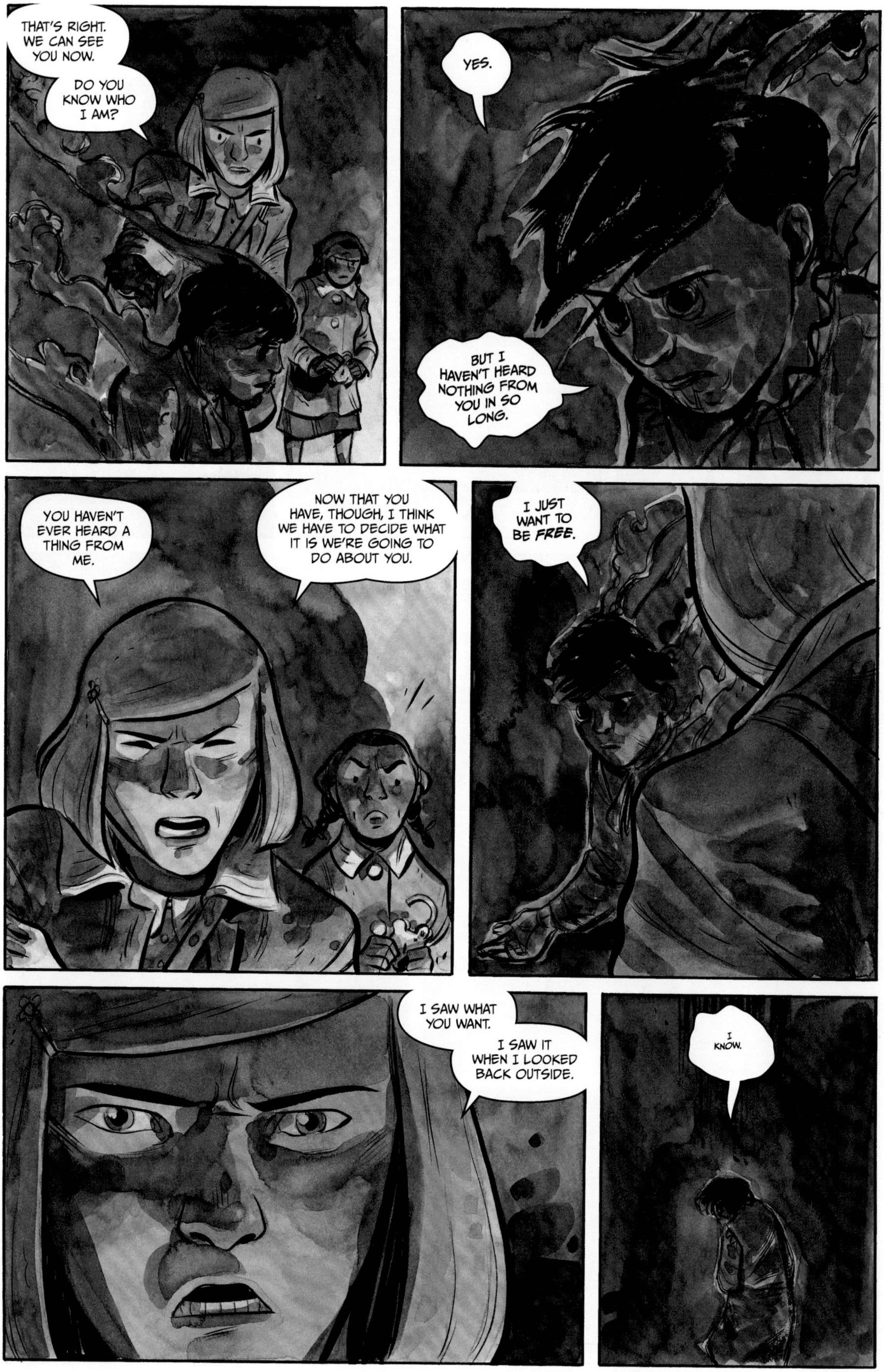
THAT'S RIGHT. WE CAN SEE YOU NOW.
DO YOU KNOW WHO I AM?
YES.
BUT I HAVEN'T HEARD NOTHING FROM YOU IN SO LONG.
YOU HAVEN'T EVER HEARD A THING FROM ME.
NOW THAT YOU HAVE, THOUGH, I THINK WE HAVE TO DECIDE WHAT IT IS WE'RE GOING TO DO ABOUT YOU.
I JUST WANT TO BE FREE.
I SAW WHAT YOU WANT.
I SAW IT WHEN I LOOKED BACK OUTSIDE.
I KNOW.

ALL RIGHT, THEN.

YOU MUST ALSO KNOW THAT I CAN'T ALLOW SOMETHING LIKE THAT TO COME TO PASS.

YOU'RE PLANNING ON HURTING PEOPLE.

YOU'VE GOT AN ILL INTENT FOR THE WORLD.

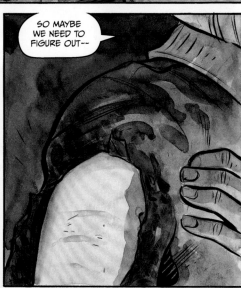

SO MAYBE WE NEED TO FIGURE OUT--

THERE AIN'T NOTHING TO FIGURE OUT.

THERE'S NO PLACE FOR A CREATURE LIKE THIS OUT IN THE WORLD.

YOU DON'T BELONG AMONG THE NATURAL WORLD.

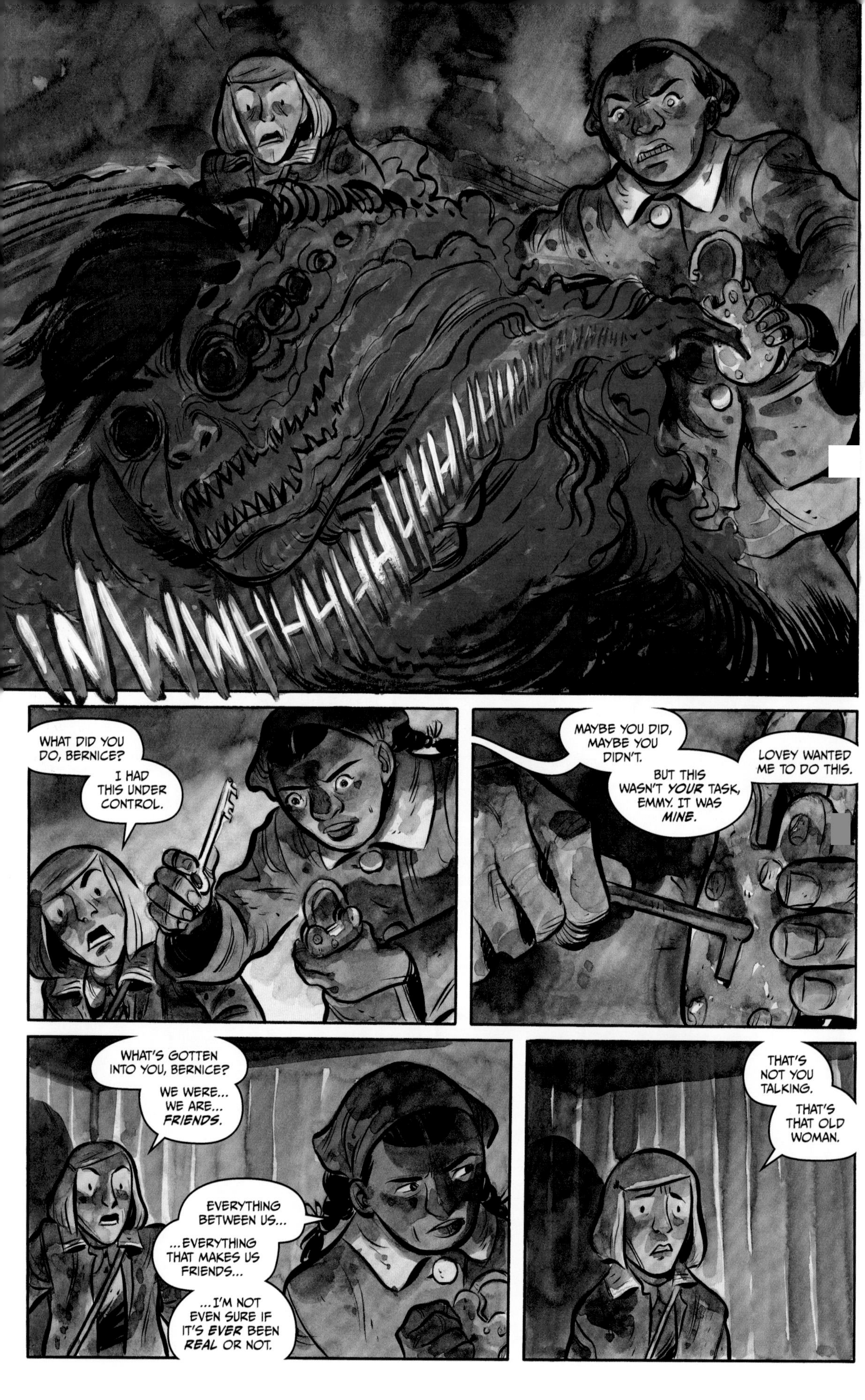
WWWHHHHHHHHHHHHHHHHHHHHH
WHAT DID YOU DO, BERNICE?
I HAD THIS UNDER CONTROL.
MAYBE YOU DID, MAYBE YOU DIDN'T.
BUT THIS WASN'T *YOUR* TASK, EMMY. IT WAS *MINE*.
LOVEY WANTED ME TO DO THIS.
WHAT'S GOTTEN INTO YOU, BERNICE?
WE WERE... WE ARE... *FRIENDS*.
EVERYTHING BETWEEN US...
...EVERYTHING THAT MAKES US FRIENDS...
...I'M NOT EVEN SURE IF IT'S *EVER* BEEN *REAL* OR NOT.
THAT'S NOT YOU TALKING.
THAT'S THAT OLD WOMAN.

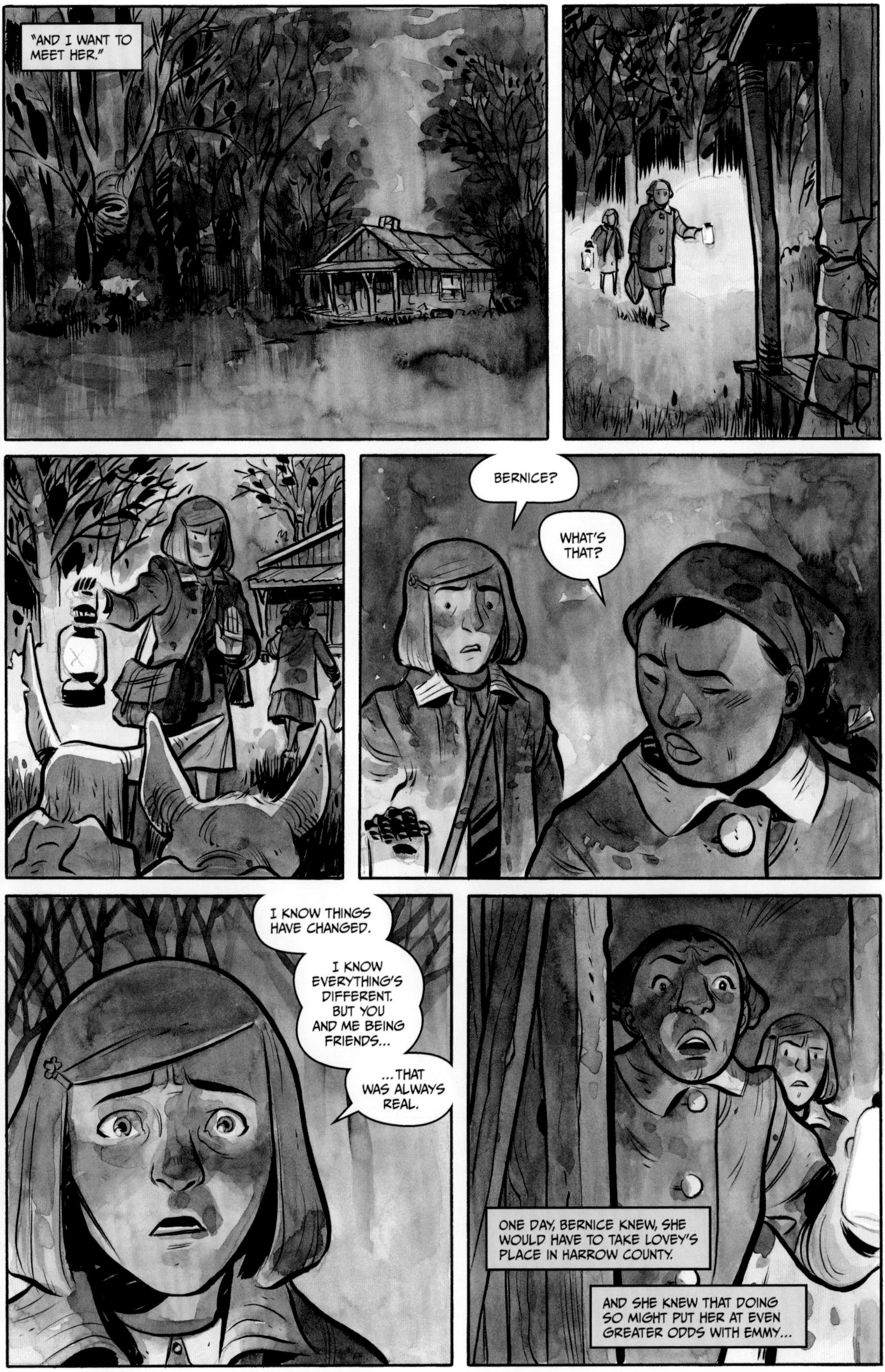
"AND I WANT TO MEET HER."
BERNICE?
WHAT'S THAT?
I KNOW THINGS HAVE CHANGED.
I KNOW EVERYTHING'S DIFFERENT. BUT YOU AND ME BEING FRIENDS...
...THAT WAS ALWAYS REAL.
ONE DAY, BERNICE KNEW, SHE WOULD HAVE TO TAKE LOVEY'S PLACE IN HARROW COUNTY.
AND SHE KNEW THAT DOING SO MIGHT PUT HER AT EVEN GREATER ODDS WITH EMMY...

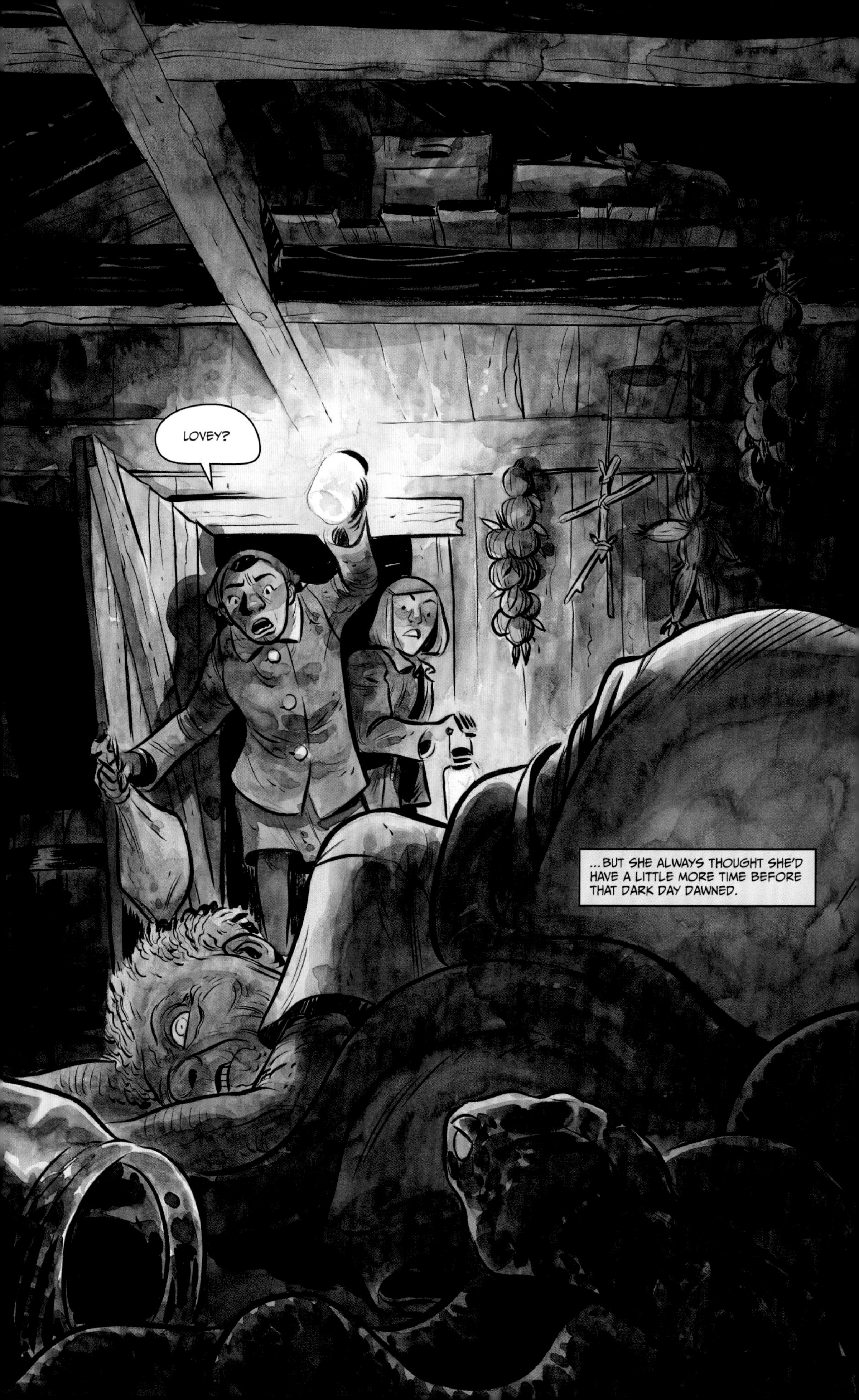
LOVEY?
...BUT SHE ALWAYS THOUGHT SHE'D HAVE A LITTLE MORE TIME BEFORE THAT DARK DAY DAWNED.

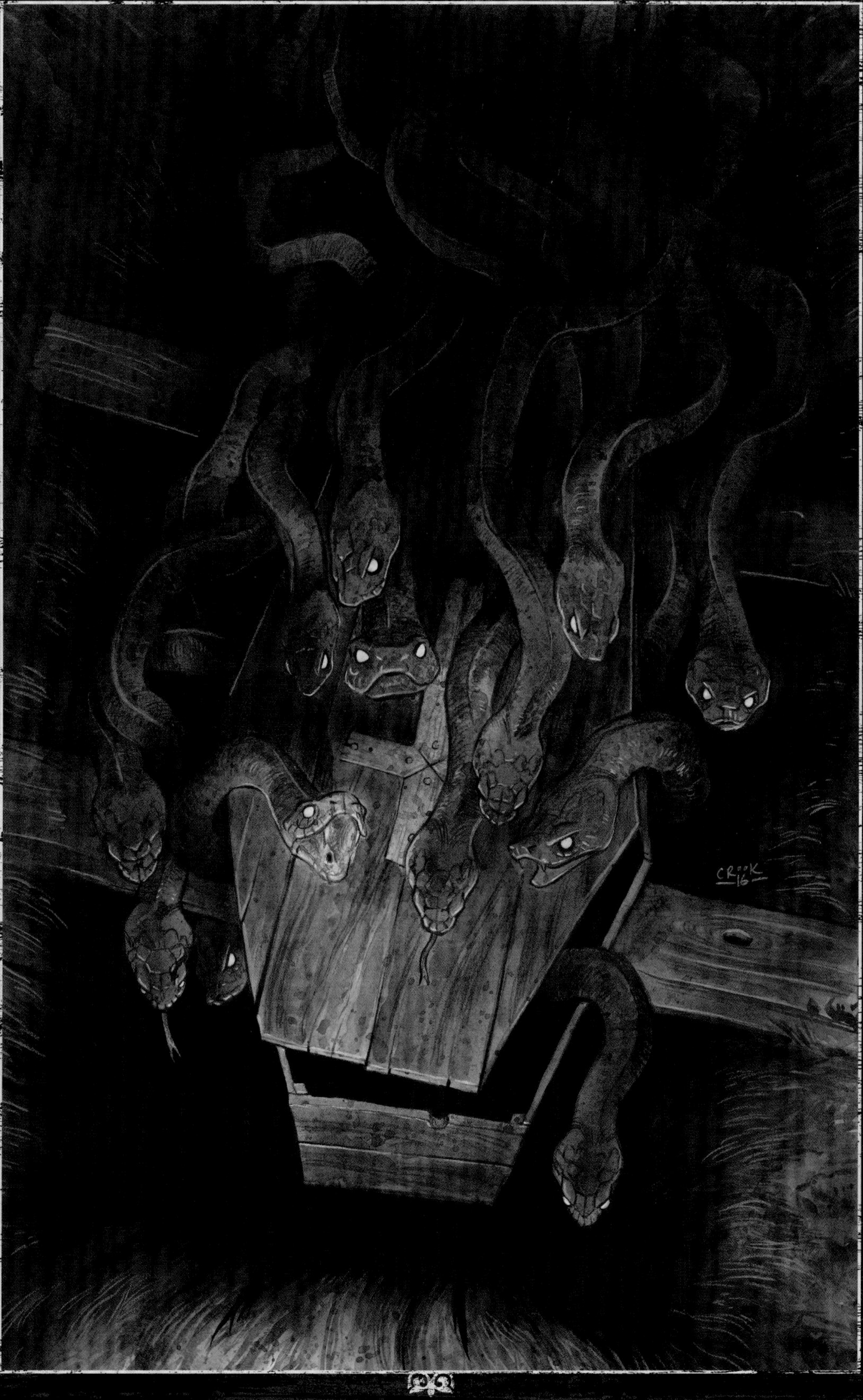
CROOK
16

THREE

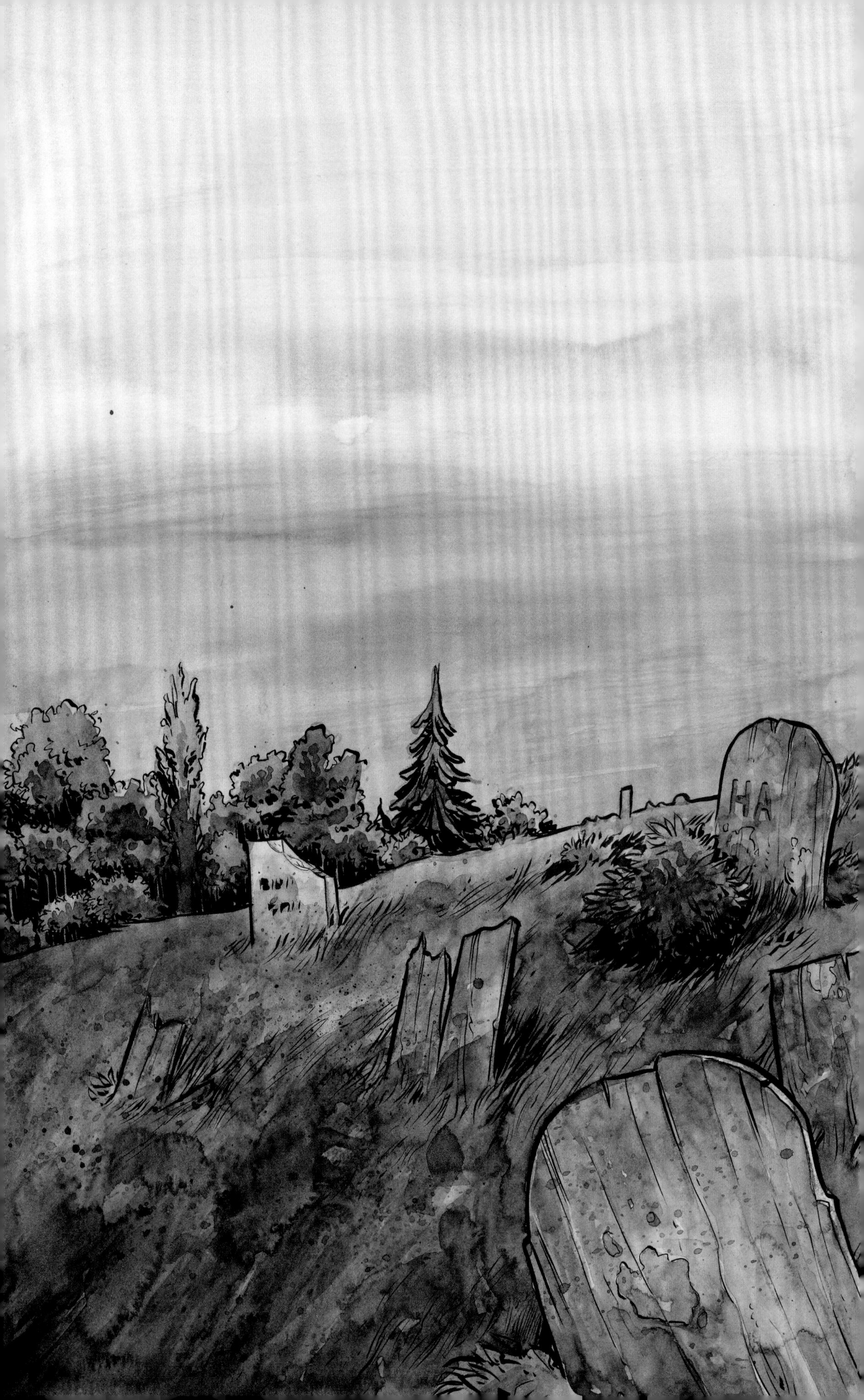
HA

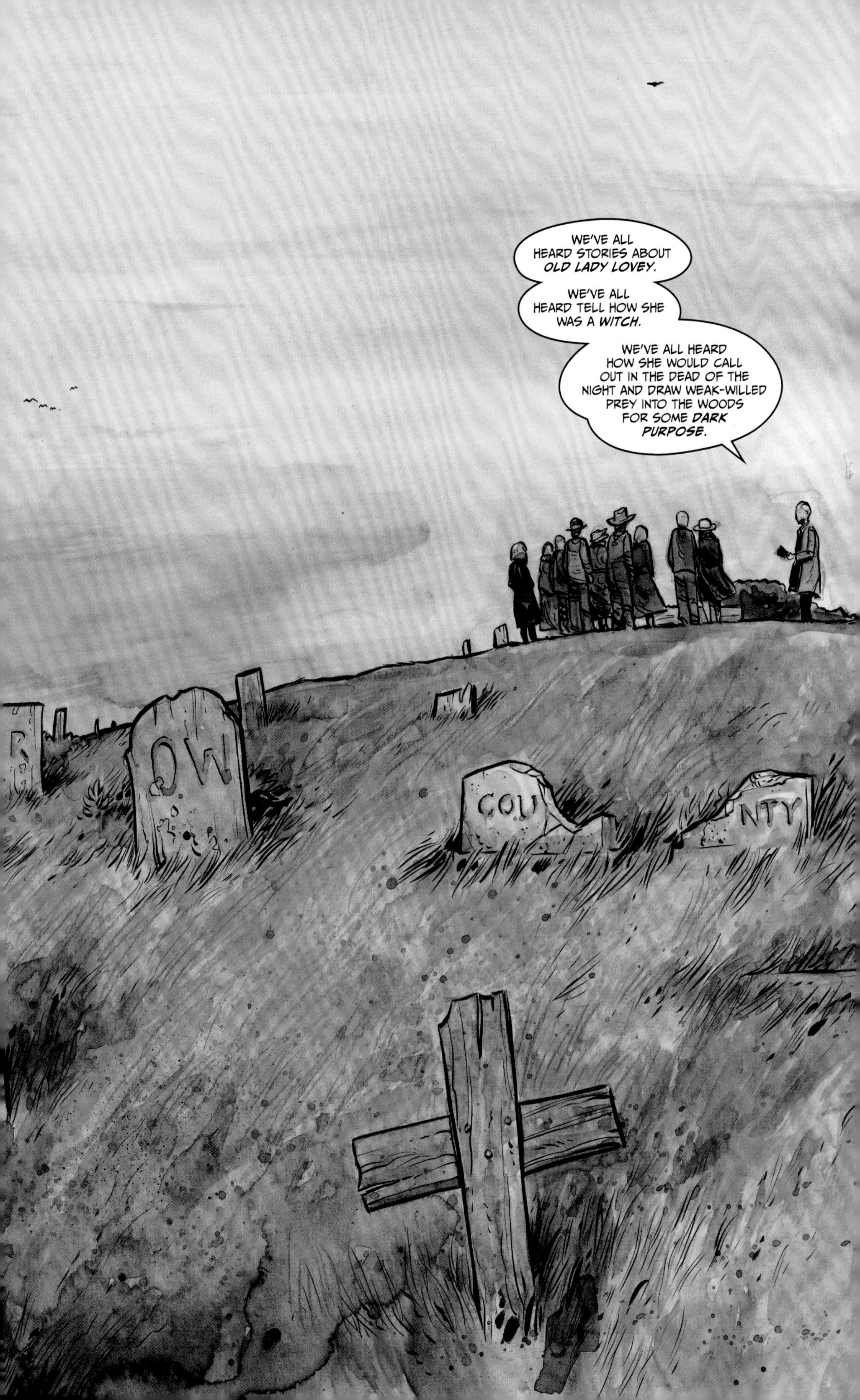
WE'VE ALL HEARD STORIES ABOUT *OLD LADY LOVEY.*
WE'VE ALL HEARD TELL HOW SHE WAS A *WITCH.*
WE'VE ALL HEARD HOW SHE WOULD CALL OUT IN THE DEAD OF THE NIGHT AND DRAW WEAK-WILLED PREY INTO THE WOODS FOR SOME *DARK PURPOSE.*
OW
COU
NTY

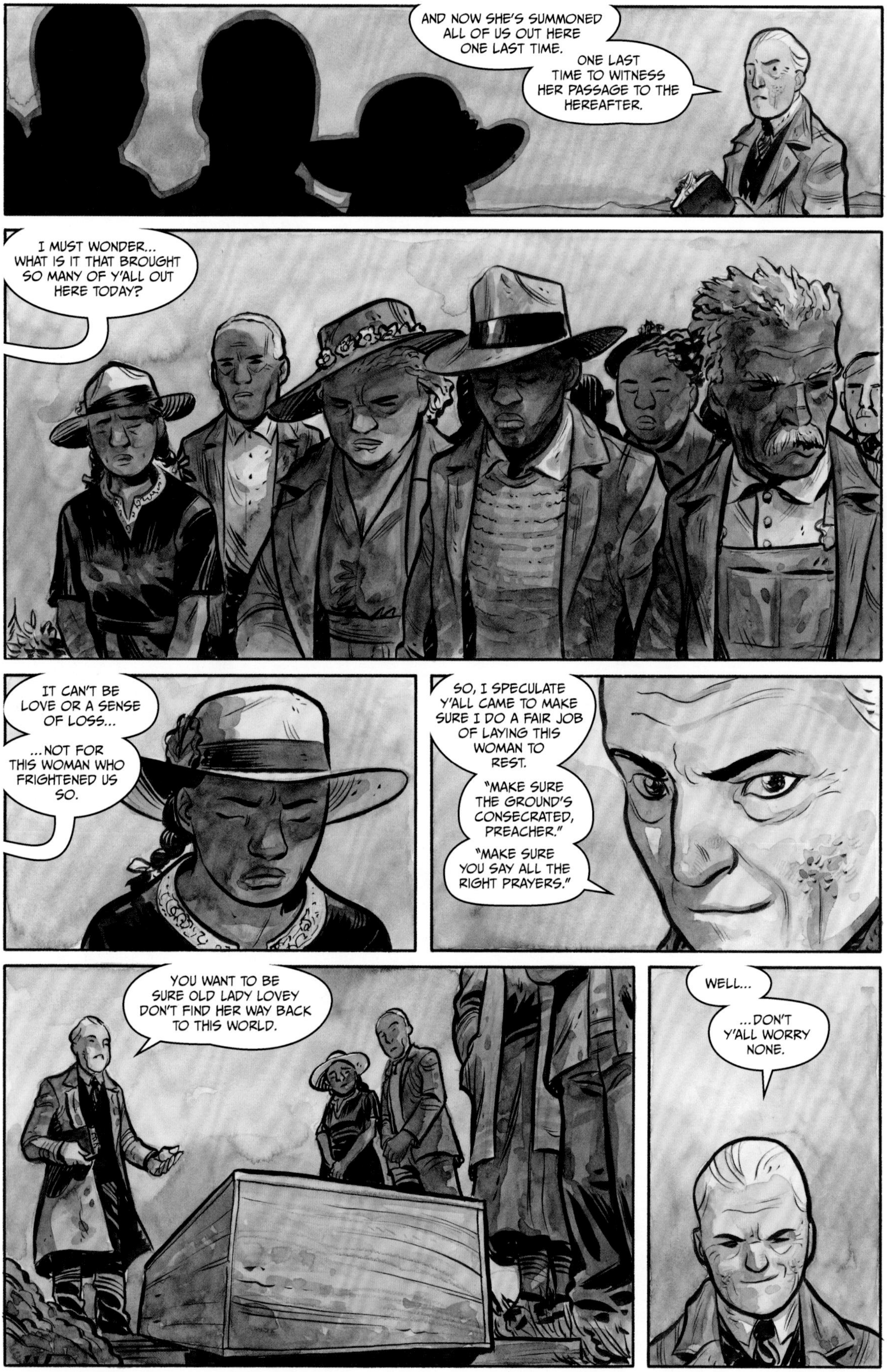
AND NOW SHE'S SUMMONED ALL OF US OUT HERE ONE LAST TIME.
ONE LAST TIME TO WITNESS HER PASSAGE TO THE HEREAFTER.
I MUST WONDER... WHAT IS IT THAT BROUGHT SO MANY OF Y'ALL OUT HERE TODAY?
IT CAN'T BE LOVE OR A SENSE OF LOSS...
...NOT FOR THIS WOMAN WHO FRIGHTENED US SO.
SO, I SPECULATE Y'ALL CAME TO MAKE SURE I DO A FAIR JOB OF LAYING THIS WOMAN TO REST.
"MAKE SURE THE GROUND'S CONSECRATED, PREACHER."
"MAKE SURE YOU SAY ALL THE RIGHT PRAYERS."
YOU WANT TO BE SURE OLD LADY LOVEY DON'T FIND HER WAY BACK TO THIS WORLD.
WELL...
...DON'T Y'ALL WORRY NONE.

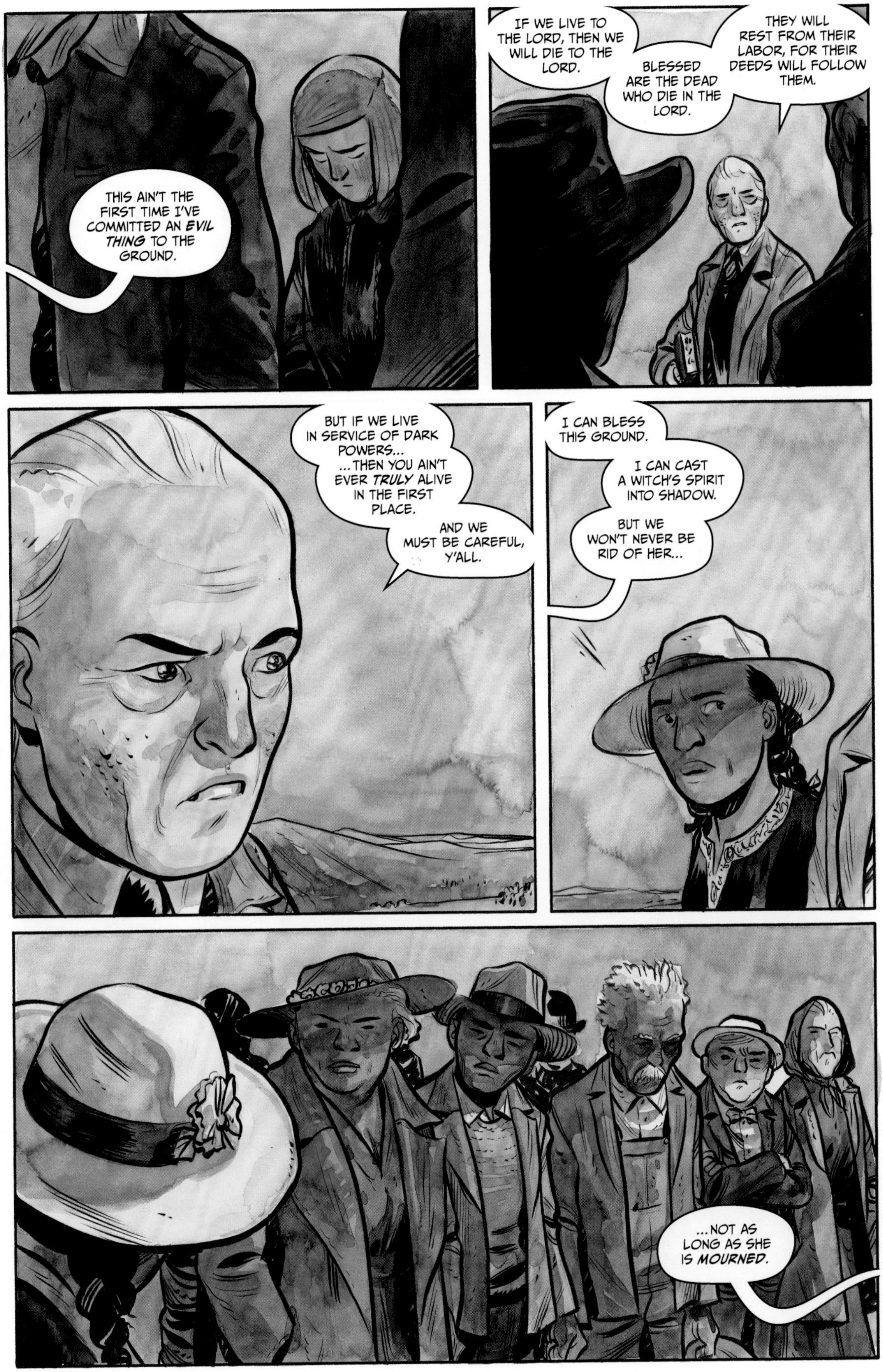
THIS AIN'T THE FIRST TIME I'VE COMMITTED AN *EVIL THING* TO THE GROUND.
IF WE LIVE TO THE LORD, THEN WE WILL DIE TO THE LORD.
BLESSED ARE THE DEAD WHO DIE IN THE LORD.
THEY WILL REST FROM THEIR LABOR, FOR THEIR DEEDS WILL FOLLOW THEM.
BUT IF WE LIVE IN SERVICE OF DARK POWERS...
...THEN YOU AIN'T EVER *TRULY* ALIVE IN THE FIRST PLACE.
AND WE MUST BE CAREFUL, Y'ALL.
I CAN BLESS THIS GROUND.
I CAN CAST A WITCH'S SPIRIT INTO SHADOW.
BUT WE WON'T NEVER BE RID OF HER...
...NOT AS LONG AS SHE IS *MOURNED*.

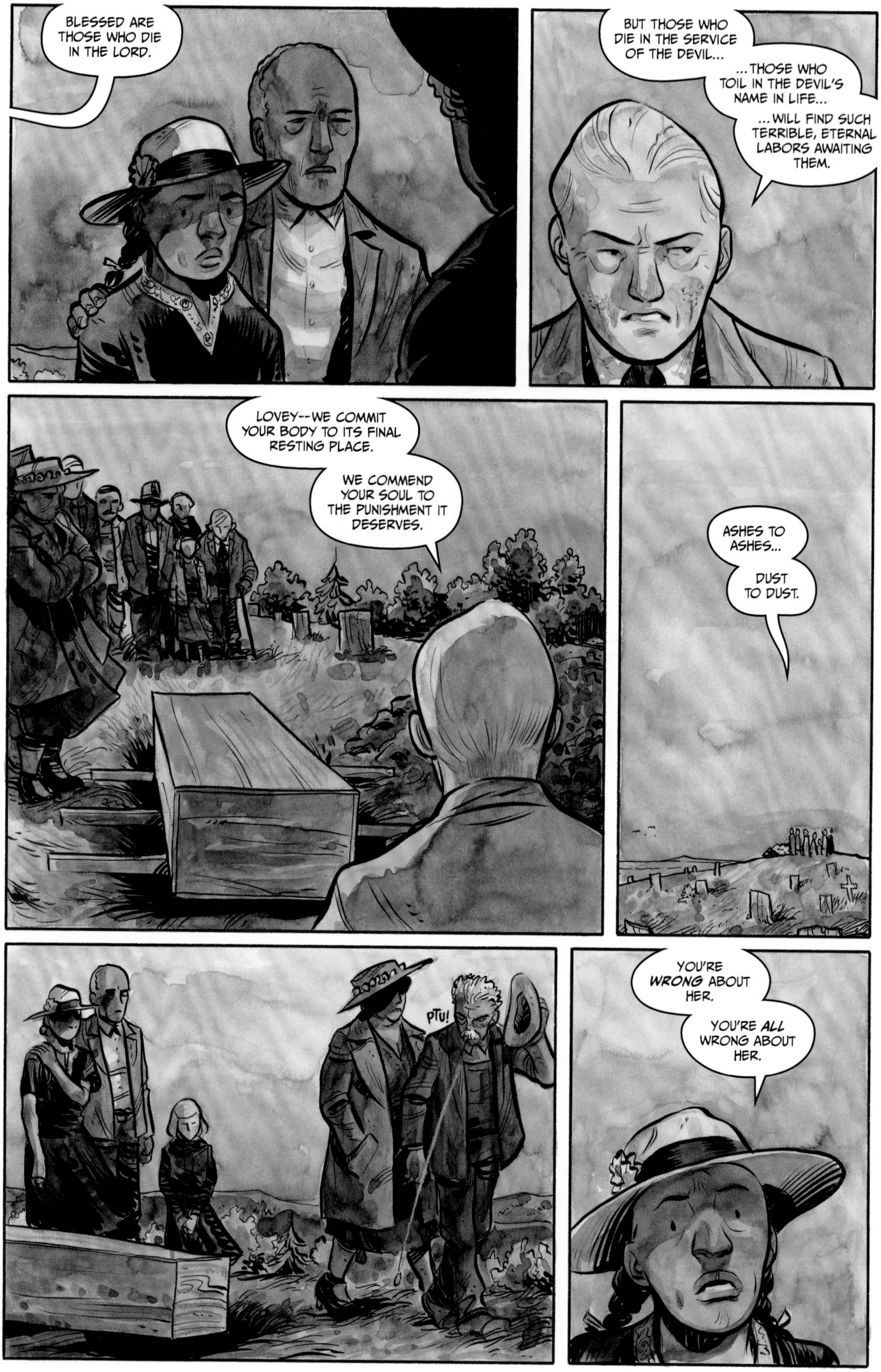
BLESSED ARE THOSE WHO DIE IN THE LORD.
BUT THOSE WHO DIE IN THE SERVICE OF THE DEVIL...
...THOSE WHO TOIL IN THE DEVIL'S NAME IN LIFE...
...WILL FIND SUCH TERRIBLE, ETERNAL LABORS AWAITING THEM.
LOVEY--WE COMMIT YOUR BODY TO ITS FINAL RESTING PLACE.
WE COMMEND YOUR SOUL TO THE PUNISHMENT IT DESERVES.
ASHES TO ASHES...
DUST TO DUST.
PTU!
YOU'RE WRONG ABOUT HER.
YOU'RE ALL WRONG ABOUT HER.

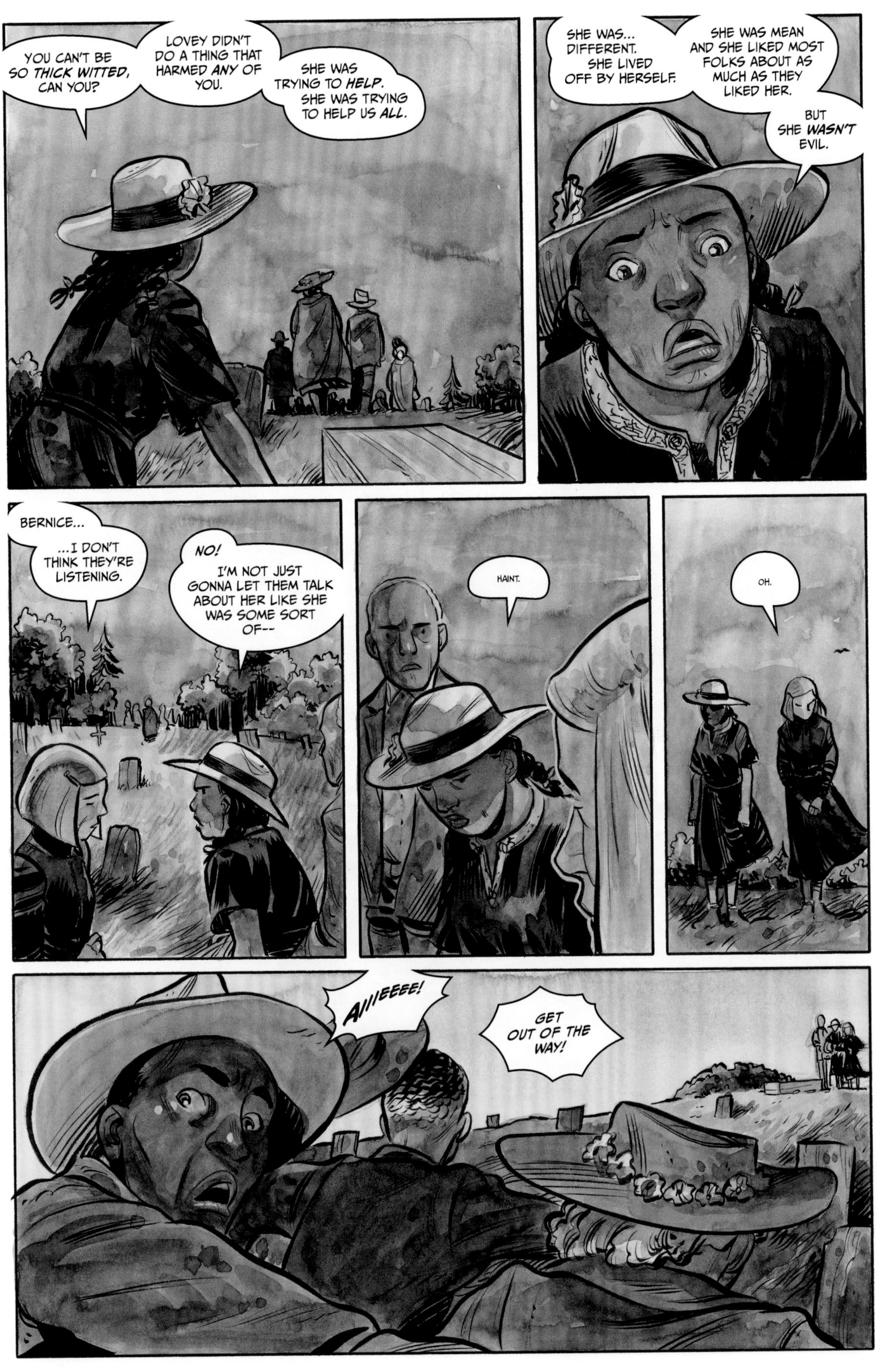

YOU CAN'T BE SO THICK WITTED, CAN YOU?
LOVEY DIDN'T DO A THING THAT HARMED ANY OF YOU.
SHE WAS TRYING TO HELP. SHE WAS TRYING TO HELP US ALL.
SHE WAS... DIFFERENT. SHE LIVED OFF BY HERSELF.
SHE WAS MEAN AND SHE LIKED MOST FOLKS ABOUT AS MUCH AS THEY LIKED HER.
BUT SHE WASN'T EVIL.
BERNICE... ...I DON'T THINK THEY'RE LISTENING.
NO! I'M NOT JUST GONNA LET THEM TALK ABOUT HER LIKE SHE WAS SOME SORT OF--
HAINT.
OH.
AIIIEEEE!
GET OUT OF THE WAY!

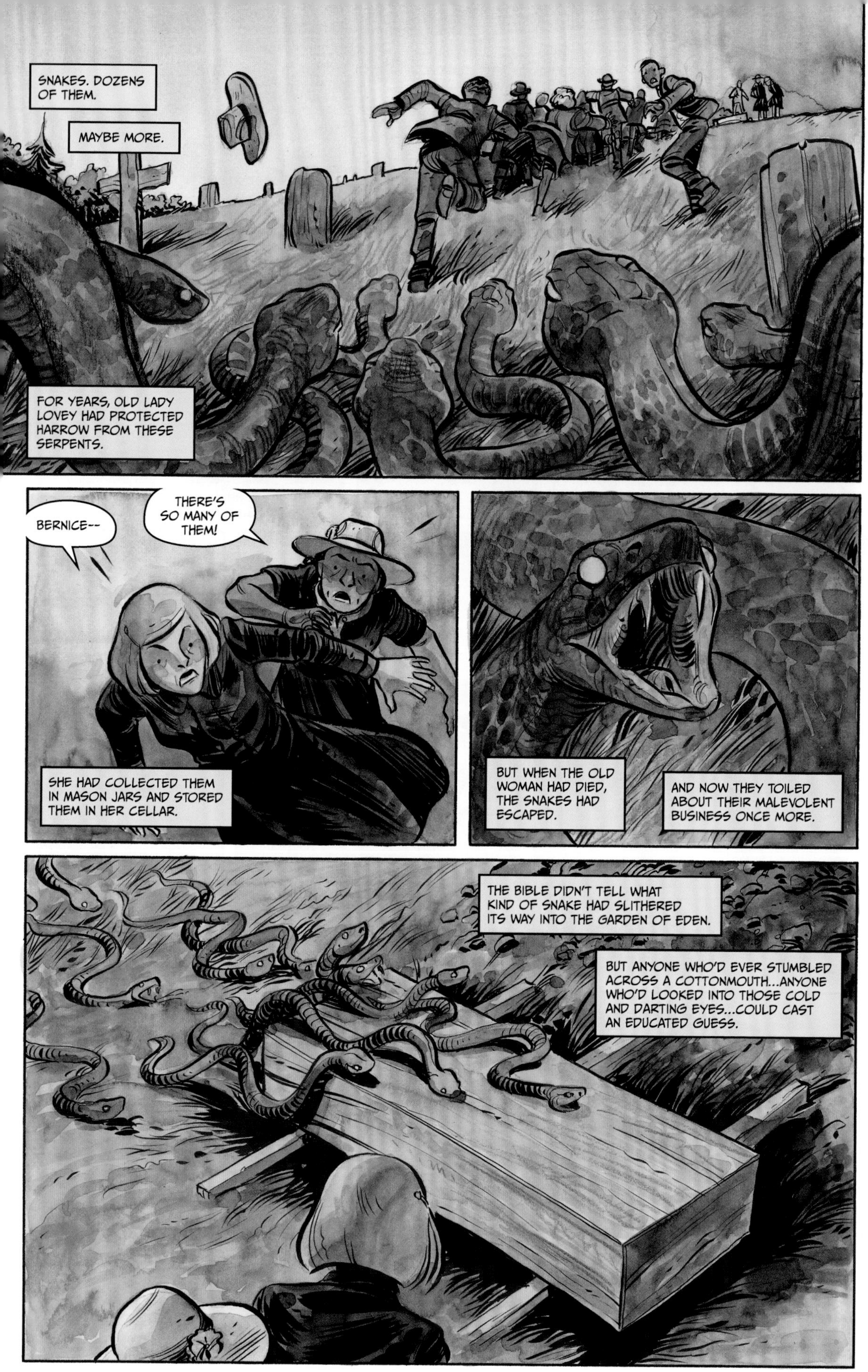
SNAKES. DOZENS OF THEM.
MAYBE MORE.
FOR YEARS, OLD LADY LOVEY HAD PROTECTED HARROW FROM THESE SERPENTS.
BERNICE--
THERE'S SO MANY OF THEM!
SHE HAD COLLECTED THEM IN MASON JARS AND STORED THEM IN HER CELLAR.
BUT WHEN THE OLD WOMAN HAD DIED, THE SNAKES HAD ESCAPED.
AND NOW THEY TOILED ABOUT THEIR MALEVOLENT BUSINESS ONCE MORE.
THE BIBLE DIDN'T TELL WHAT KIND OF SNAKE HAD SLITHERED ITS WAY INTO THE GARDEN OF EDEN.
BUT ANYONE WHO'D EVER STUMBLED ACROSS A COTTONMOUTH...ANYONE WHO'D LOOKED INTO THOSE COLD AND DARTING EYES...COULD CAST AN EDUCATED GUESS.

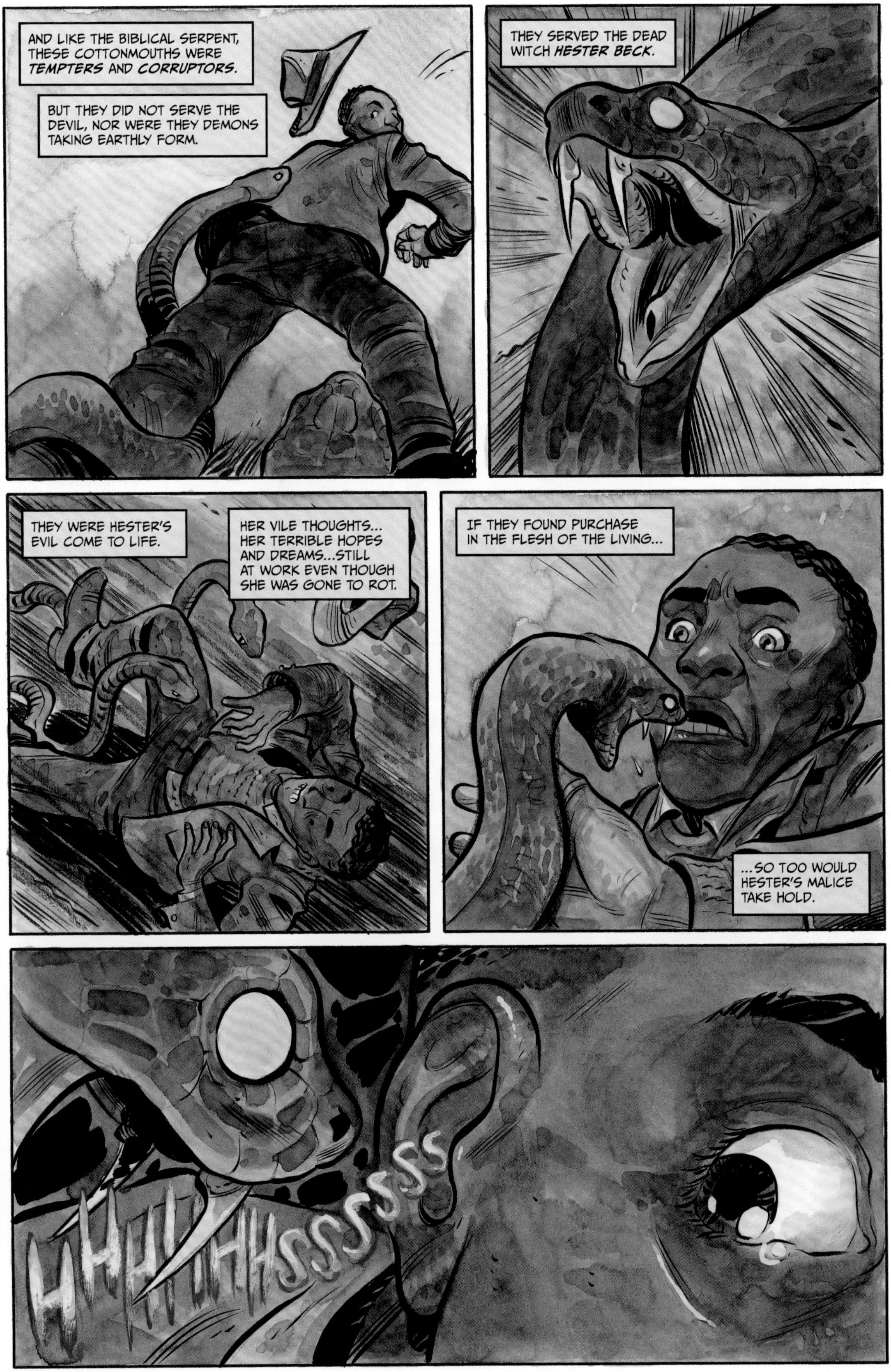
AND LIKE THE BIBLICAL SERPENT, THESE COTTONMOUTHS WERE *TEMPTERS* AND *CORRUPTORS.*
BUT THEY DID NOT SERVE THE DEVIL, NOR WERE THEY DEMONS TAKING EARTHLY FORM.
THEY SERVED THE DEAD WITCH *HESTER BECK.*
THEY WERE HESTER'S EVIL COME TO LIFE.
HER VILE THOUGHTS... HER TERRIBLE HOPES AND DREAMS...STILL AT WORK EVEN THOUGH SHE WAS GONE TO ROT.
IF THEY FOUND PURCHASE IN THE FLESH OF THE LIVING...
...SO TOO WOULD HESTER'S MALICE TAKE HOLD.
HHHHHHSSSSSSSS

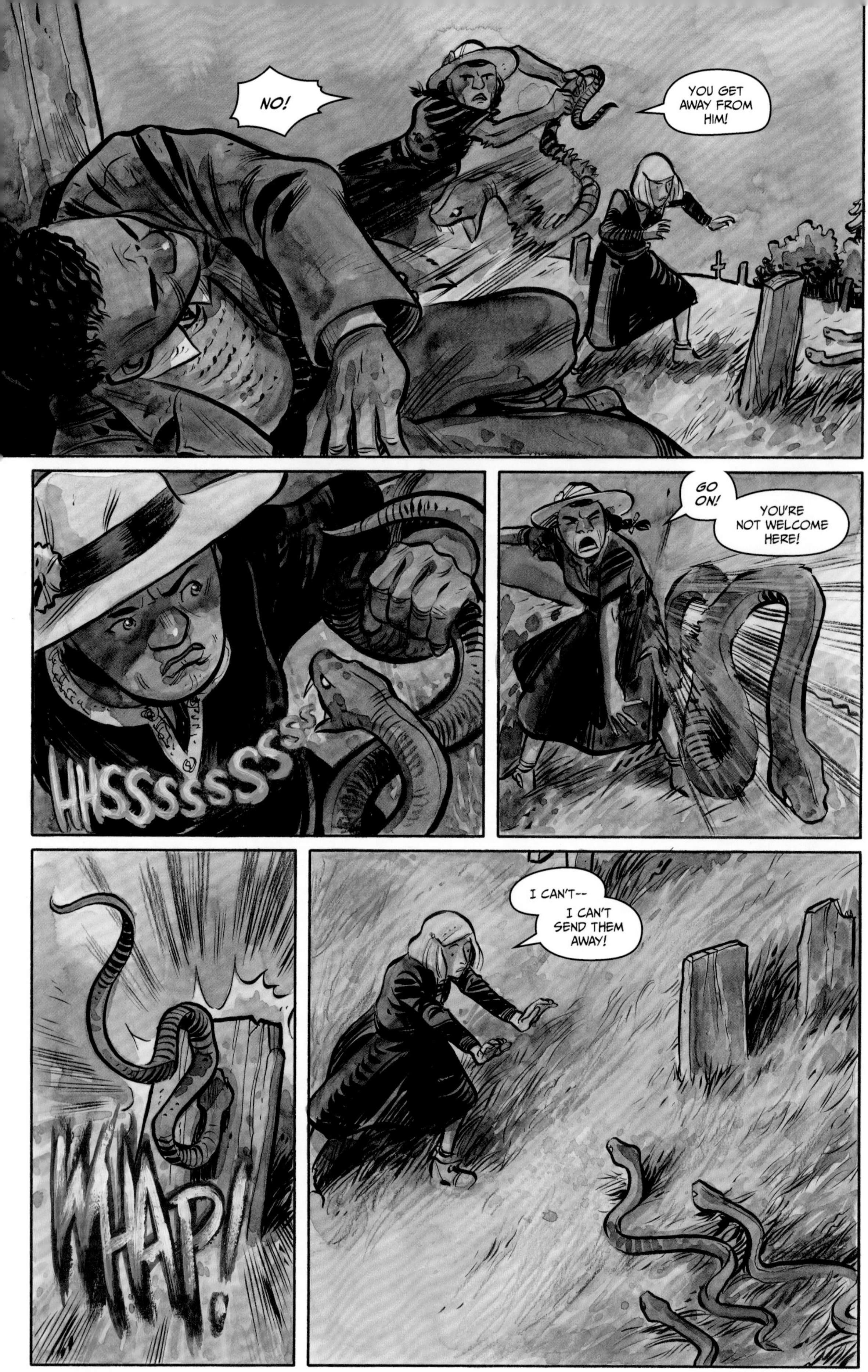
NO!
YOU GET AWAY FROM HIM!
HHSSSSSSSS
GO ON!
YOU'RE NOT WELCOME HERE!
WHAP!
I CAN'T--
I CAN'T SEND THEM AWAY!

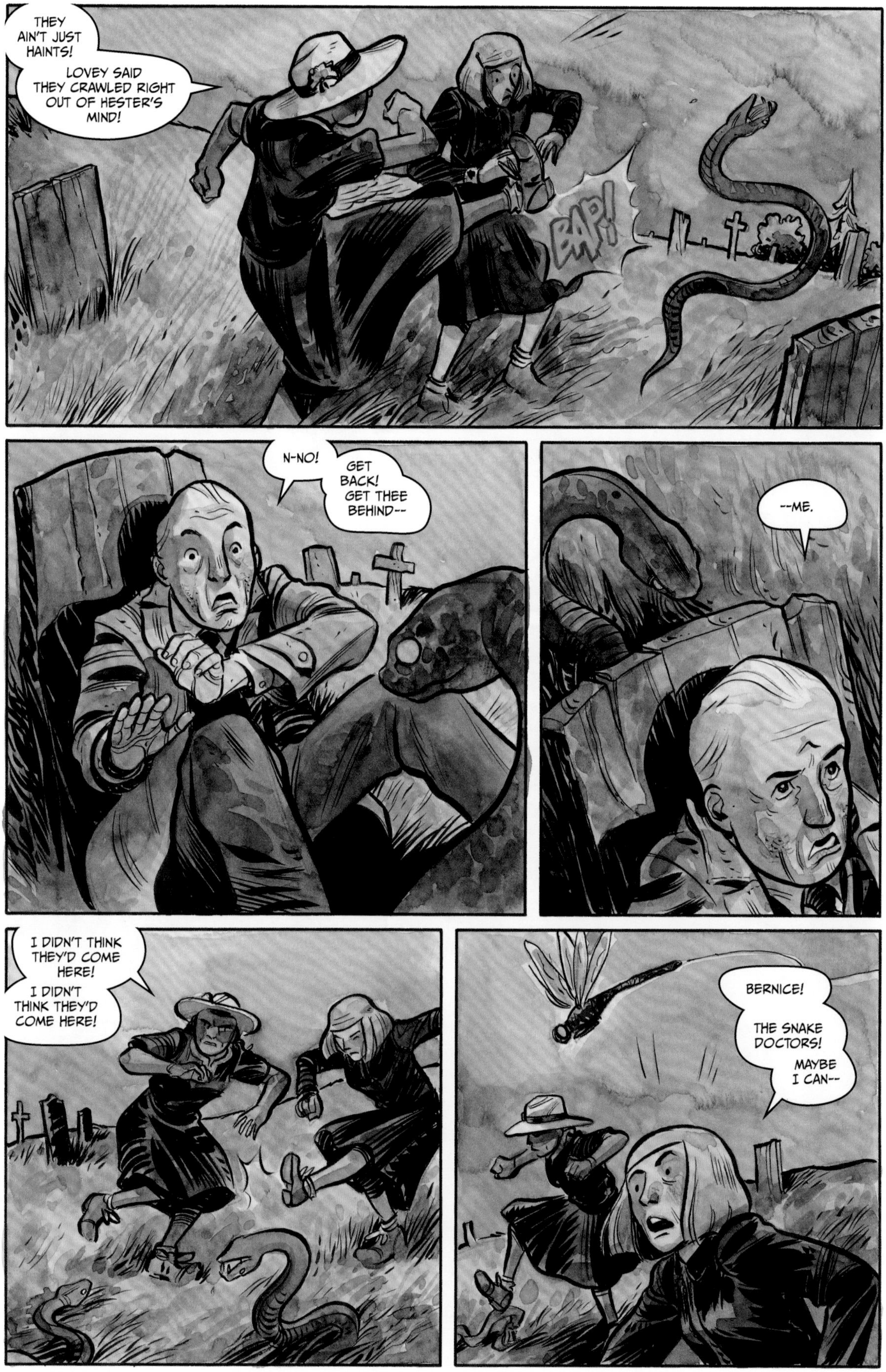
THEY AIN'T JUST HAINTS!
LOVEY SAID THEY CRAWLED RIGHT OUT OF HESTER'S MIND!
BAP!
N-NO!
GET BACK! GET THEE BEHIND--
--ME.
I DIDN'T THINK THEY'D COME HERE!
I DIDN'T THINK THEY'D COME HERE!
BERNICE!
THE SNAKE DOCTORS!
MAYBE I CAN--

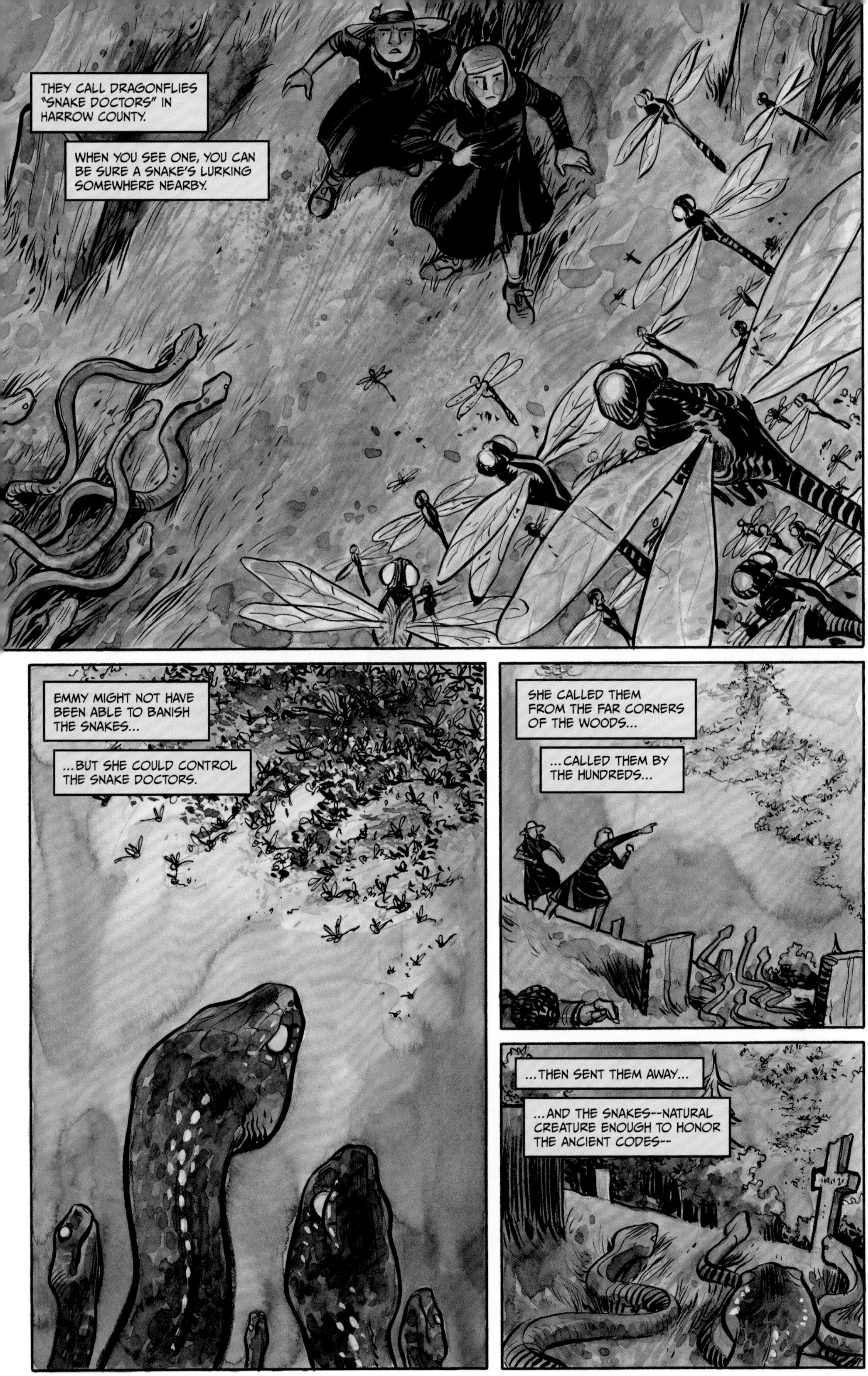
THEY CALL DRAGONFLIES "SNAKE DOCTORS" IN HARROW COUNTY.
WHEN YOU SEE ONE, YOU CAN BE SURE A SNAKE'S LURKING SOMEWHERE NEARBY.
EMMY MIGHT NOT HAVE BEEN ABLE TO BANISH THE SNAKES...
...BUT SHE COULD CONTROL THE SNAKE DOCTORS.
SHE CALLED THEM FROM THE FAR CORNERS OF THE WOODS...
...CALLED THEM BY THE HUNDREDS...
...THEN SENT THEM AWAY...
...AND THE SNAKES--NATURAL CREATURE ENOUGH TO HONOR THE ANCIENT CODES--

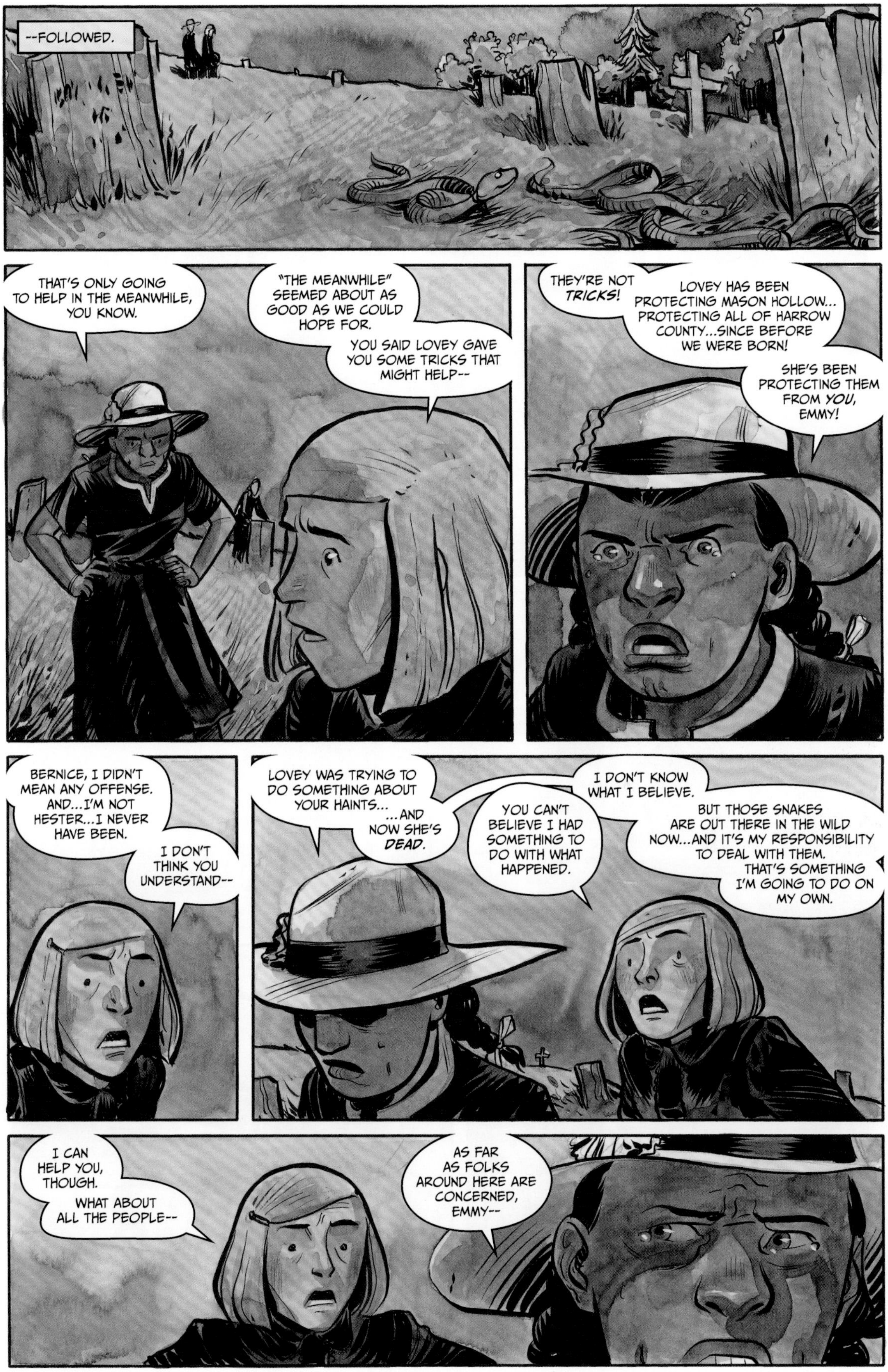
--FOLLOWED.
THAT'S ONLY GOING TO HELP IN THE MEANWHILE, YOU KNOW.
"THE MEANWHILE" SEEMED ABOUT AS GOOD AS WE COULD HOPE FOR.
YOU SAID LOVEY GAVE YOU SOME TRICKS THAT MIGHT HELP--
THEY'RE NOT *TRICKS!*
LOVEY HAS BEEN PROTECTING MASON HOLLOW... PROTECTING ALL OF HARROW COUNTY...SINCE BEFORE WE WERE BORN!
SHE'S BEEN PROTECTING THEM FROM *YOU*, EMMY!
BERNICE, I DIDN'T MEAN ANY OFFENSE. AND...I'M NOT HESTER...I NEVER HAVE BEEN.
I DON'T THINK YOU UNDERSTAND--
LOVEY WAS TRYING TO DO SOMETHING ABOUT YOUR HAINTS...
...AND NOW SHE'S *DEAD*.
YOU CAN'T BELIEVE I HAD SOMETHING TO DO WITH WHAT HAPPENED.
I DON'T KNOW WHAT I BELIEVE.
BUT THOSE SNAKES ARE OUT THERE IN THE WILD NOW...AND IT'S MY RESPONSIBILITY TO DEAL WITH THEM.
THAT'S SOMETHING I'M GOING TO DO ON MY OWN.
I CAN HELP YOU, THOUGH.
WHAT ABOUT ALL THE PEOPLE--
AS FAR AS FOLKS AROUND HERE ARE CONCERNED, EMMY--

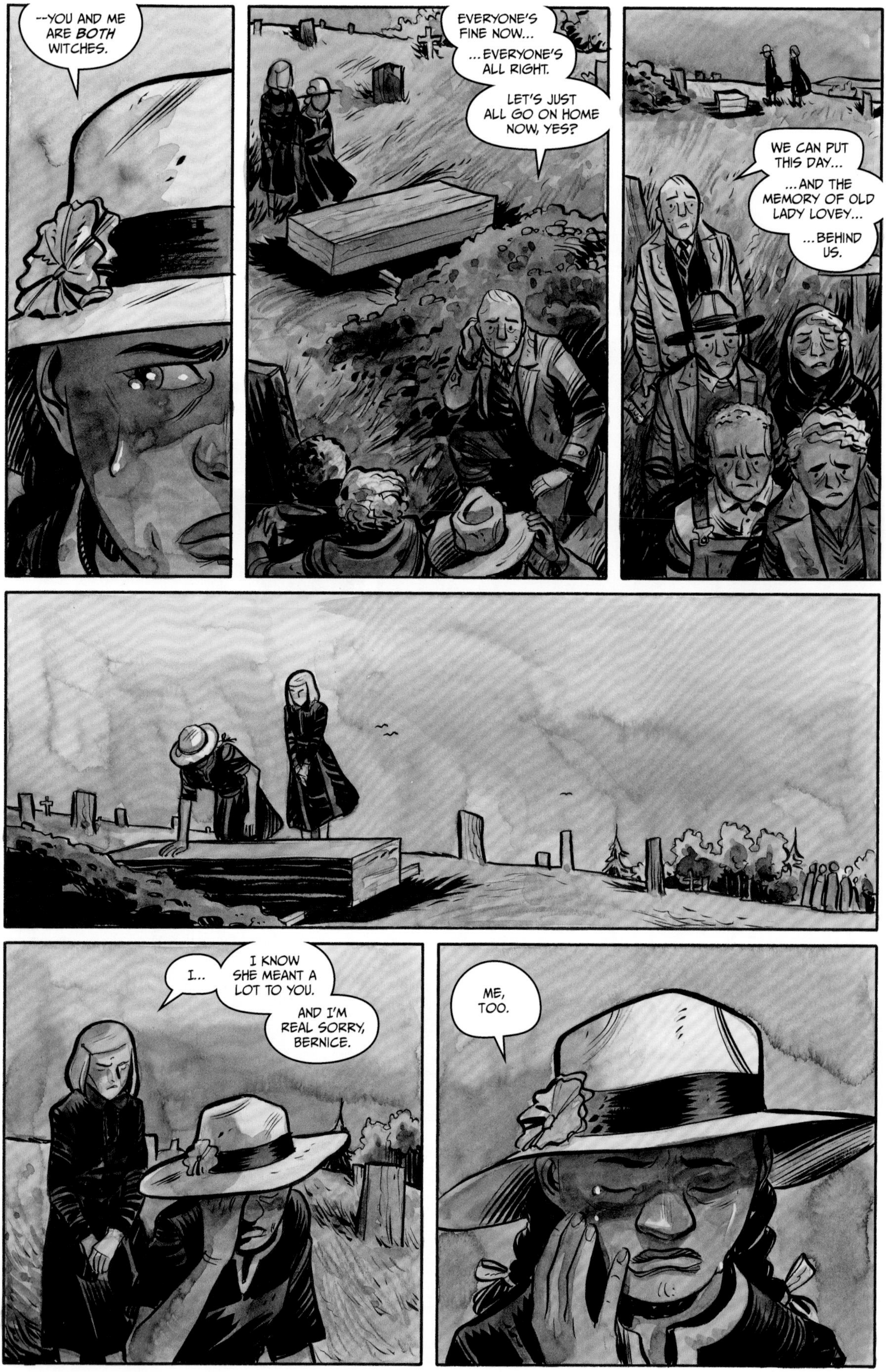
--YOU AND ME ARE *BOTH* WITCHES.
EVERYONE'S FINE NOW...
...EVERYONE'S ALL RIGHT.
LET'S JUST ALL GO ON HOME NOW, YES?
WE CAN PUT THIS DAY...
...AND THE MEMORY OF OLD LADY LOVEY...
...BEHIND US.
I...
I KNOW SHE MEANT A LOT TO YOU.
AND I'M REAL SORRY, BERNICE.
ME, TOO.

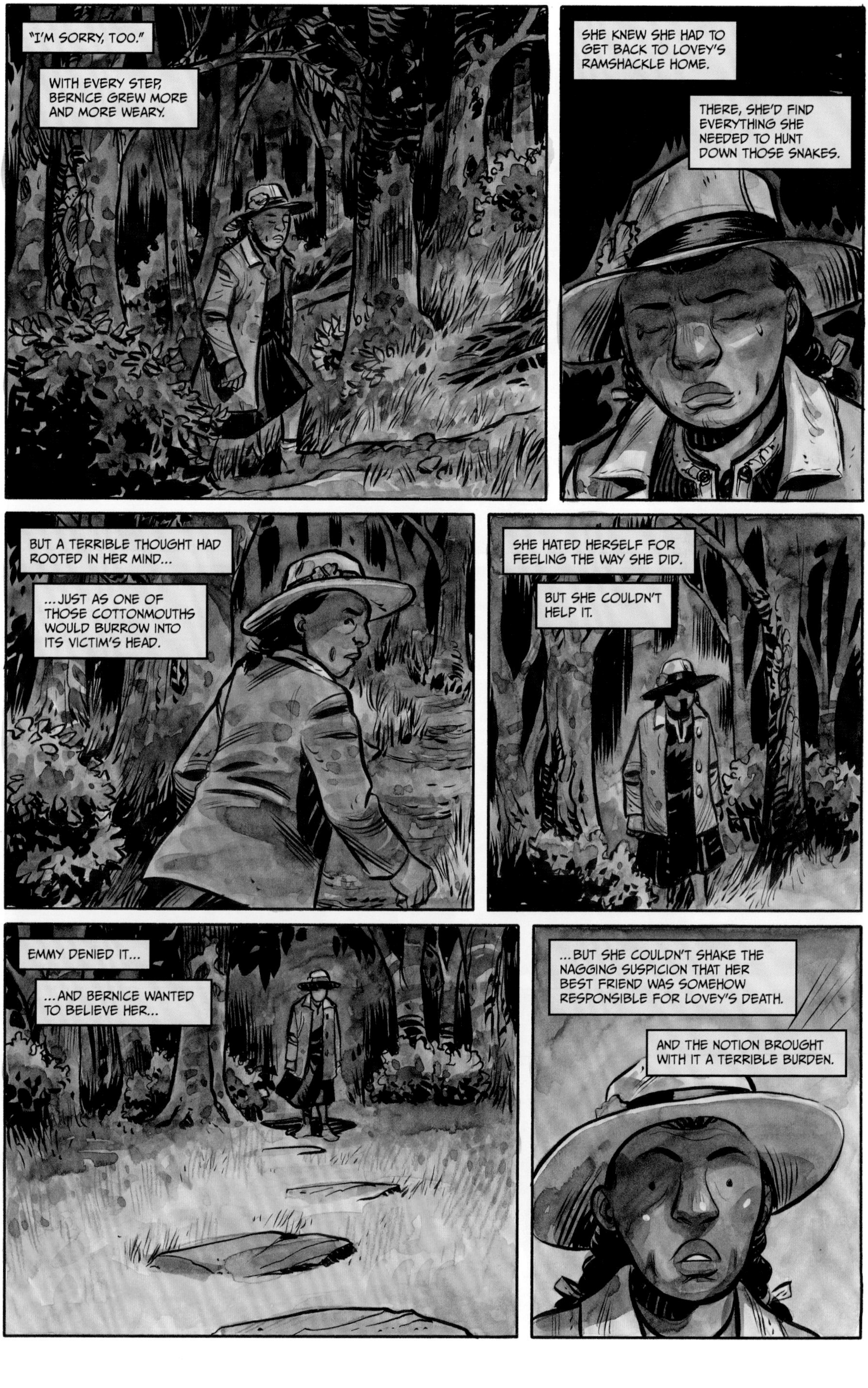
"I'M SORRY, TOO."
WITH EVERY STEP, BERNICE GREW MORE AND MORE WEARY.
SHE KNEW SHE HAD TO GET BACK TO LOVEY'S RAMSHACKLE HOME.
THERE, SHE'D FIND EVERYTHING SHE NEEDED TO HUNT DOWN THOSE SNAKES.
BUT A TERRIBLE THOUGHT HAD ROOTED IN HER MIND...
...JUST AS ONE OF THOSE COTTONMOUTHS WOULD BURROW INTO ITS VICTIM'S HEAD.
SHE HATED HERSELF FOR FEELING THE WAY SHE DID.
BUT SHE COULDN'T HELP IT.
EMMY DENIED IT...
...AND BERNICE WANTED TO BELIEVE HER...
...BUT SHE COULDN'T SHAKE THE NAGGING SUSPICION THAT HER BEST FRIEND WAS SOMEHOW RESPONSIBLE FOR LOVEY'S DEATH.
AND THE NOTION BROUGHT WITH IT A TERRIBLE BURDEN.

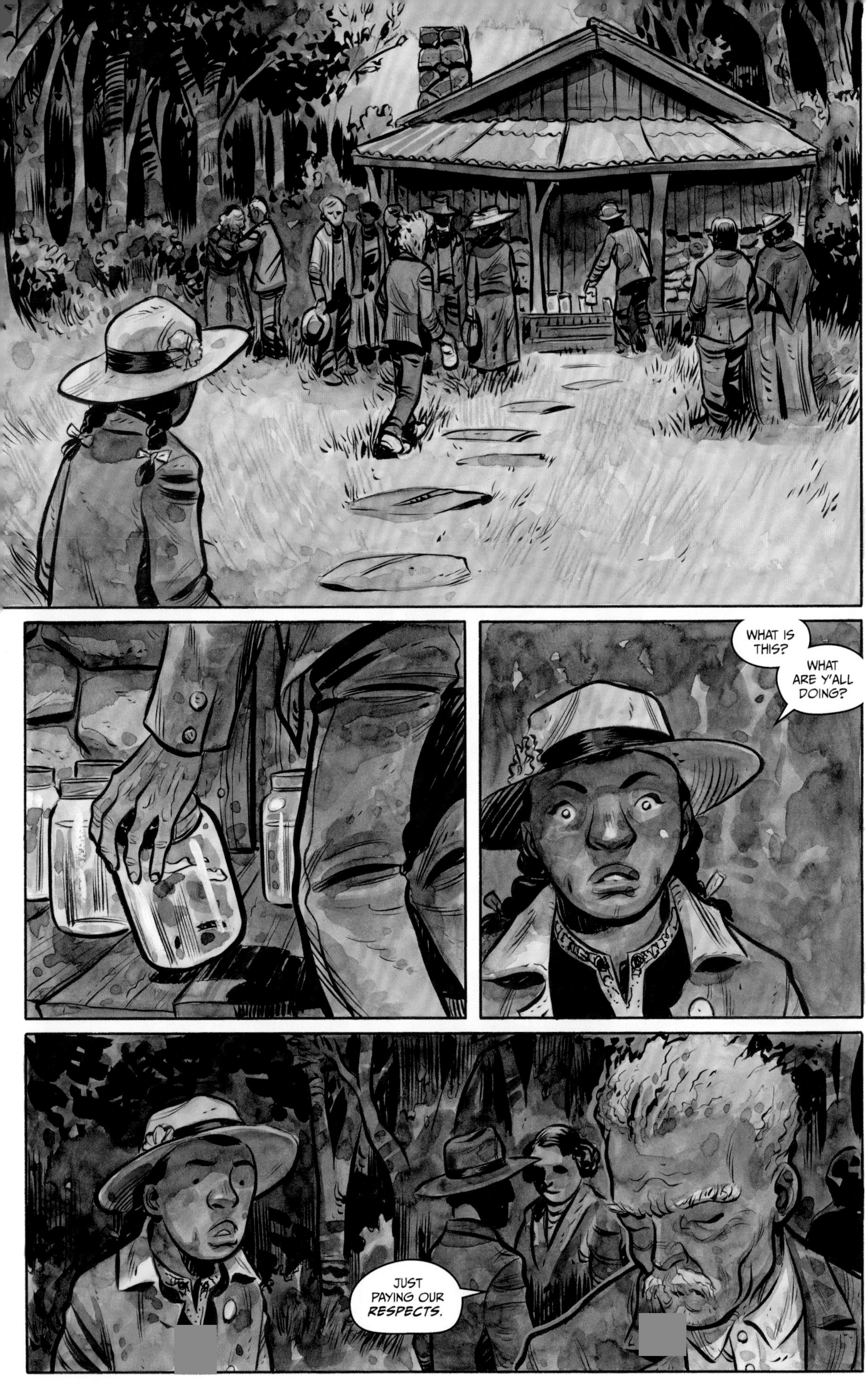
WHAT IS THIS?
WHAT ARE Y'ALL DOING?
JUST PAYING OUR *RESPECTS.*

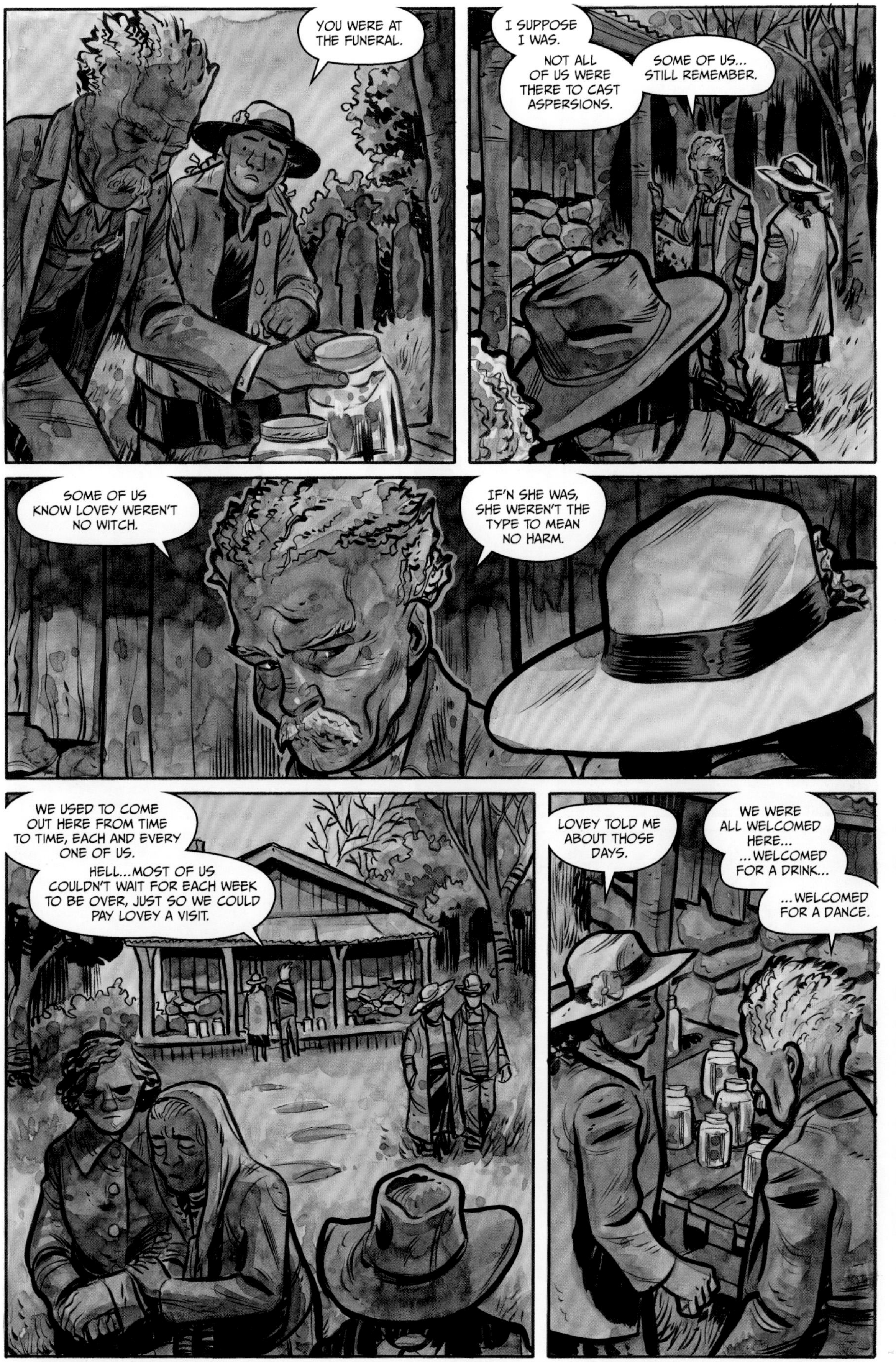
YOU WERE AT THE FUNERAL.
I SUPPOSE I WAS.
NOT ALL OF US WERE THERE TO CAST ASPERSIONS.
SOME OF US... STILL REMEMBER.
SOME OF US KNOW LOVEY WEREN'T NO WITCH.
IF'N SHE WAS, SHE WEREN'T THE TYPE TO MEAN NO HARM.
WE USED TO COME OUT HERE FROM TIME TO TIME, EACH AND EVERY ONE OF US.
HELL...MOST OF US COULDN'T WAIT FOR EACH WEEK TO BE OVER, JUST SO WE COULD PAY LOVEY A VISIT.
LOVEY TOLD ME ABOUT THOSE DAYS.
WE WERE ALL WELCOMED HERE... ...WELCOMED FOR A DRINK...
...WELCOMED FOR A DANCE.

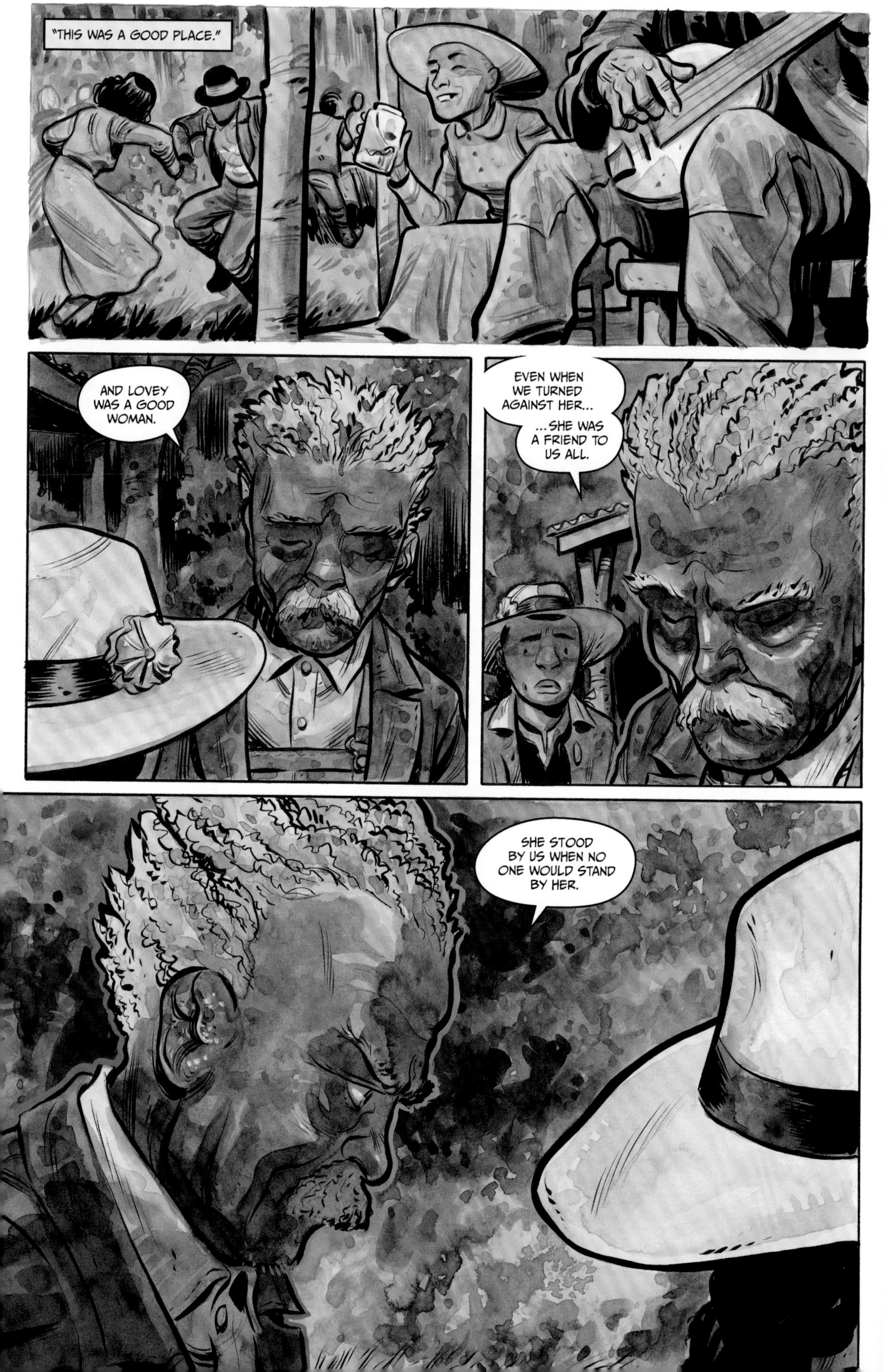
"THIS WAS A GOOD PLACE."
AND LOVEY WAS A GOOD WOMAN.
EVEN WHEN WE TURNED AGAINST HER...
...SHE WAS A FRIEND TO US ALL.
SHE STOOD BY US WHEN NO ONE WOULD STAND BY HER.

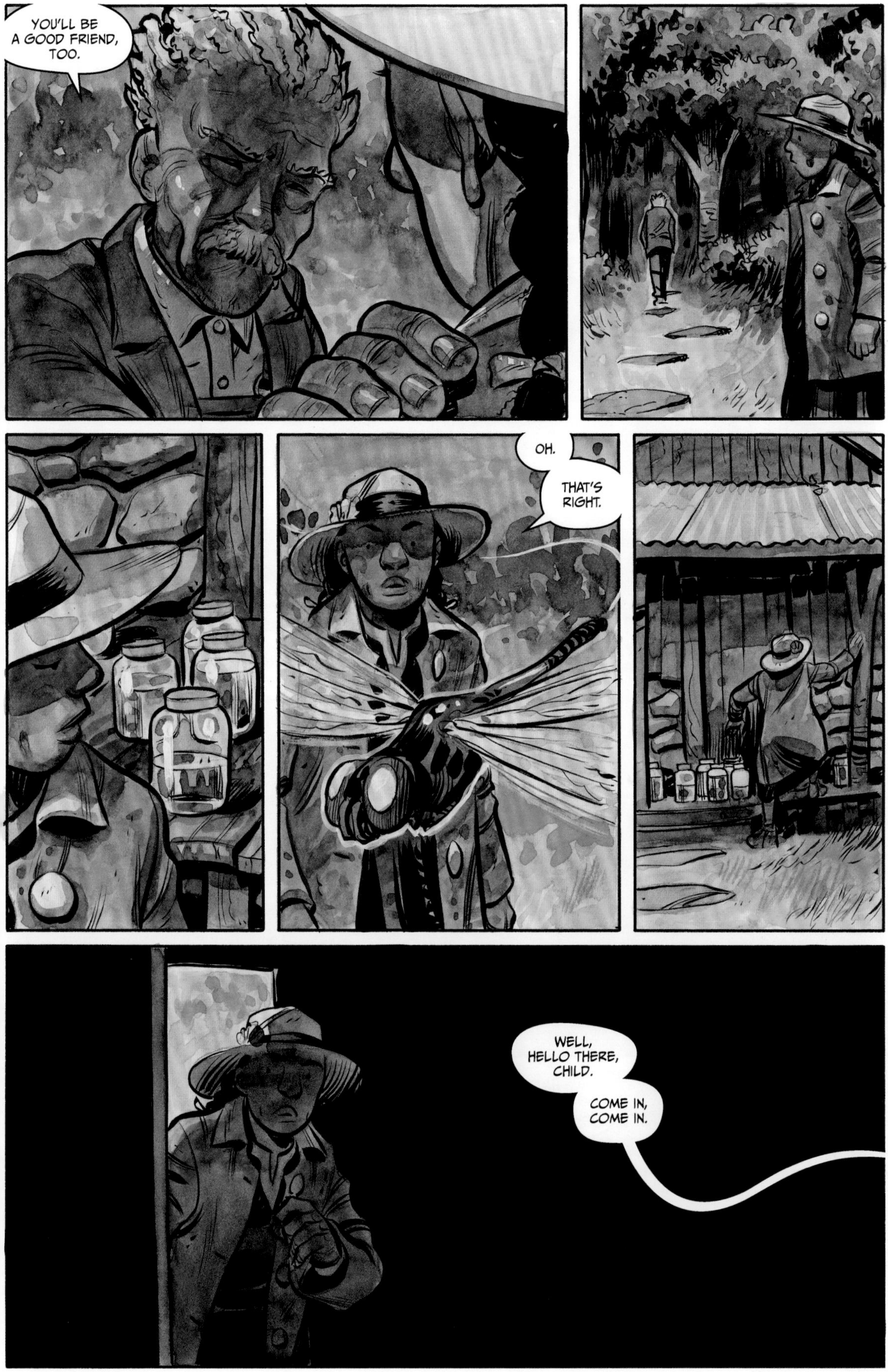
YOU'LL BE A GOOD FRIEND, TOO.
OH.
THAT'S RIGHT.
WELL, HELLO THERE, CHILD.
COME IN, COME IN.

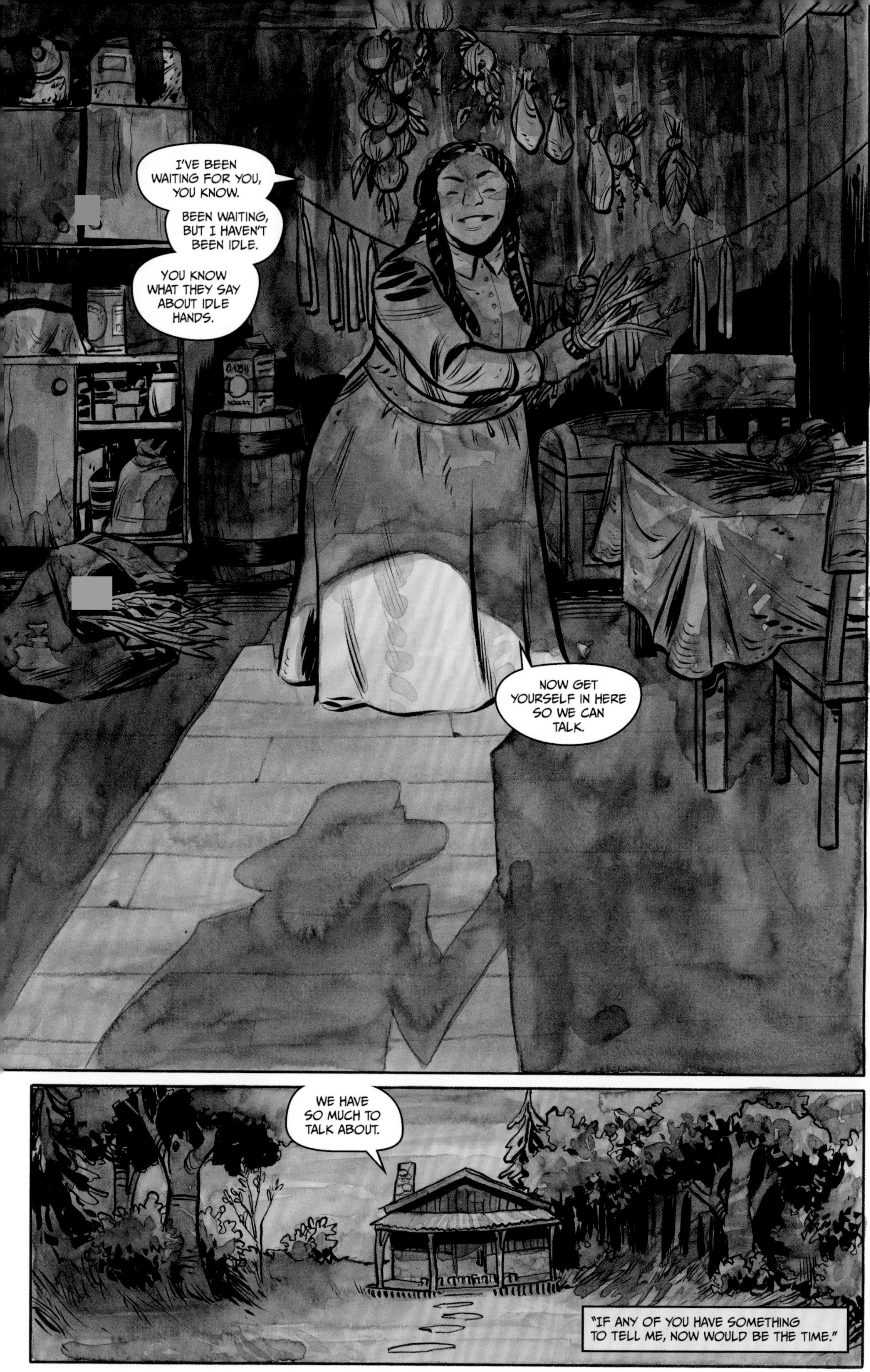
I'VE BEEN WAITING FOR YOU, YOU KNOW.
BEEN WAITING, BUT I HAVEN'T BEEN IDLE.
YOU KNOW WHAT THEY SAY ABOUT IDLE HANDS.
NOW GET YOURSELF IN HERE SO WE CAN TALK.
WE HAVE SO MUCH TO TALK ABOUT.
"IF ANY OF YOU HAVE SOMETHING TO TELL ME, NOW WOULD BE THE TIME."

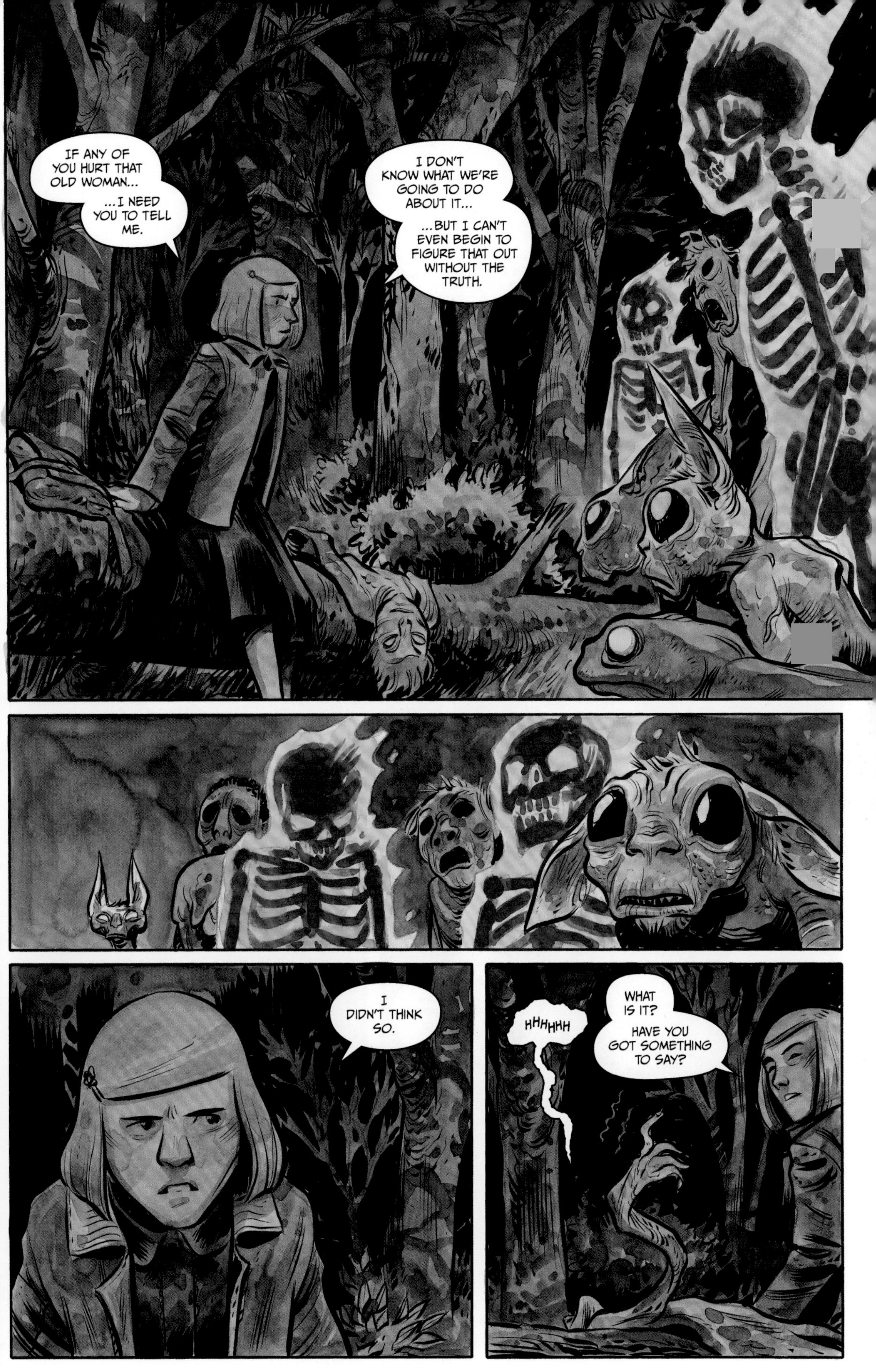
IF ANY OF YOU HURT THAT OLD WOMAN...
...I NEED YOU TO TELL ME.
I DON'T KNOW WHAT WE'RE GOING TO DO ABOUT IT...
...BUT I CAN'T EVEN BEGIN TO FIGURE THAT OUT WITHOUT THE TRUTH.
I DIDN'T THINK SO.
HHHHHH
WHAT IS IT?
HAVE YOU GOT SOMETHING TO SAY?

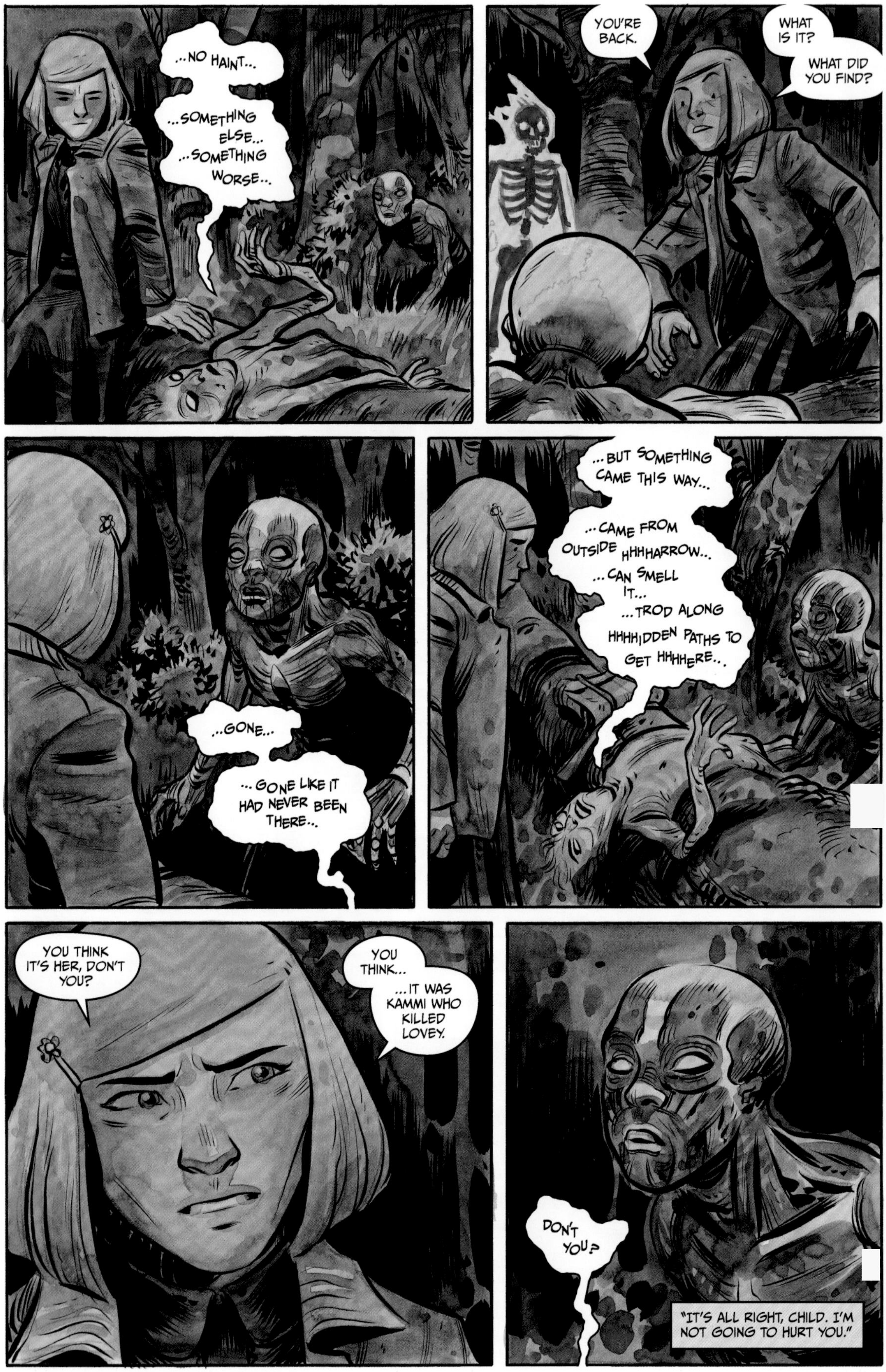
...NO HAINT...
...SOMETHING ELSE... ...SOMETHING WORSE...
YOU'RE BACK.
WHAT IS IT?
WHAT DID YOU FIND?
...GONE...
...GONE LIKE IT HAD NEVER BEEN THERE...
...BUT SOMETHING CAME THIS WAY...
...CAME FROM OUTSIDE HHHHARROW...
...CAN SMELL IT...
...TROD ALONG HHHHIDDEN PATHS TO GET HHHHERE...
YOU THINK IT'S HER, DON'T YOU?
YOU THINK...
...IT WAS KAMMI WHO KILLED LOVEY.
DON'T YOU?
"IT'S ALL RIGHT, CHILD. I'M NOT GOING TO HURT YOU."

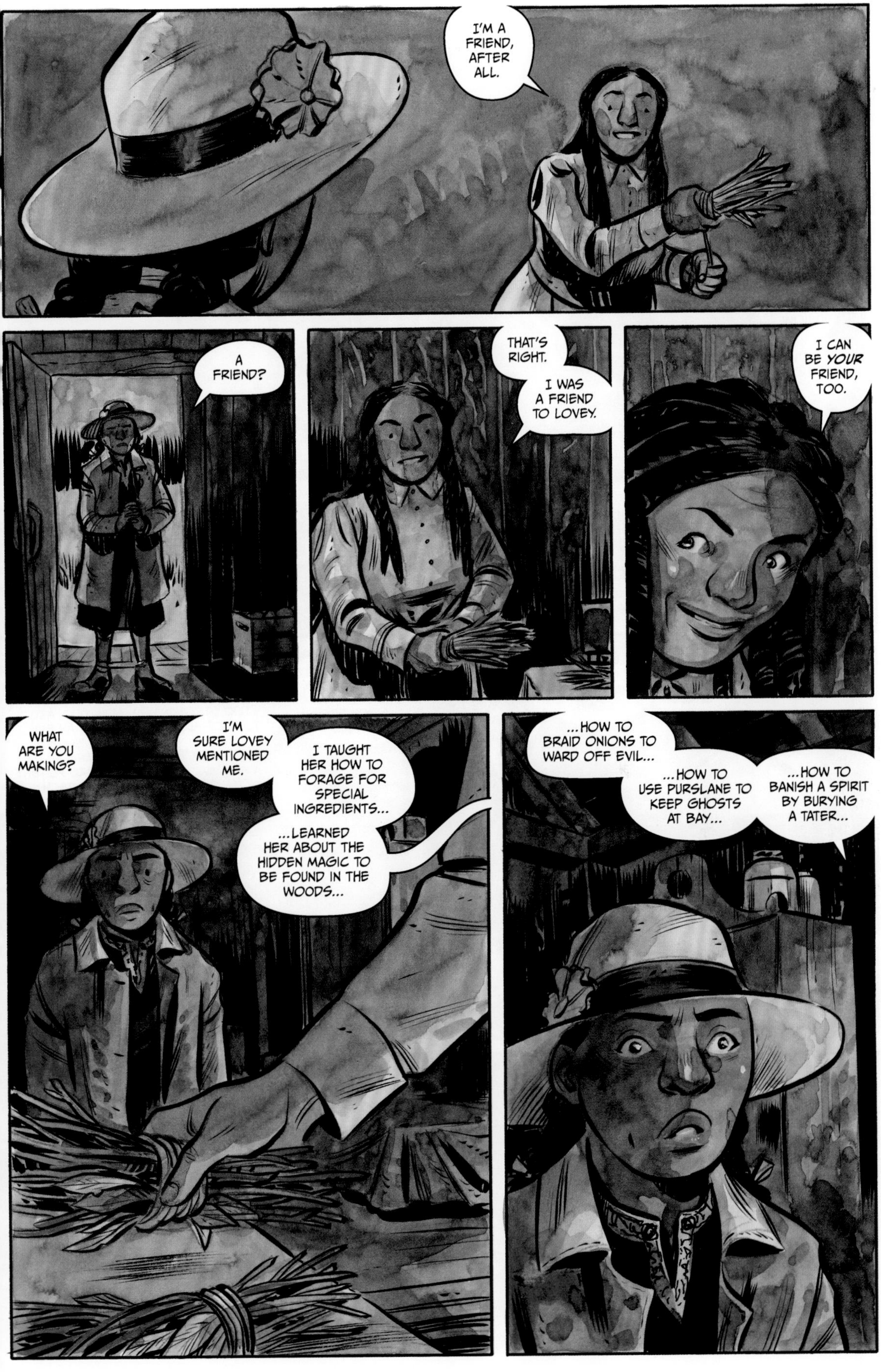
I'M A FRIEND, AFTER ALL.
A FRIEND?
THAT'S RIGHT.
I WAS A FRIEND TO LOVEY.
I CAN BE *YOUR* FRIEND, TOO.
WHAT ARE YOU MAKING?
I'M SURE LOVEY MENTIONED ME.
I TAUGHT HER HOW TO FORAGE FOR SPECIAL INGREDIENTS...
...LEARNED HER ABOUT THE HIDDEN MAGIC TO BE FOUND IN THE WOODS...
...HOW TO BRAID ONIONS TO WARD OFF EVIL...
...HOW TO USE PURSLANE TO KEEP GHOSTS AT BAY...
...HOW TO BANISH A SPIRIT BY BURYING A TATER...

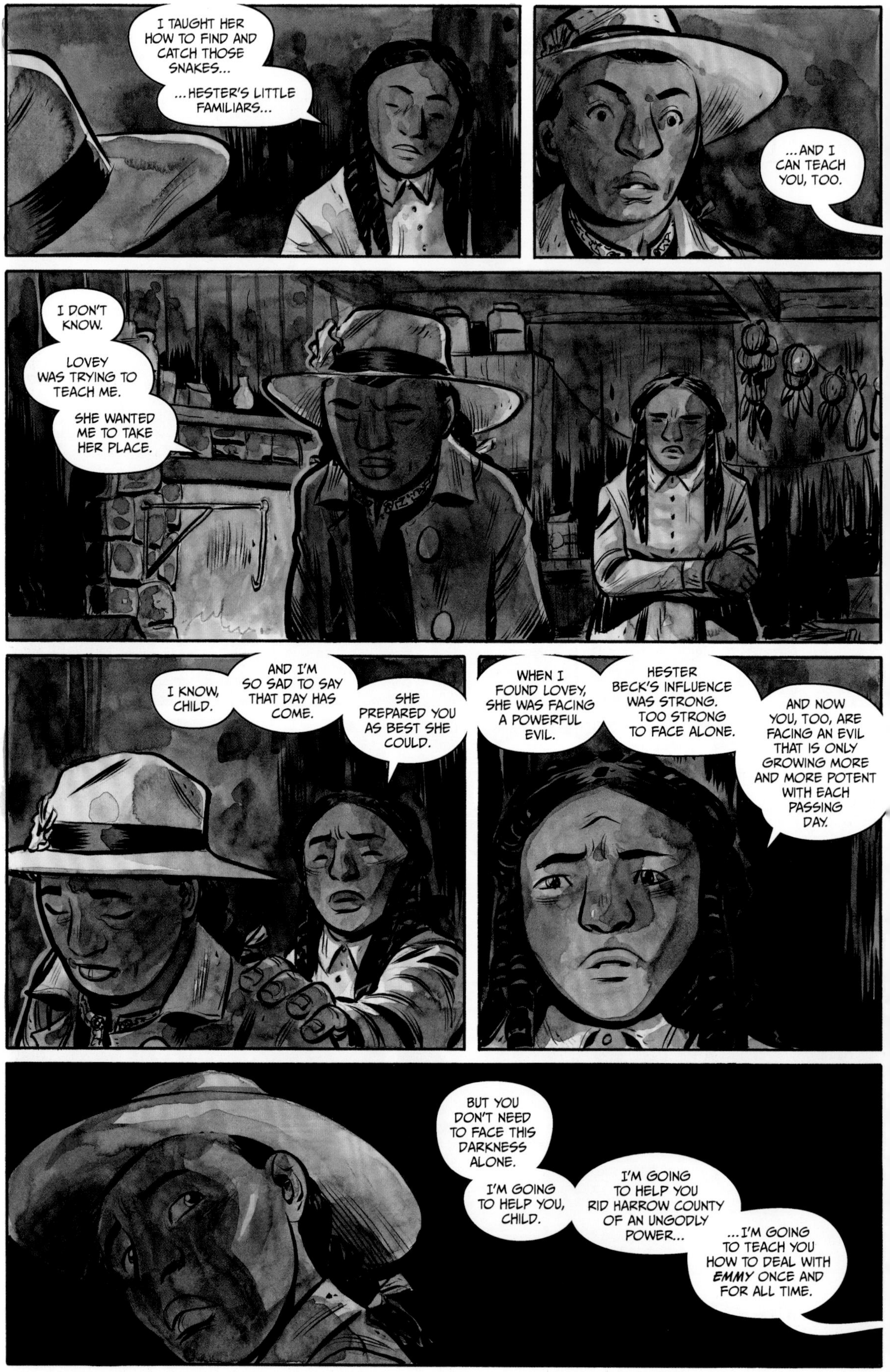
I TAUGHT HER HOW TO FIND AND CATCH THOSE SNAKES...
...HESTER'S LITTLE FAMILIARS...
...AND I CAN TEACH YOU, TOO.
I DON'T KNOW.
LOVEY WAS TRYING TO TEACH ME.
SHE WANTED ME TO TAKE HER PLACE.
I KNOW, CHILD.
AND I'M SO SAD TO SAY THAT DAY HAS COME.
SHE PREPARED YOU AS BEST SHE COULD.
WHEN I FOUND LOVEY, SHE WAS FACING A POWERFUL EVIL.
HESTER BECK'S INFLUENCE WAS STRONG. TOO STRONG TO FACE ALONE.
AND NOW YOU, TOO, ARE FACING AN EVIL THAT IS ONLY GROWING MORE AND MORE POTENT WITH EACH PASSING DAY.
BUT YOU DON'T NEED TO FACE THIS DARKNESS ALONE.
I'M GOING TO HELP YOU, CHILD.
I'M GOING TO HELP YOU RID HARROW COUNTY OF AN UNGODLY POWER...
...I'M GOING TO TEACH YOU HOW TO DEAL WITH *EMMY* ONCE AND FOR ALL TIME.

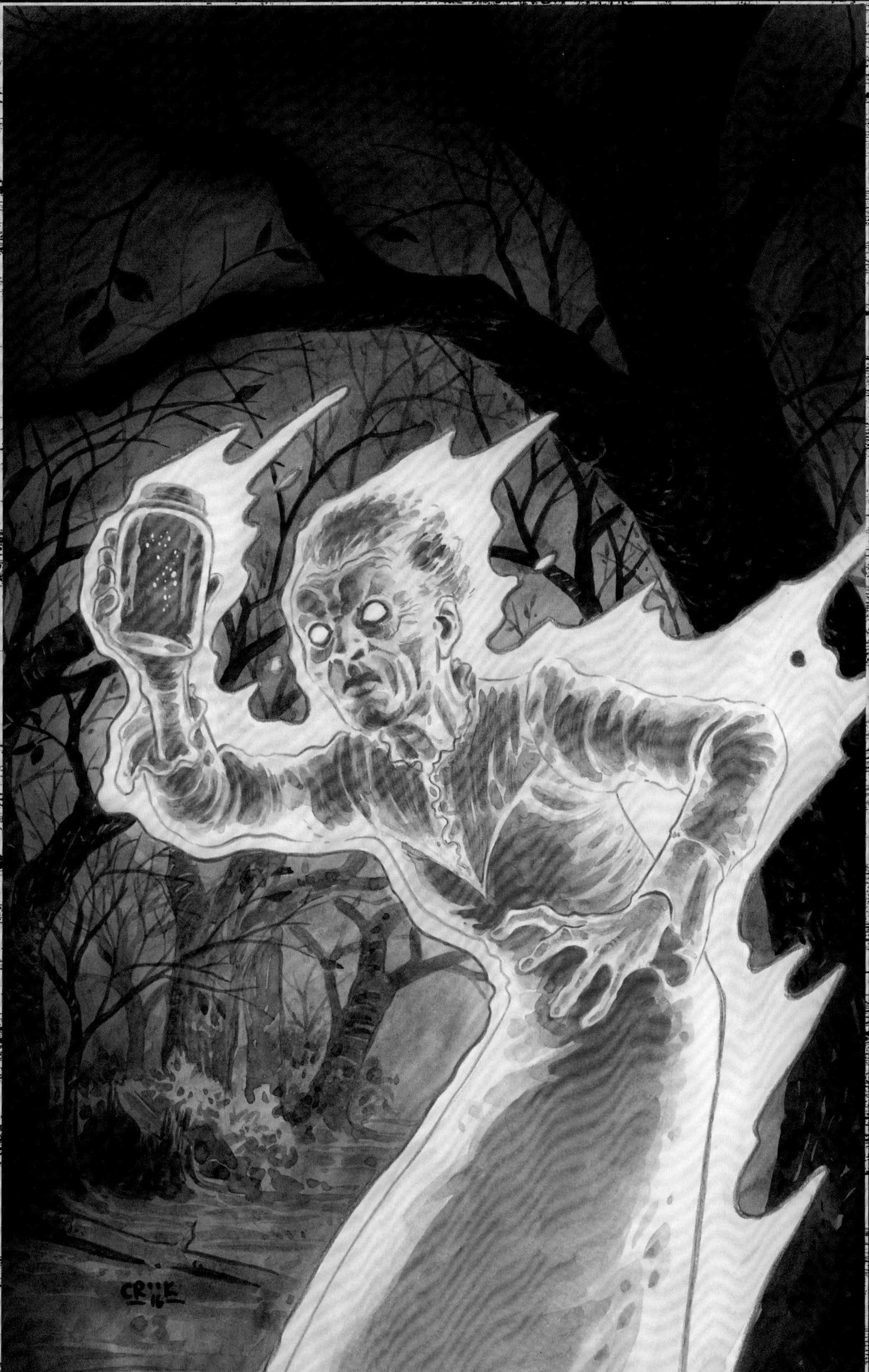

FOUR

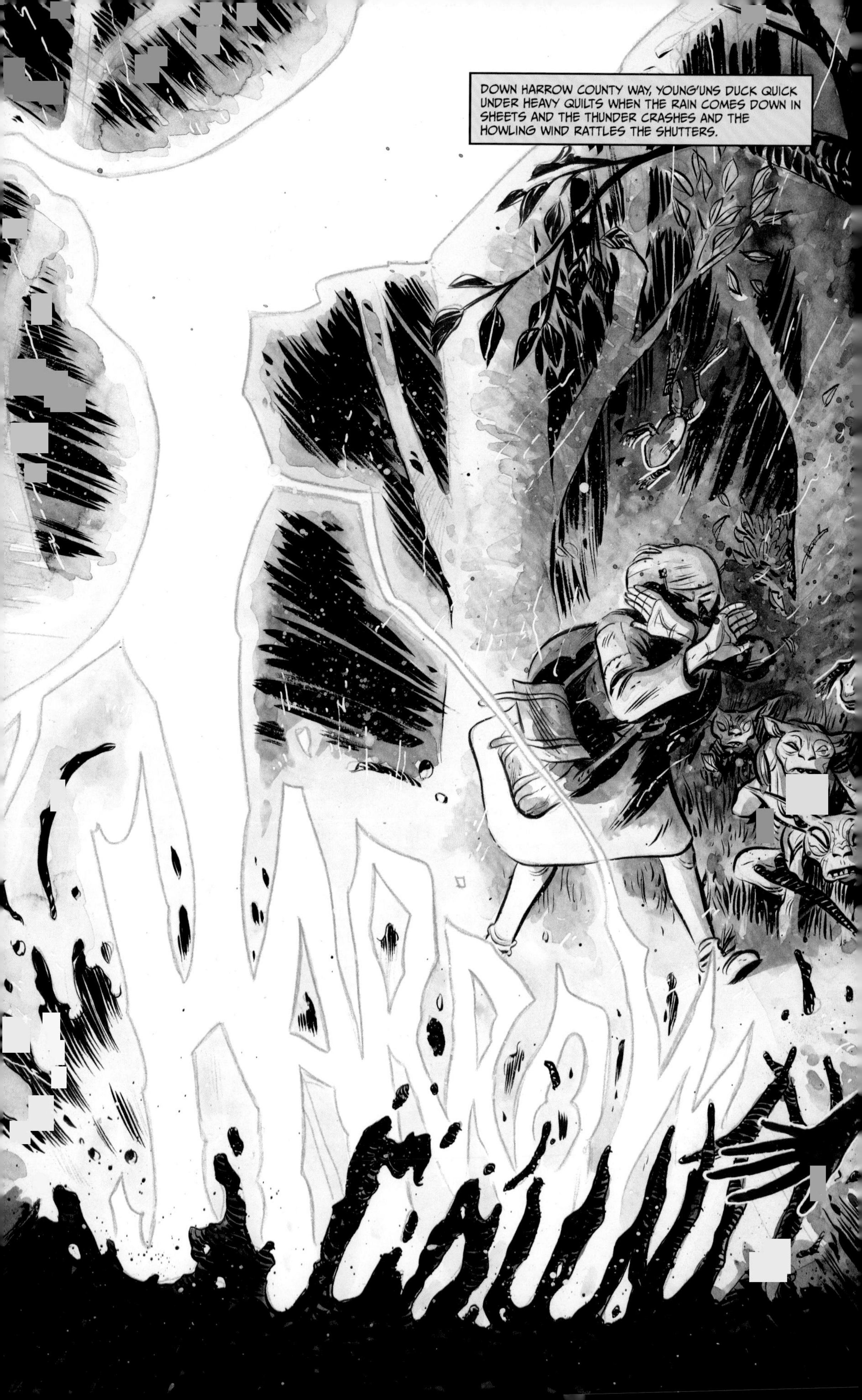
DOWN HARROW COUNTY WAY, YOUNG'UNS DUCK QUICK UNDER HEAVY QUILTS WHEN THE RAIN COMES DOWN IN SHEETS AND THE THUNDER CRASHES AND THE HOWLING WIND RATTLES THE SHUTTERS.
HARROW COUNTY

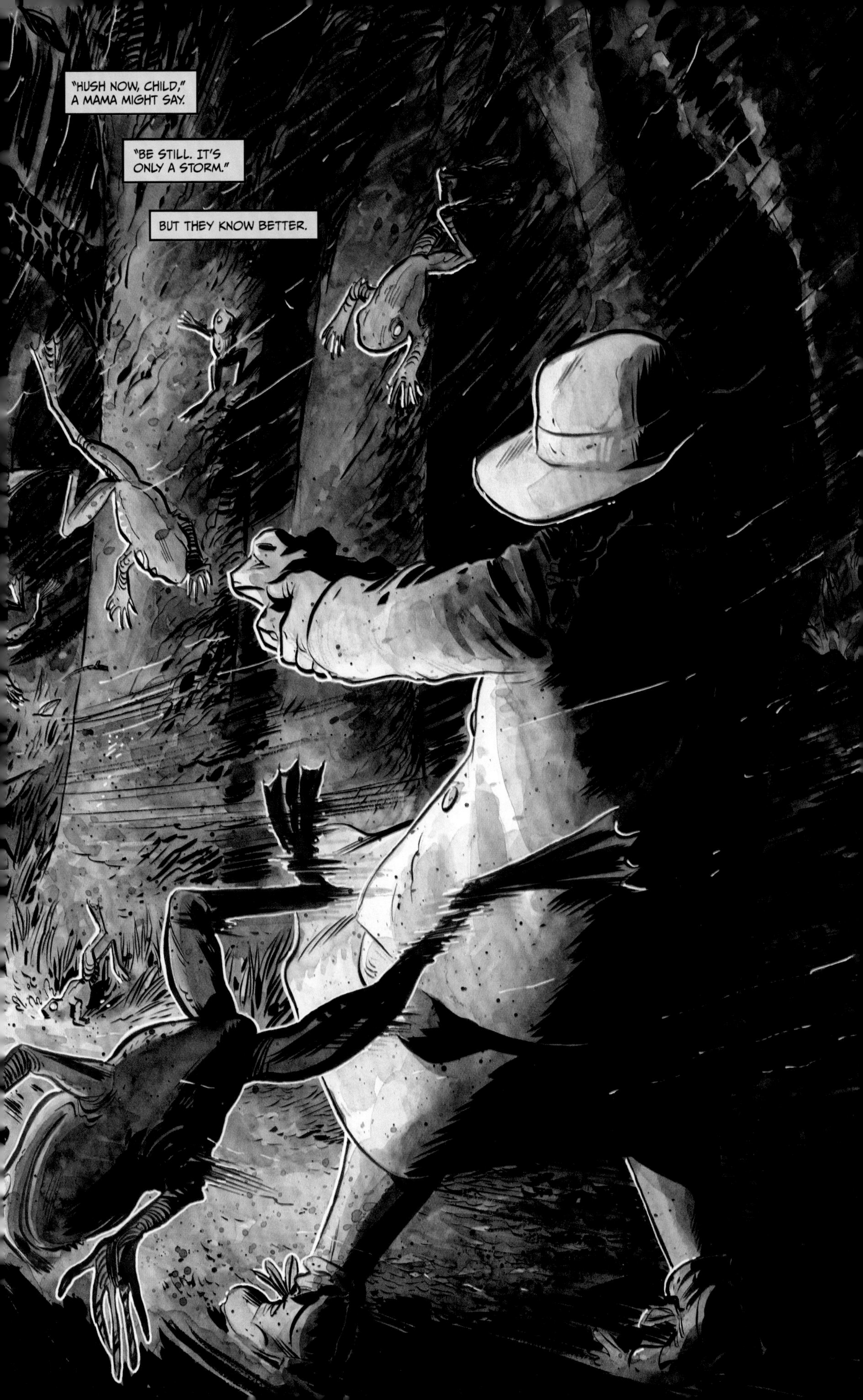
"HUSH NOW, CHILD," A MAMA MIGHT SAY.
"BE STILL. IT'S ONLY A STORM."
BUT THEY KNOW BETTER.

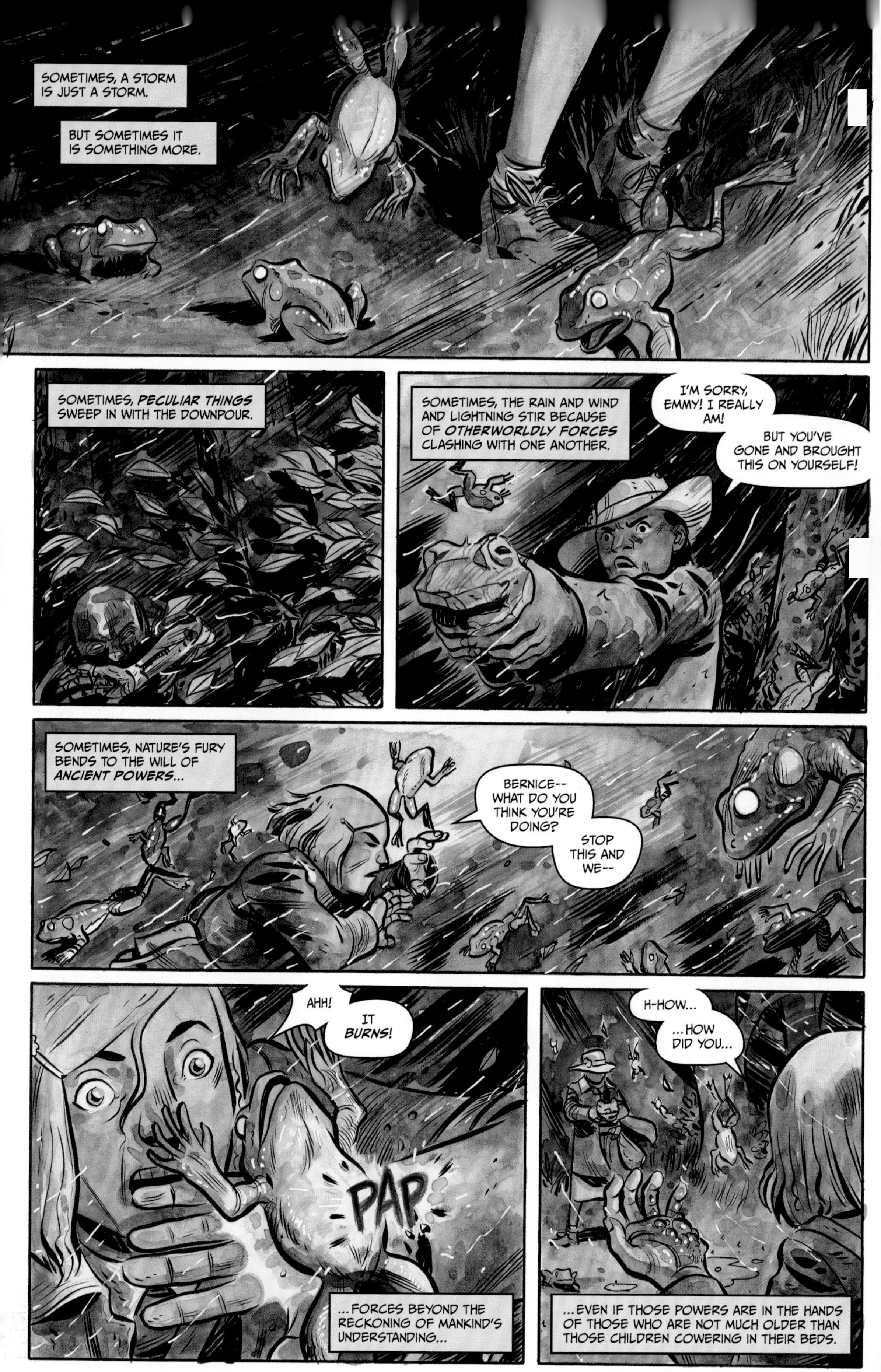
SOMETIMES, A STORM IS JUST A STORM.
BUT SOMETIMES IT IS SOMETHING MORE.
SOMETIMES, PECULIAR THINGS SWEEP IN WITH THE DOWNPOUR.
SOMETIMES, THE RAIN AND WIND AND LIGHTNING STIR BECAUSE OF OTHERWORLDLY FORCES CLASHING WITH ONE ANOTHER.
I'M SORRY, EMMY! I REALLY AM!
BUT YOU'VE GONE AND BROUGHT THIS ON YOURSELF!
SOMETIMES, NATURE'S FURY BENDS TO THE WILL OF ANCIENT POWERS...
BERNICE-- WHAT DO YOU THINK YOU'RE DOING?
STOP THIS AND WE--
AHH!
IT BURNS!
PAP
...FORCES BEYOND THE RECKONING OF MANKIND'S UNDERSTANDING...
H-HOW...
...HOW DID YOU...
...EVEN IF THOSE POWERS ARE IN THE HANDS OF THOSE WHO ARE NOT MUCH OLDER THAN THOSE CHILDREN COWERING IN THEIR BEDS.

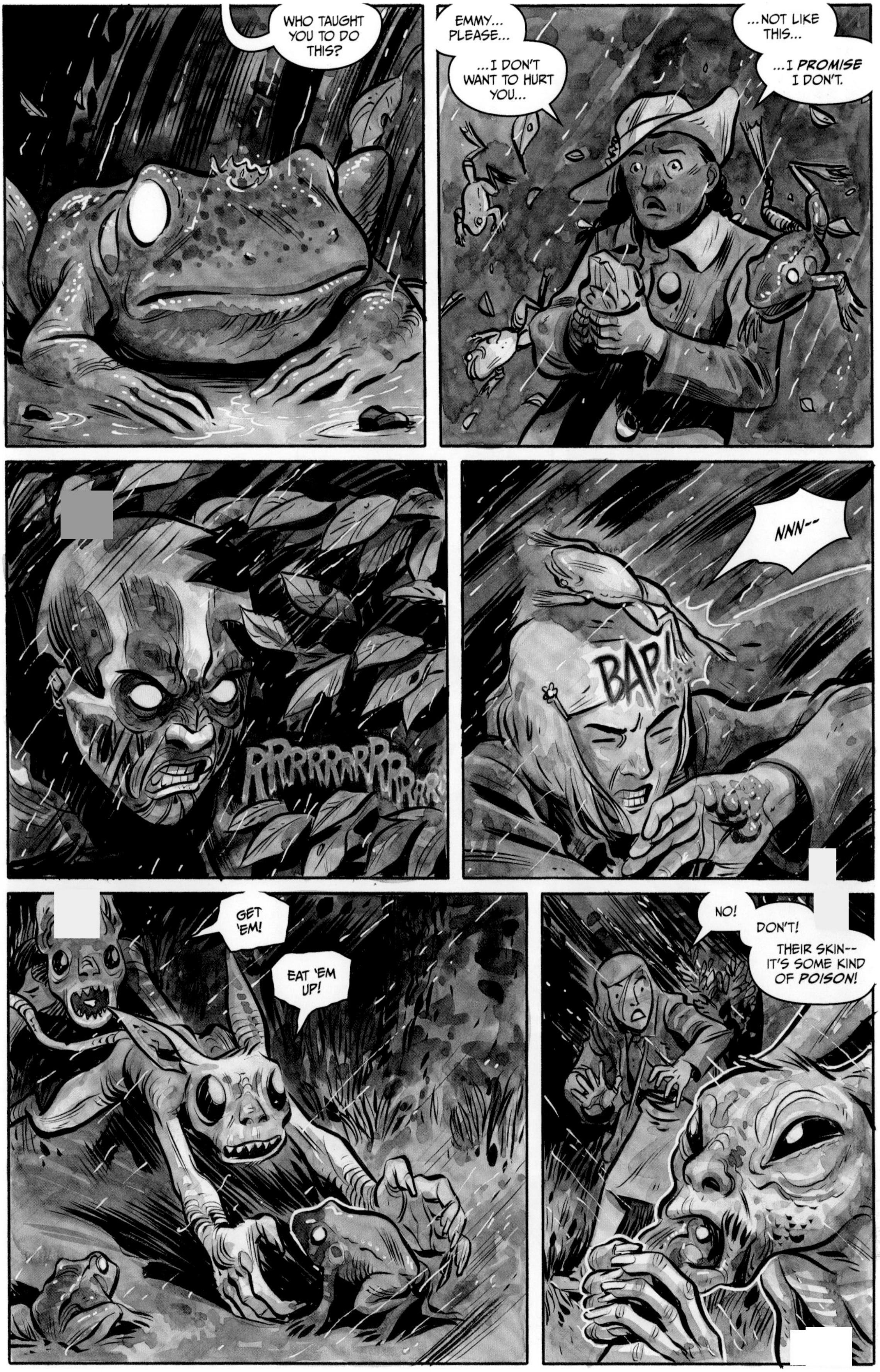
WHO TAUGHT YOU TO DO THIS?
EMMY... PLEASE...
...I DON'T WANT TO HURT YOU...
...NOT LIKE THIS...
...I PROMISE I DON'T.
RRRRRRRRRRRRR
NNN--
BAP!
GET 'EM!
EAT 'EM UP!
NO!
DON'T!
THEIR SKIN-- IT'S SOME KIND OF POISON!

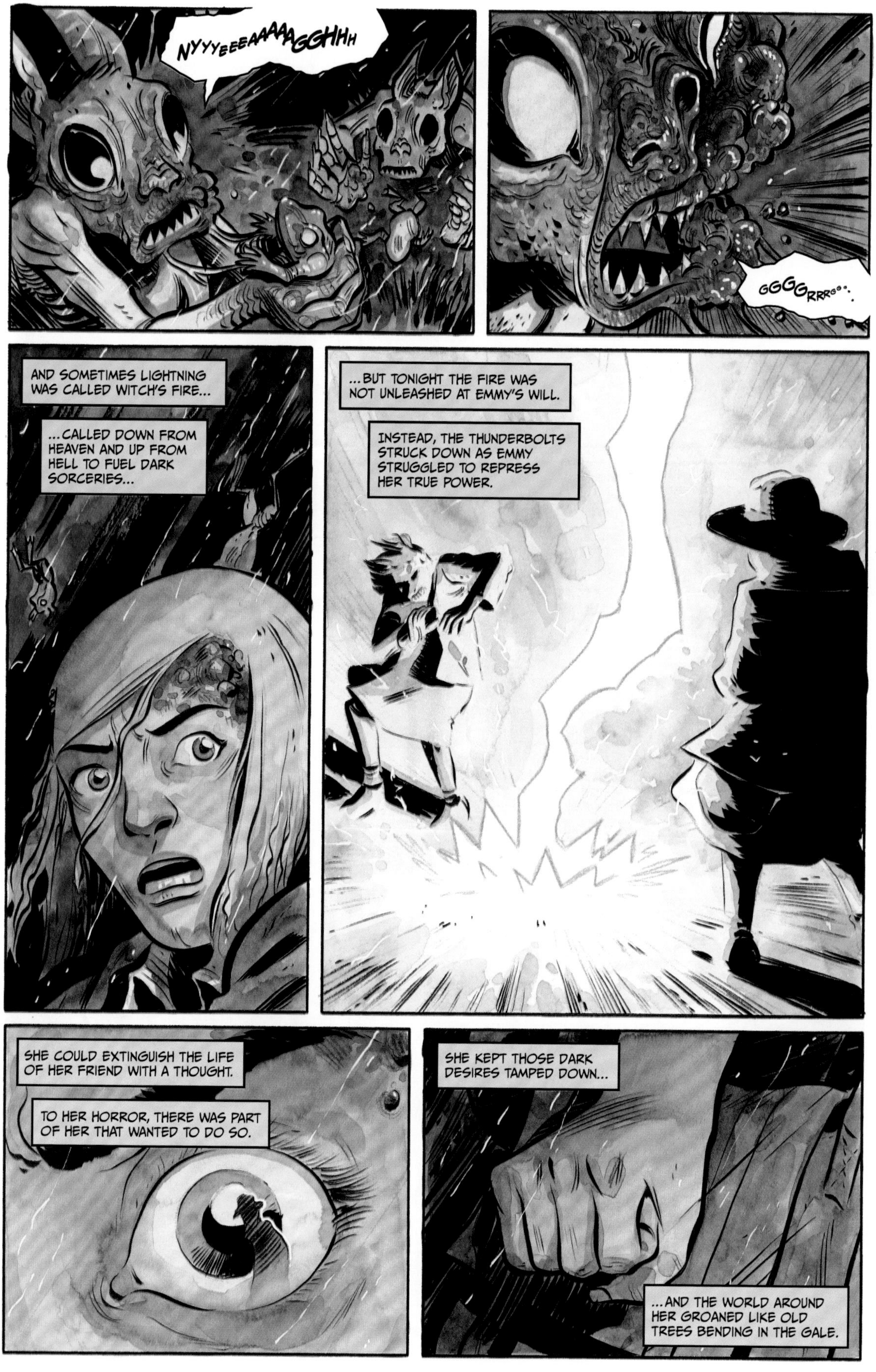
NYYYEEEAAAAAGGHHH
GGGGRRRGGG...
AND SOMETIMES LIGHTNING WAS CALLED WITCH'S FIRE...
...CALLED DOWN FROM HEAVEN AND UP FROM HELL TO FUEL DARK SORCERIES...
...BUT TONIGHT THE FIRE WAS NOT UNLEASHED AT EMMY'S WILL.
INSTEAD, THE THUNDERBOLTS STRUCK DOWN AS EMMY STRUGGLED TO REPRESS HER TRUE POWER.
SHE COULD EXTINGUISH THE LIFE OF HER FRIEND WITH A THOUGHT.
TO HER HORROR, THERE WAS PART OF HER THAT WANTED TO DO SO.
SHE KEPT THOSE DARK DESIRES TAMPED DOWN...
...AND THE WORLD AROUND HER GROANED LIKE OLD TREES BENDING IN THE GALE.

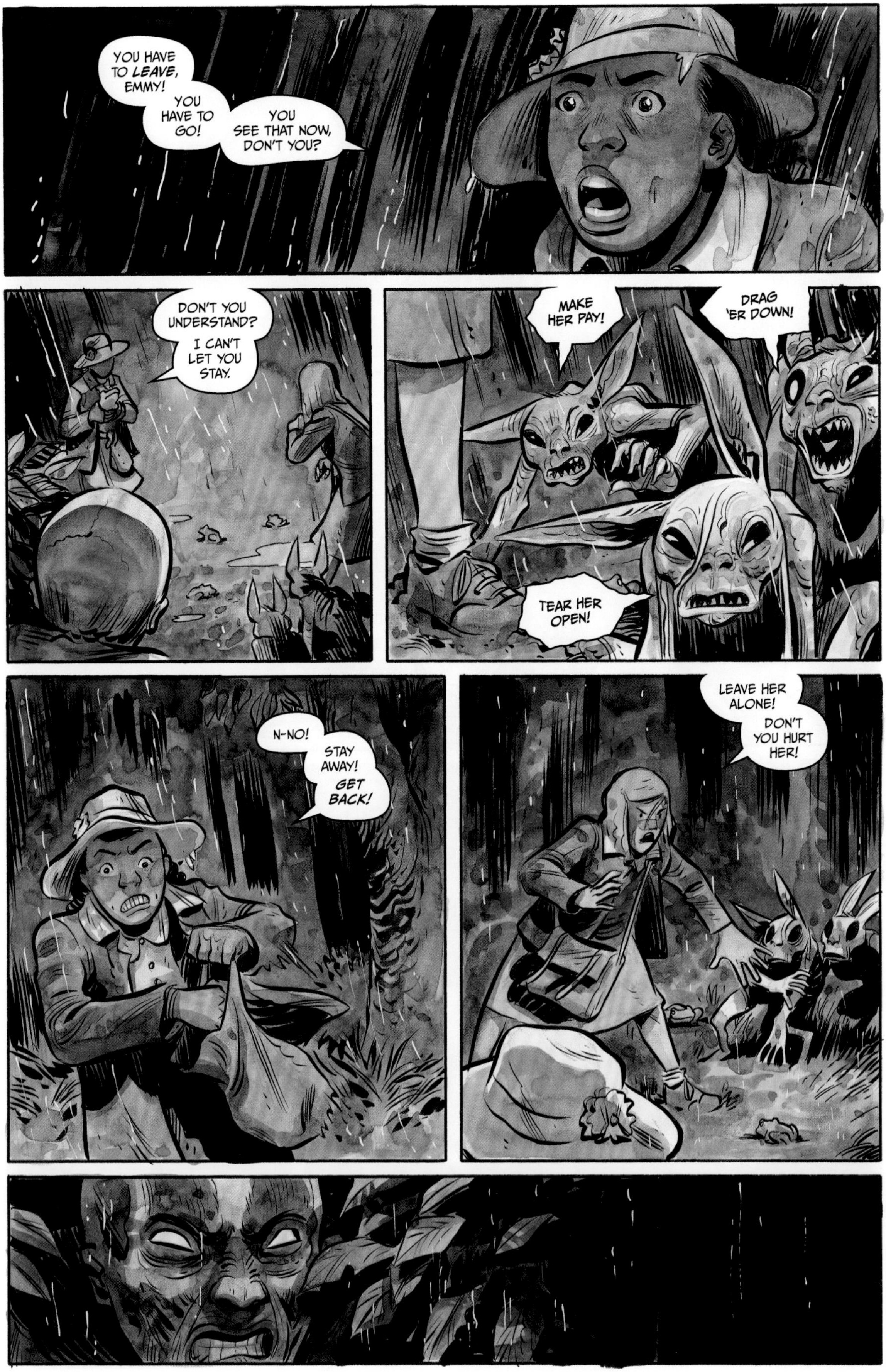
YOU HAVE TO LEAVE, EMMY!
YOU HAVE TO GO!
YOU SEE THAT NOW, DON'T YOU?
DON'T YOU UNDERSTAND?
I CAN'T LET YOU STAY.
MAKE HER PAY!
DRAG 'ER DOWN!
TEAR HER OPEN!
N-NO!
STAY AWAY!
GET BACK!
LEAVE HER ALONE!
DON'T YOU HURT HER!

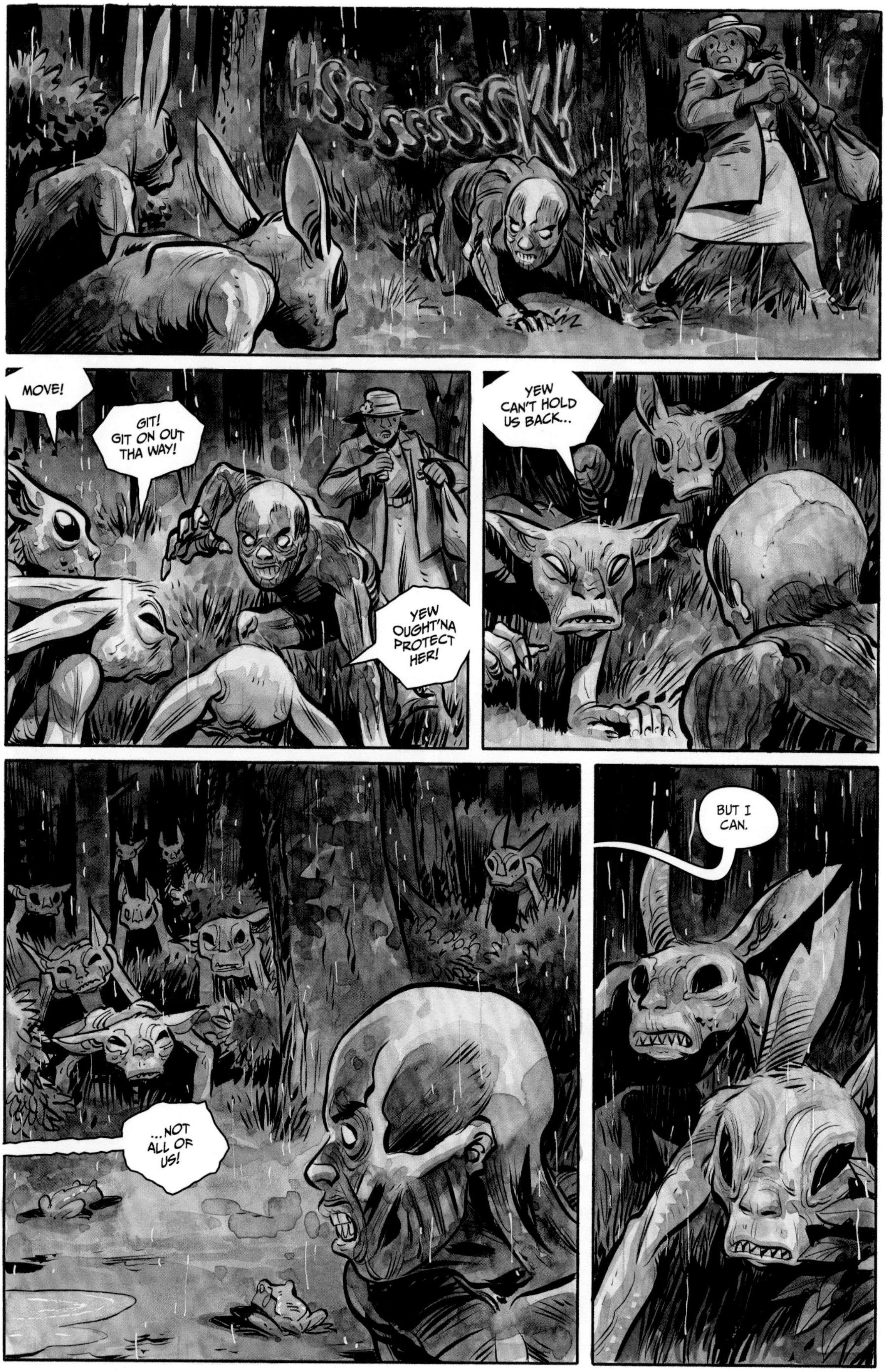
HSSSSSSSK!!
MOVE!
GIT! GIT ON OUT THA WAY!
YEW OUGHT'NA PROTECT HER!
YEW CAN'T HOLD US BACK..
...NOT ALL OF US!
BUT I CAN.

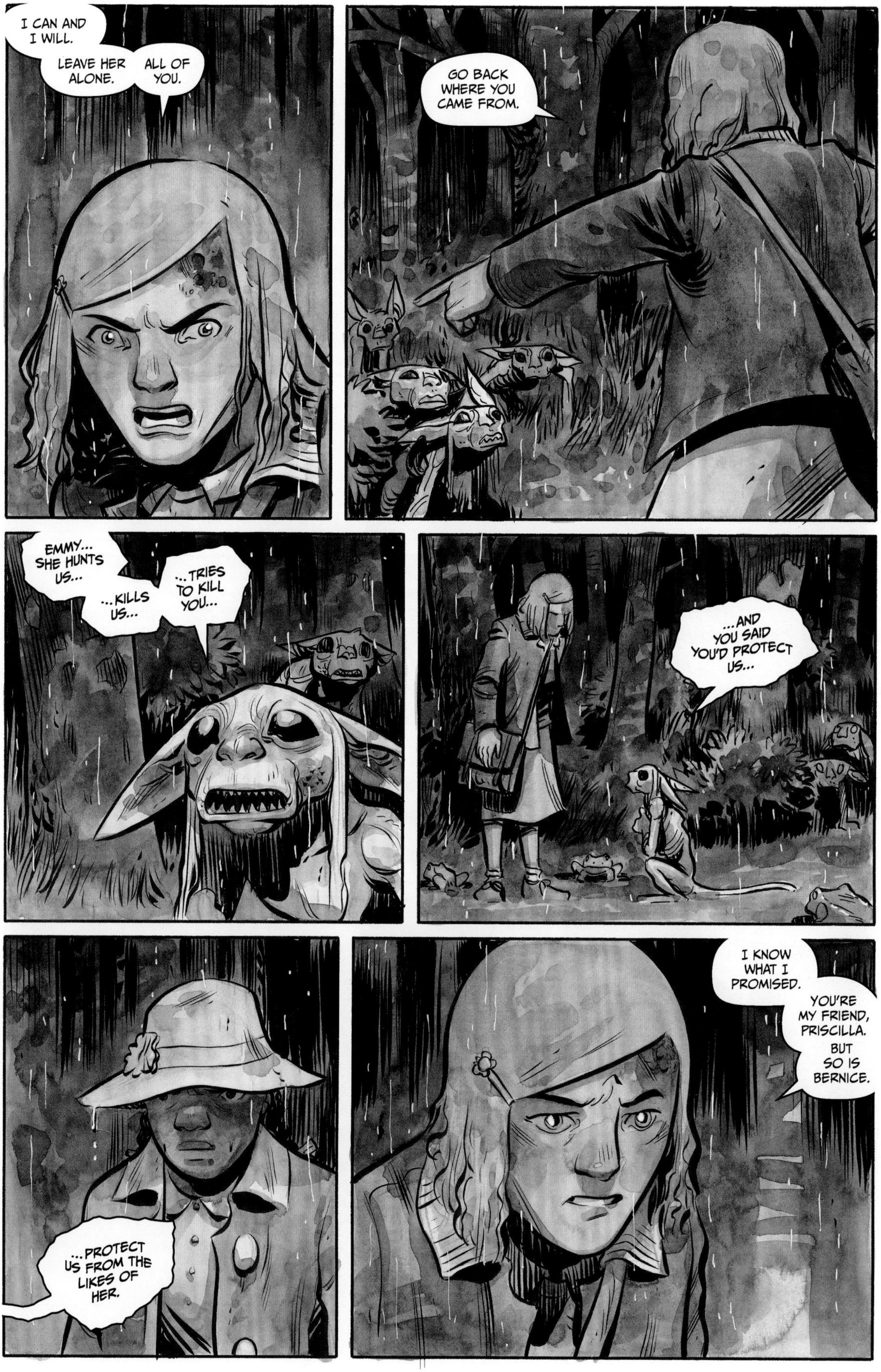
I CAN AND I WILL.
LEAVE HER ALONE.
ALL OF YOU.
GO BACK WHERE YOU CAME FROM.
EMMY... SHE HUNTS US...
...KILLS US...
...TRIES TO KILL YOU...
...AND YOU SAID YOU'D PROTECT US...
...PROTECT US FROM THE LIKES OF HER.
I KNOW WHAT I PROMISED.
YOU'RE MY FRIEND, PRISCILLA.
BUT SO IS BERNICE.

AND I'M NOT GOING TO LET FRIENDS HURT EACH OTHER.

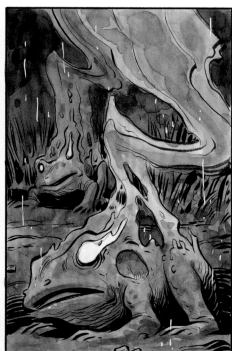

AM I UNDERSTOOD?

HHUHH--

--YES, MA'AM.

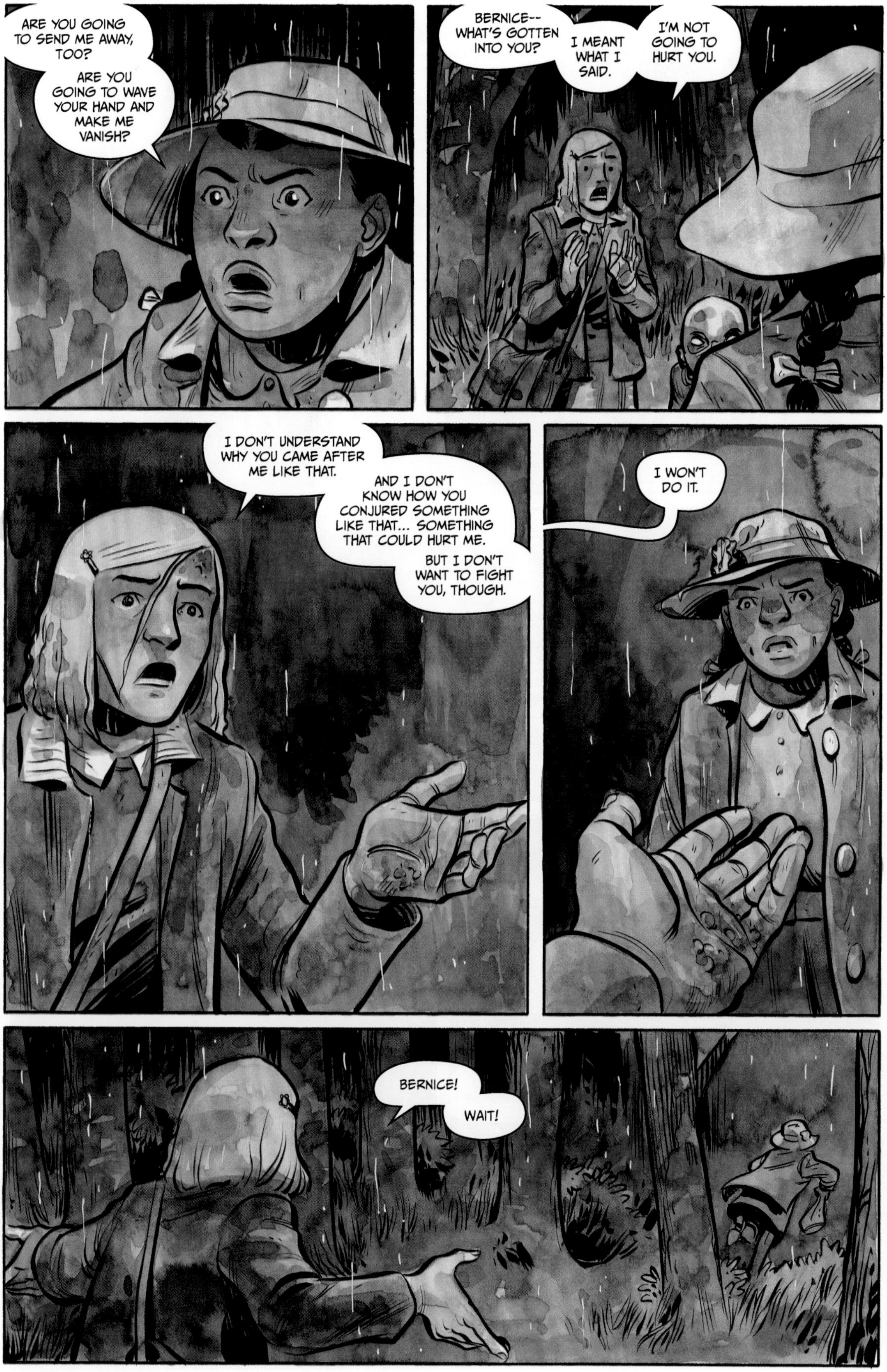
ARE YOU GOING TO SEND ME AWAY, TOO?
ARE YOU GOING TO WAVE YOUR HAND AND MAKE ME VANISH?
BERNICE-- WHAT'S GOTTEN INTO YOU?
I MEANT WHAT I SAID.
I'M NOT GOING TO HURT YOU.
I DON'T UNDERSTAND WHY YOU CAME AFTER ME LIKE THAT.
AND I DON'T KNOW HOW YOU CONJURED SOMETHING LIKE THAT... SOMETHING THAT COULD HURT ME.
BUT I DON'T WANT TO FIGHT YOU, THOUGH.
I WON'T DO IT.
BERNICE!
WAIT!

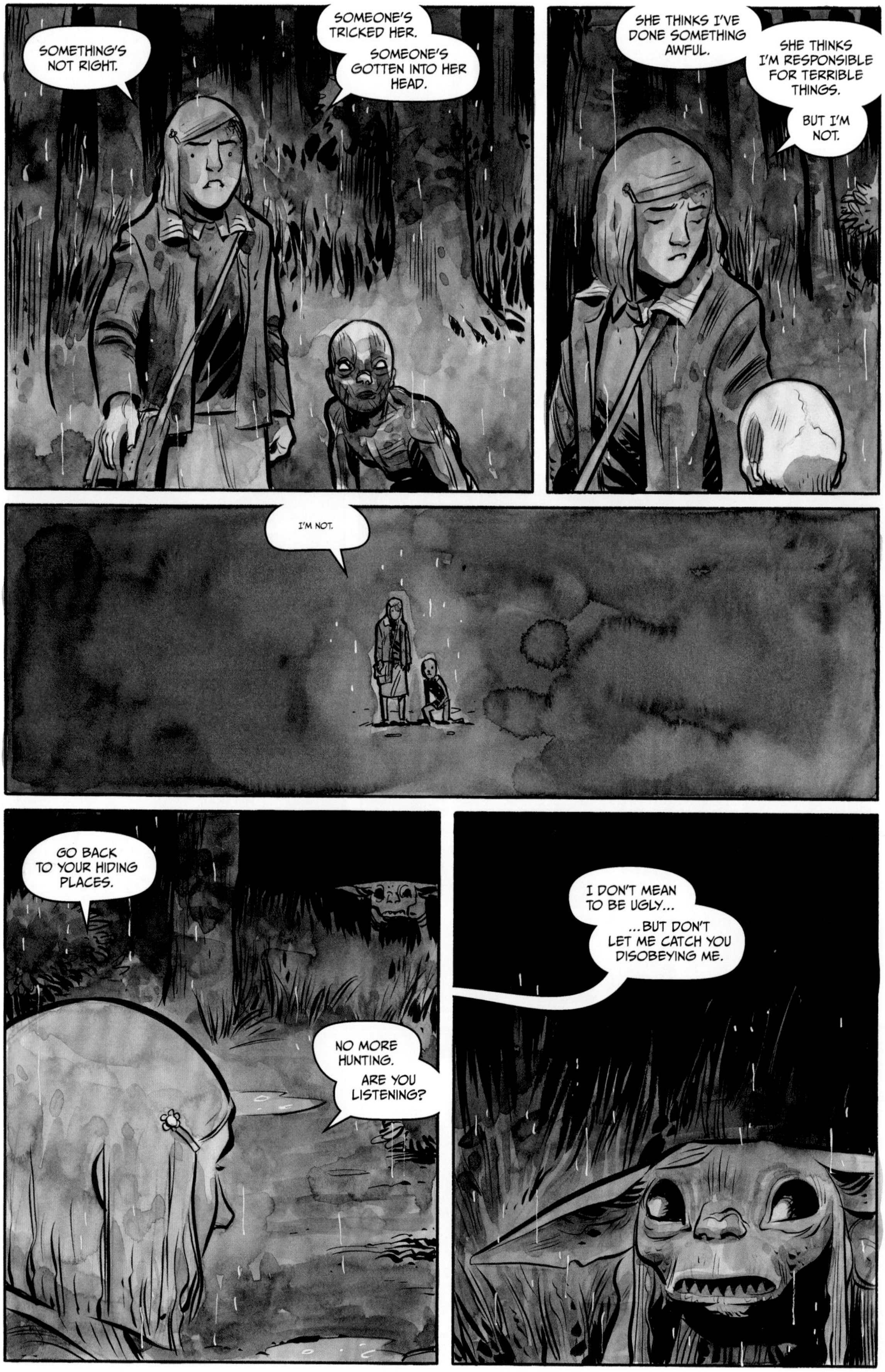
SOMETHING'S NOT RIGHT.
SOMEONE'S TRICKED HER.
SOMEONE'S GOTTEN INTO HER HEAD.
SHE THINKS I'VE DONE SOMETHING AWFUL.
SHE THINKS I'M RESPONSIBLE FOR TERRIBLE THINGS.
BUT I'M NOT.
I'M NOT.
GO BACK TO YOUR HIDING PLACES.
NO MORE HUNTING.
ARE YOU LISTENING?
I DON'T MEAN TO BE UGLY...
...BUT DON'T LET ME CATCH YOU DISOBEYING ME.

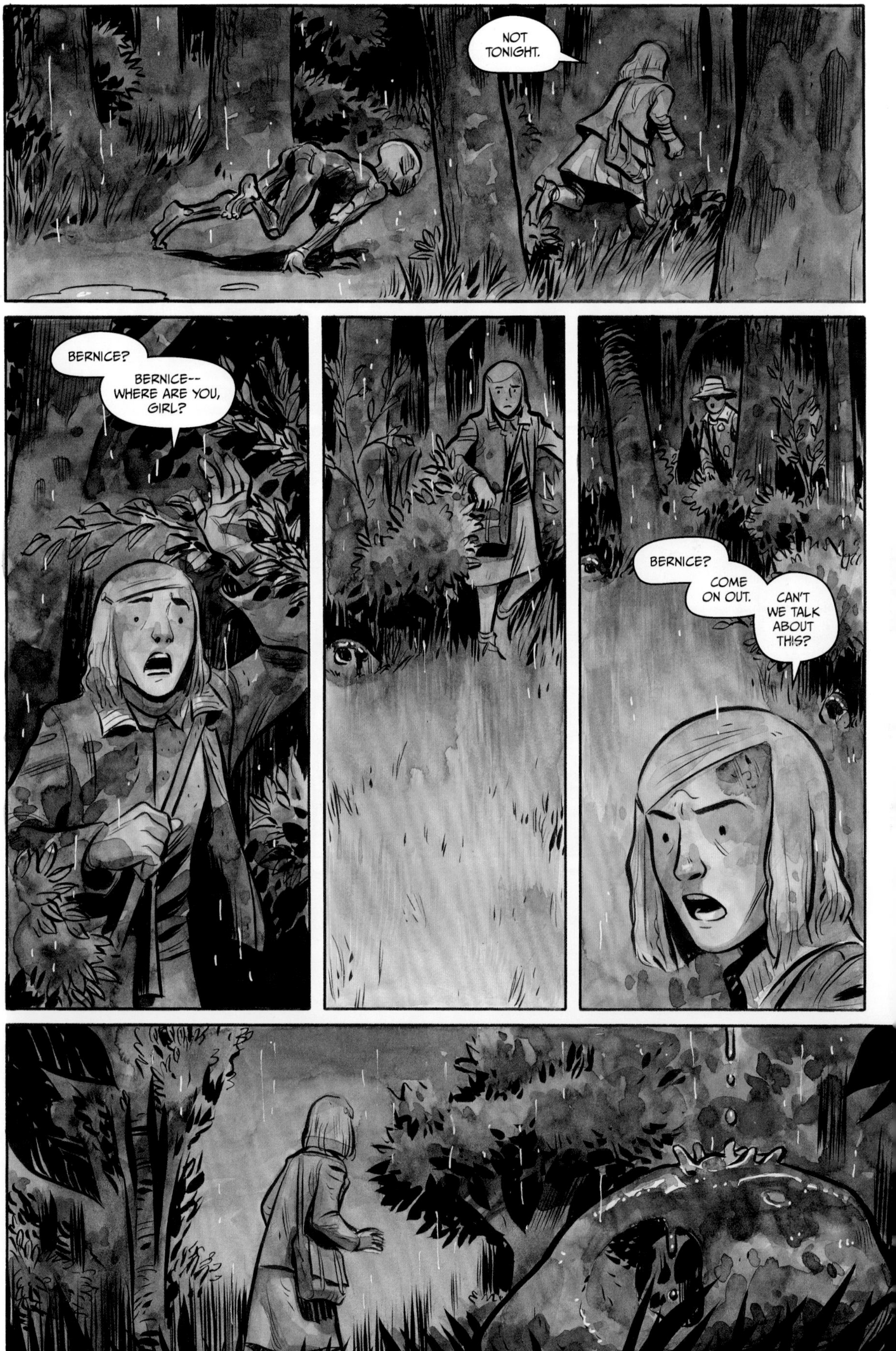
NOT TONIGHT.
BERNICE?
BERNICE-- WHERE ARE YOU, GIRL?
BERNICE?
COME ON OUT.
CAN'T WE TALK ABOUT THIS?

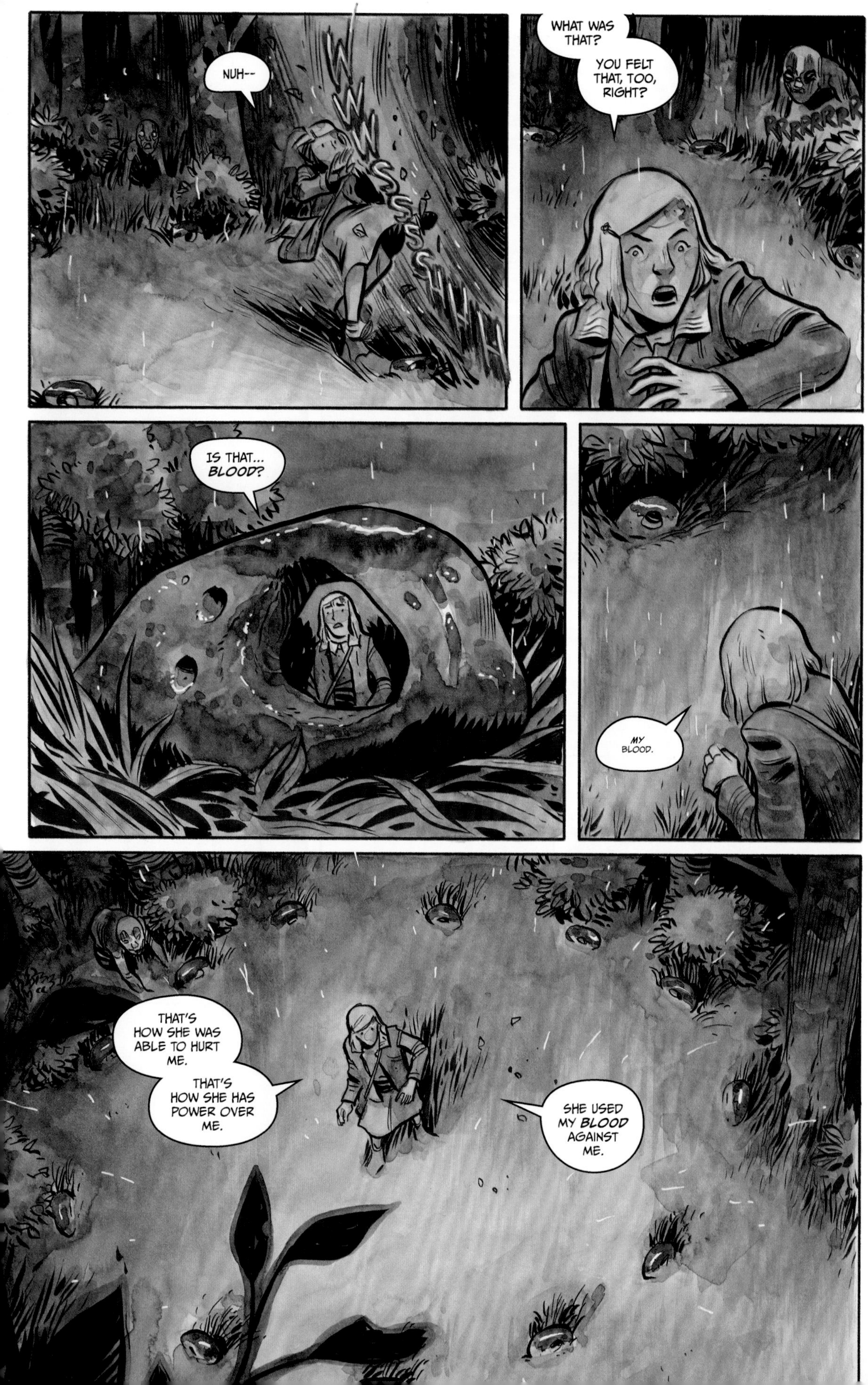
NUH--
WWWSSSSHHH
WHAT WAS THAT?
YOU FELT THAT, TOO, RIGHT?
RRRRRRRR
IS THAT... *BLOOD?*
MY BLOOD.
THAT'S HOW SHE WAS ABLE TO HURT ME.
THAT'S HOW SHE HAS POWER OVER ME.
SHE USED MY *BLOOD* AGAINST ME.

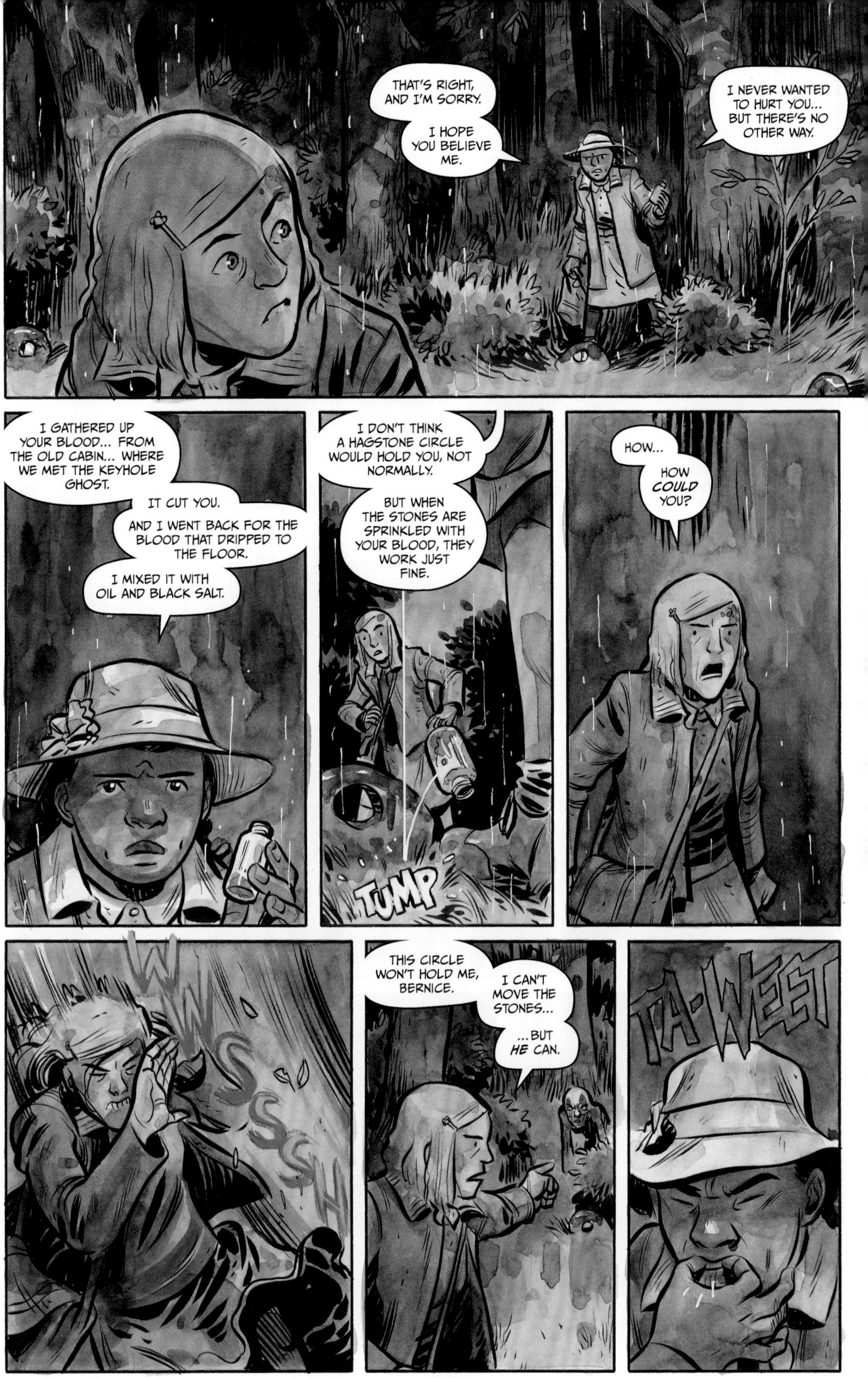
THAT'S RIGHT, AND I'M SORRY.
I HOPE YOU BELIEVE ME.
I NEVER WANTED TO HURT YOU... BUT THERE'S NO OTHER WAY.
I GATHERED UP YOUR BLOOD... FROM THE OLD CABIN... WHERE WE MET THE KEYHOLE GHOST.
IT CUT YOU.
AND I WENT BACK FOR THE BLOOD THAT DRIPPED TO THE FLOOR.
I MIXED IT WITH OIL AND BLACK SALT.
I DON'T THINK A HAGSTONE CIRCLE WOULD HOLD YOU, NOT NORMALLY.
BUT WHEN THE STONES ARE SPRINKLED WITH YOUR BLOOD, THEY WORK JUST FINE.
TUMP
HOW...
HOW COULD YOU?
WWWSSSSH
THIS CIRCLE WON'T HOLD ME, BERNICE.
I CAN'T MOVE THE STONES...
...BUT HE CAN.
TA-WEET

SKRRRAAAA

KHHKKHKK

RRREEEK

STOP IT! GET OFF OF THEM! LET HIM UP!

YOU HEARD HER. THAT'S ENOUGH NOW.

LEAVE HIM ALONE.

RRNNNRNNNRRNNN

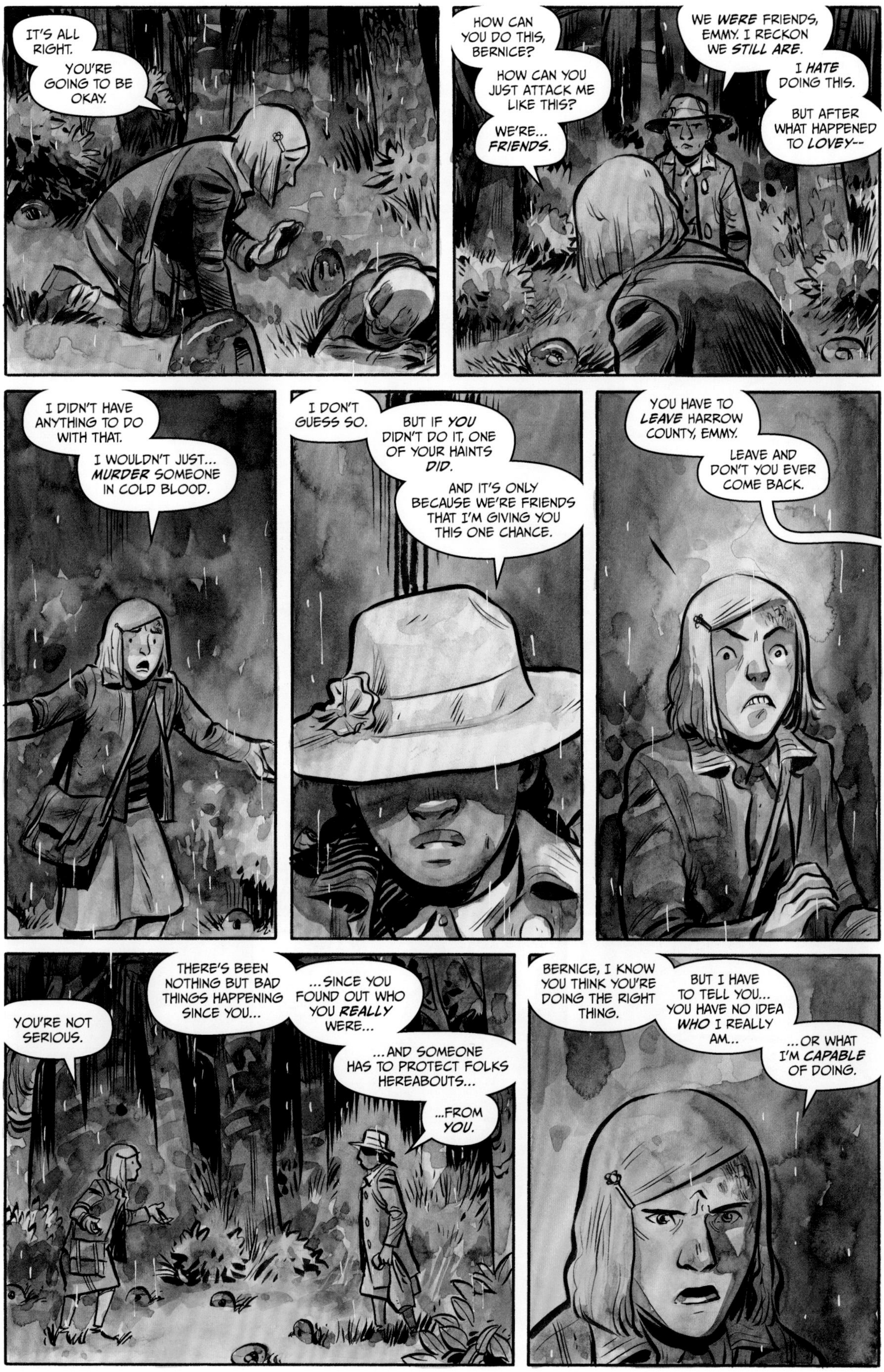
IT'S ALL RIGHT.
YOU'RE GOING TO BE OKAY.
HOW CAN YOU DO THIS, BERNICE?
HOW CAN YOU JUST ATTACK ME LIKE THIS?
WE'RE... FRIENDS.
WE WERE FRIENDS, EMMY. I RECKON WE STILL ARE.
I HATE DOING THIS.
BUT AFTER WHAT HAPPENED TO LOVEY--
I DIDN'T HAVE ANYTHING TO DO WITH THAT.
I WOULDN'T JUST... MURDER SOMEONE IN COLD BLOOD.
I DON'T GUESS SO.
BUT IF YOU DIDN'T DO IT, ONE OF YOUR HAINTS DID.
AND IT'S ONLY BECAUSE WE'RE FRIENDS THAT I'M GIVING YOU THIS ONE CHANCE.
YOU HAVE TO LEAVE HARROW COUNTY, EMMY.
LEAVE AND DON'T YOU EVER COME BACK.
YOU'RE NOT SERIOUS.
THERE'S BEEN NOTHING BUT BAD THINGS HAPPENING SINCE YOU...
...SINCE YOU FOUND OUT WHO YOU REALLY WERE...
...AND SOMEONE HAS TO PROTECT FOLKS HEREABOUTS...
...FROM YOU.
BERNICE, I KNOW YOU THINK YOU'RE DOING THE RIGHT THING.
BUT I HAVE TO TELL YOU... YOU HAVE NO IDEA WHO I REALLY AM...
...OR WHAT I'M CAPABLE OF DOING.

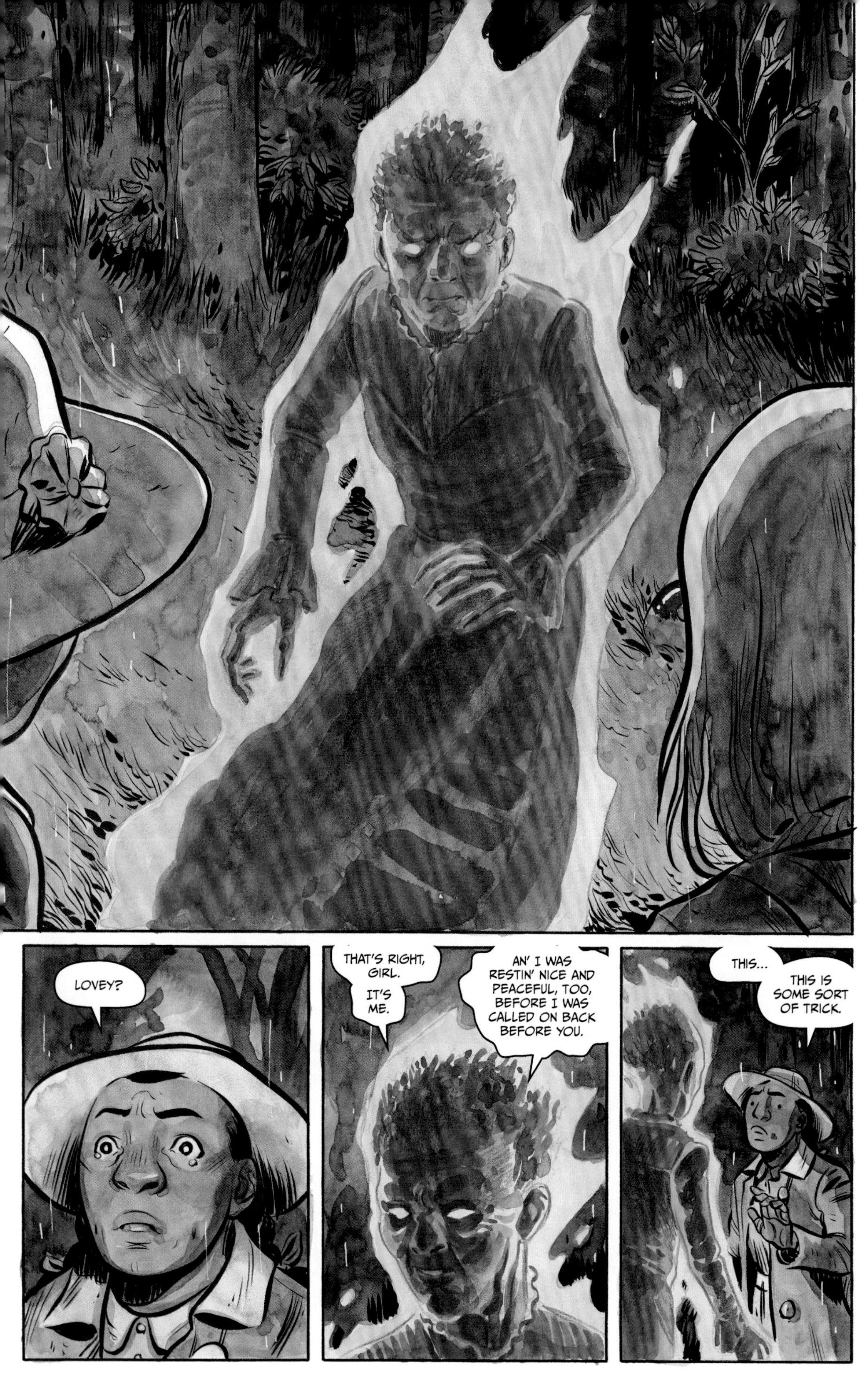
LOVEY?
THAT'S RIGHT, GIRL.
IT'S ME.
AN' I WAS RESTIN' NICE AND PEACEFUL, TOO, BEFORE I WAS CALLED ON BACK BEFORE YOU.
THIS...
THIS IS SOME SORT OF TRICK.

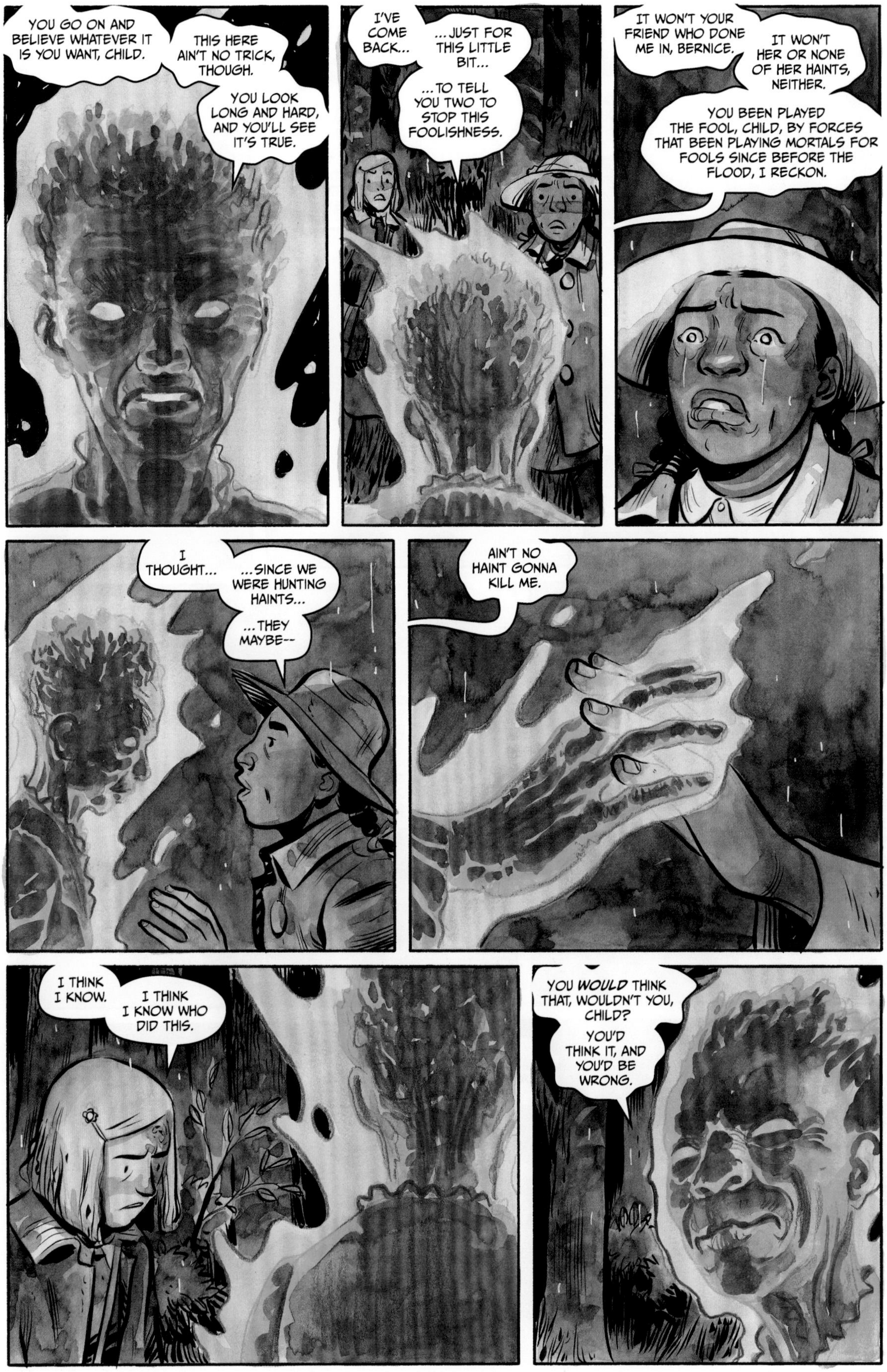
YOU GO ON AND BELIEVE WHATEVER IT IS YOU WANT, CHILD.
THIS HERE AIN'T NO TRICK, THOUGH.
YOU LOOK LONG AND HARD, AND YOU'LL SEE IT'S TRUE.
I'VE COME BACK...
...JUST FOR THIS LITTLE BIT...
...TO TELL YOU TWO TO STOP THIS FOOLISHNESS.
IT WON'T YOUR FRIEND WHO DONE ME IN, BERNICE.
IT WON'T HER OR NONE OF HER HAINTS, NEITHER.
YOU BEEN PLAYED THE FOOL, CHILD, BY FORCES THAT BEEN PLAYING MORTALS FOR FOOLS SINCE BEFORE THE FLOOD, I RECKON.
I THOUGHT...
...SINCE WE WERE HUNTING HAINTS...
...THEY MAYBE--
AIN'T NO HAINT GONNA KILL ME.
I THINK I KNOW.
I THINK I KNOW WHO DID THIS.
YOU *WOULD* THINK THAT, WOULDN'T YOU, CHILD?
YOU'D THINK IT, AND YOU'D BE WRONG.

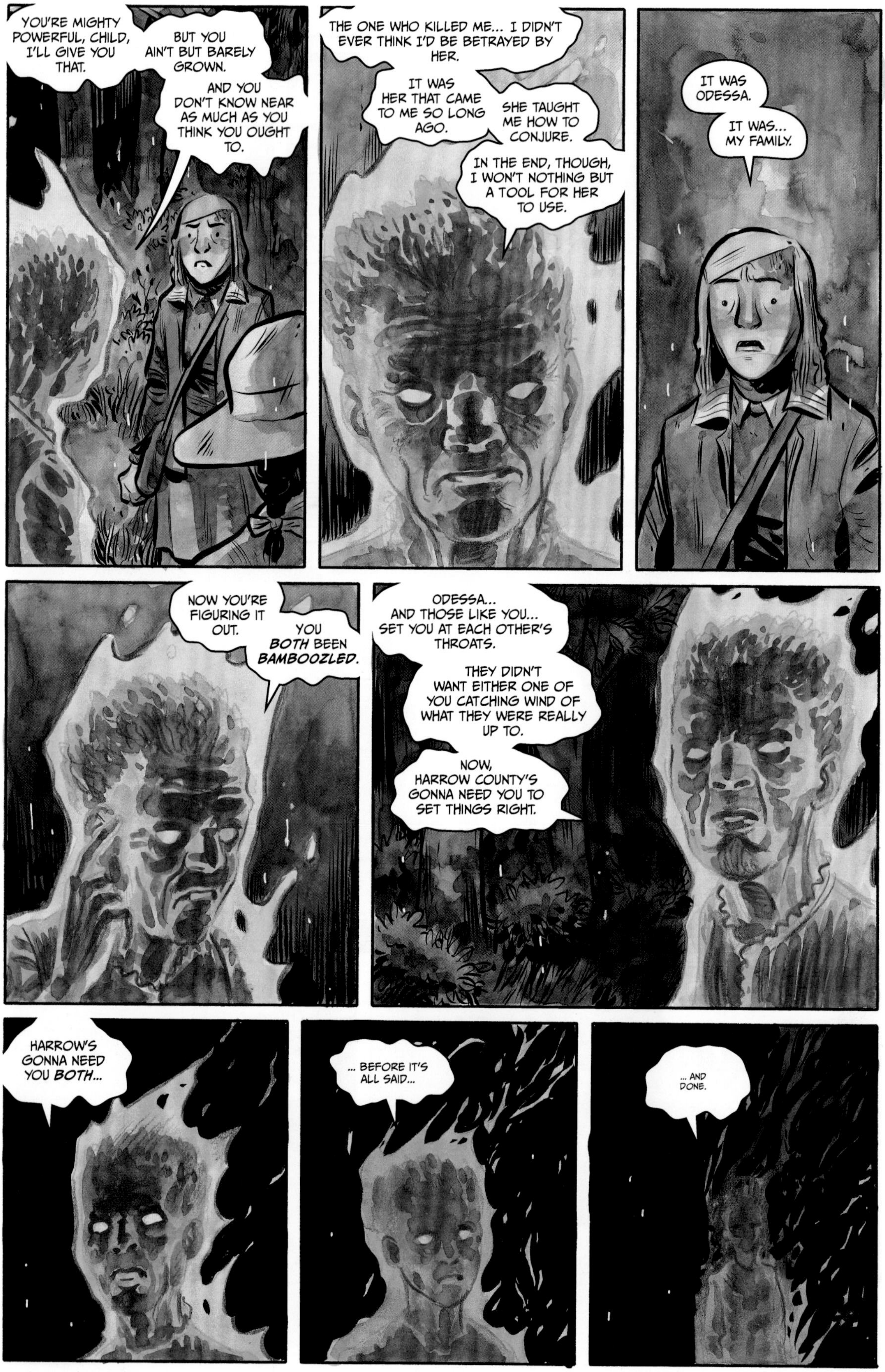
YOU'RE MIGHTY POWERFUL, CHILD, I'LL GIVE YOU THAT.
BUT YOU AIN'T BUT BARELY GROWN.
AND YOU DON'T KNOW NEAR AS MUCH AS YOU THINK YOU OUGHT TO.
THE ONE WHO KILLED ME... I DIDN'T EVER THINK I'D BE BETRAYED BY HER.
IT WAS HER THAT CAME TO ME SO LONG AGO.
SHE TAUGHT ME HOW TO CONJURE.
IN THE END, THOUGH, I WON'T NOTHING BUT A TOOL FOR HER TO USE.
IT WAS ODESSA.
IT WAS... MY FAMILY.
NOW YOU'RE FIGURING IT OUT.
YOU *BOTH* BEEN *BAMBOOZLED*.
ODESSA... AND THOSE LIKE YOU... SET YOU AT EACH OTHER'S THROATS.
THEY DIDN'T WANT EITHER ONE OF YOU CATCHING WIND OF WHAT THEY WERE REALLY UP TO.
NOW, HARROW COUNTY'S GONNA NEED YOU TO SET THINGS RIGHT.
HARROW'S GONNA NEED YOU *BOTH*...
... BEFORE IT'S ALL SAID...
... AND DONE.

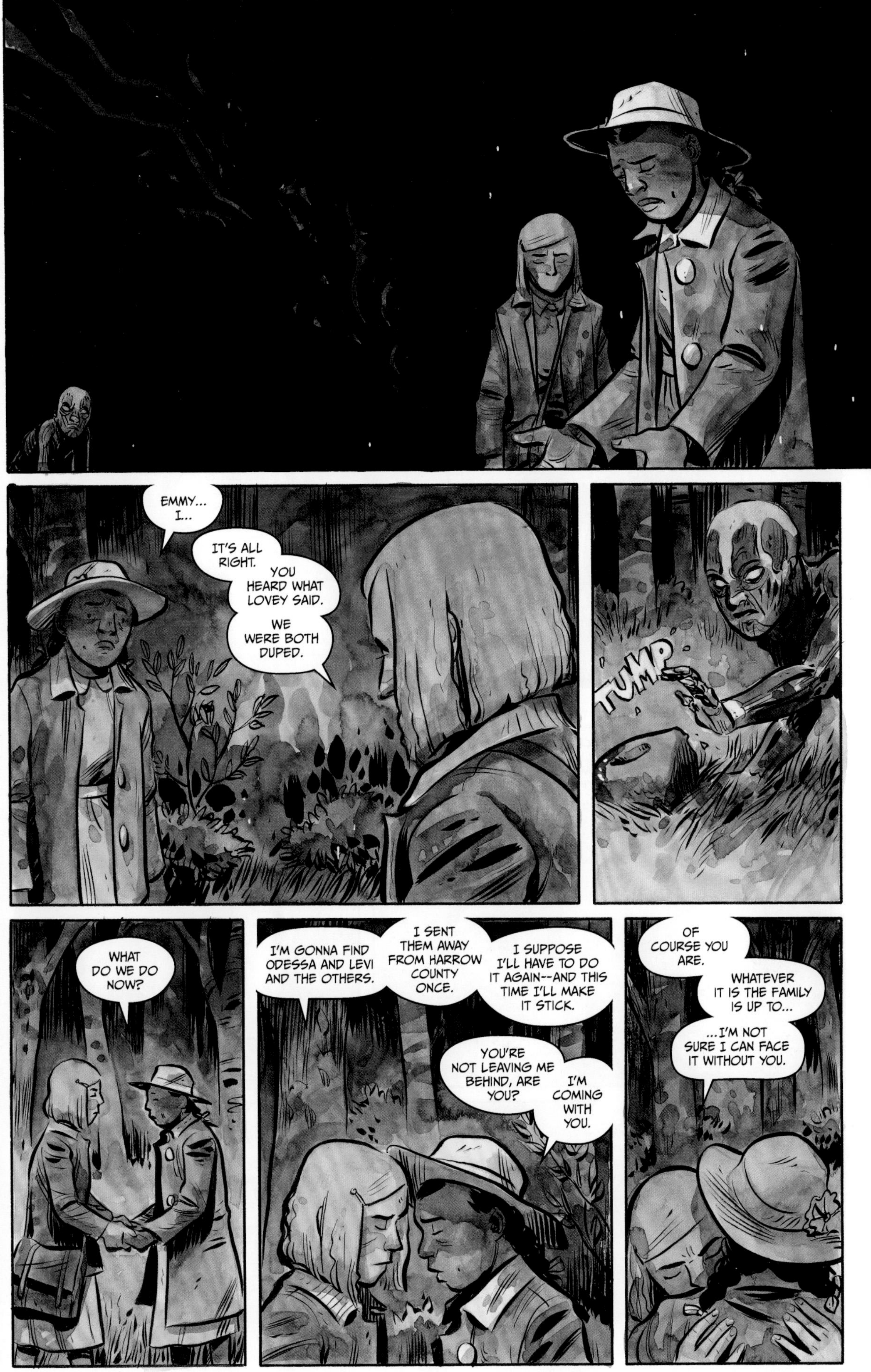
EMMY... I...
IT'S ALL RIGHT.
YOU HEARD WHAT LOVEY SAID.
WE WERE BOTH DUPED.
TUMP
WHAT DO WE DO NOW?
I'M GONNA FIND ODESSA AND LEVI AND THE OTHERS.
I SENT THEM AWAY FROM HARROW COUNTY ONCE.
I SUPPOSE I'LL HAVE TO DO IT AGAIN--AND THIS TIME I'LL MAKE IT STICK.
YOU'RE NOT LEAVING ME BEHIND, ARE YOU?
I'M COMING WITH YOU.
OF COURSE YOU ARE.
WHATEVER IT IS THE FAMILY IS UP TO...
...I'M NOT SURE I CAN FACE IT WITHOUT YOU.

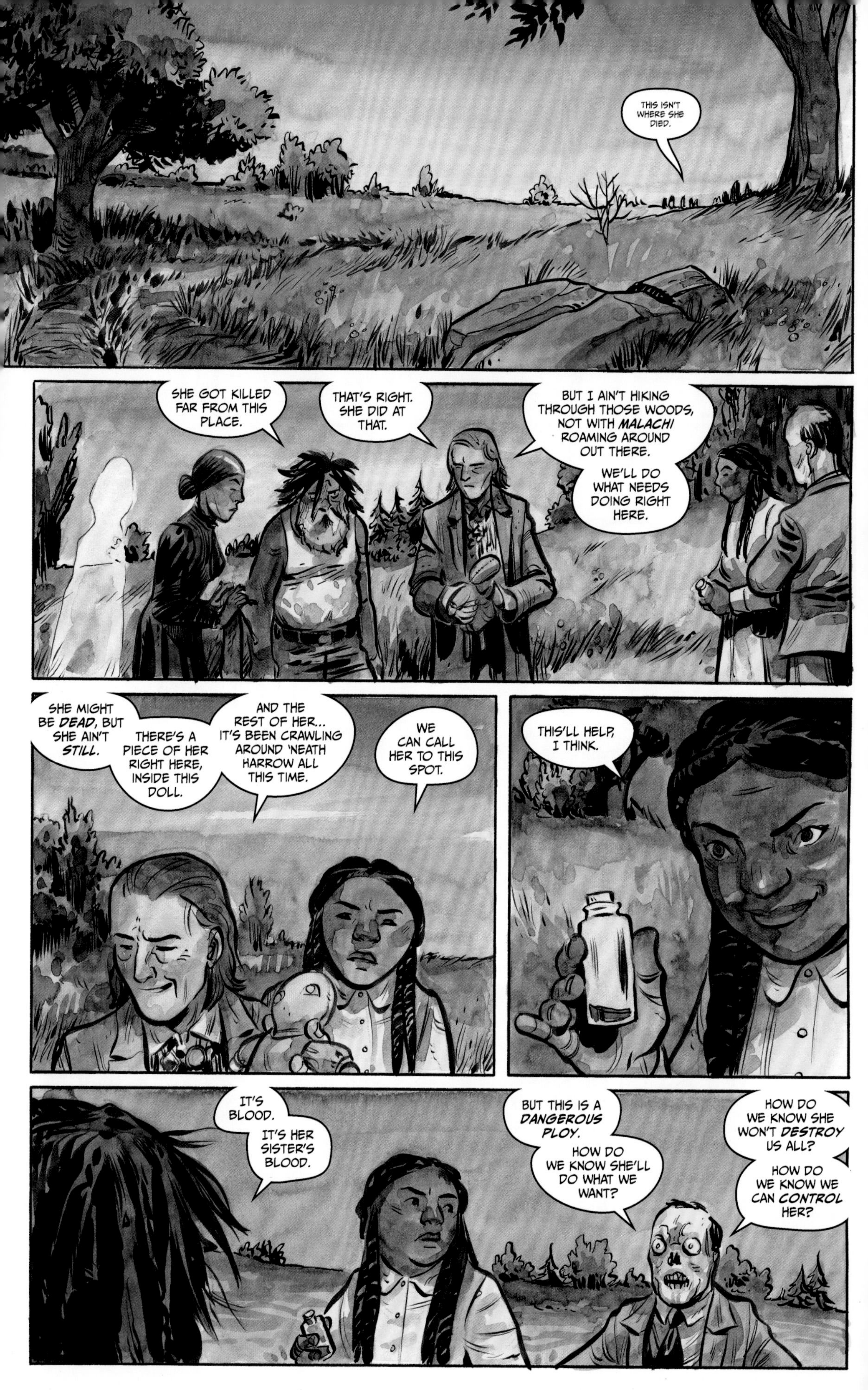
THIS ISN'T WHERE SHE DIED.
SHE GOT KILLED FAR FROM THIS PLACE.
THAT'S RIGHT. SHE DID AT THAT.
BUT I AIN'T HIKING THROUGH THOSE WOODS, NOT WITH MALACHI ROAMING AROUND OUT THERE.
WE'LL DO WHAT NEEDS DOING RIGHT HERE.
SHE MIGHT BE DEAD, BUT SHE AIN'T STILL.
THERE'S A PIECE OF HER RIGHT HERE, INSIDE THIS DOLL.
AND THE REST OF HER... IT'S BEEN CRAWLING AROUND 'NEATH HARROW ALL THIS TIME.
WE CAN CALL HER TO THIS SPOT.
THIS'LL HELP, I THINK.
IT'S BLOOD.
IT'S HER SISTER'S BLOOD.
BUT THIS IS A DANGEROUS PLOY.
HOW DO WE KNOW SHE'LL DO WHAT WE WANT?
HOW DO WE KNOW SHE WON'T DESTROY US ALL?
HOW DO WE KNOW WE CAN CONTROL HER?

AIN'T NO CONTROLLING HER.

WE OUGHT TO KNOW THAT BETTER'N JUST ABOUT ANYONE.

BUT SHE'LL OWE US, WON'T SHE?

DON'T THAT COUNT FOR SOMETHING?

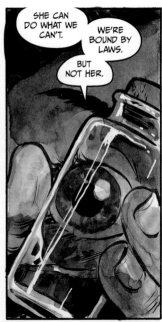

SHE CAN DO WHAT WE CAN'T.

WE'RE BOUND BY LAWS.

BUT NOT HER.

SHE'S NEVER CARED ABOUT SUCH THINGS.

ALL OF US NOW...

...FOCUS ON BRINGING HER BACK... WAKING HER UP...

...ME GUIDING HER SPIRIT BACK...

TK-TK-TAK

...ODESSA COAXING THE GRUBS AND WORMS OUT OF HER WAY...

...KAINE CALLING UP NIGHTMARES AND CORBIN CAUSING HER GHOST TO STIR...

...WILLA KNITTING A DARK FATE...

TK-TAK-TK-TK-TK-TAK-TK-TK-TAK-TK

...AND MILDRED DWELLING ON THE MISFORTUNE SHE'LL BRING.

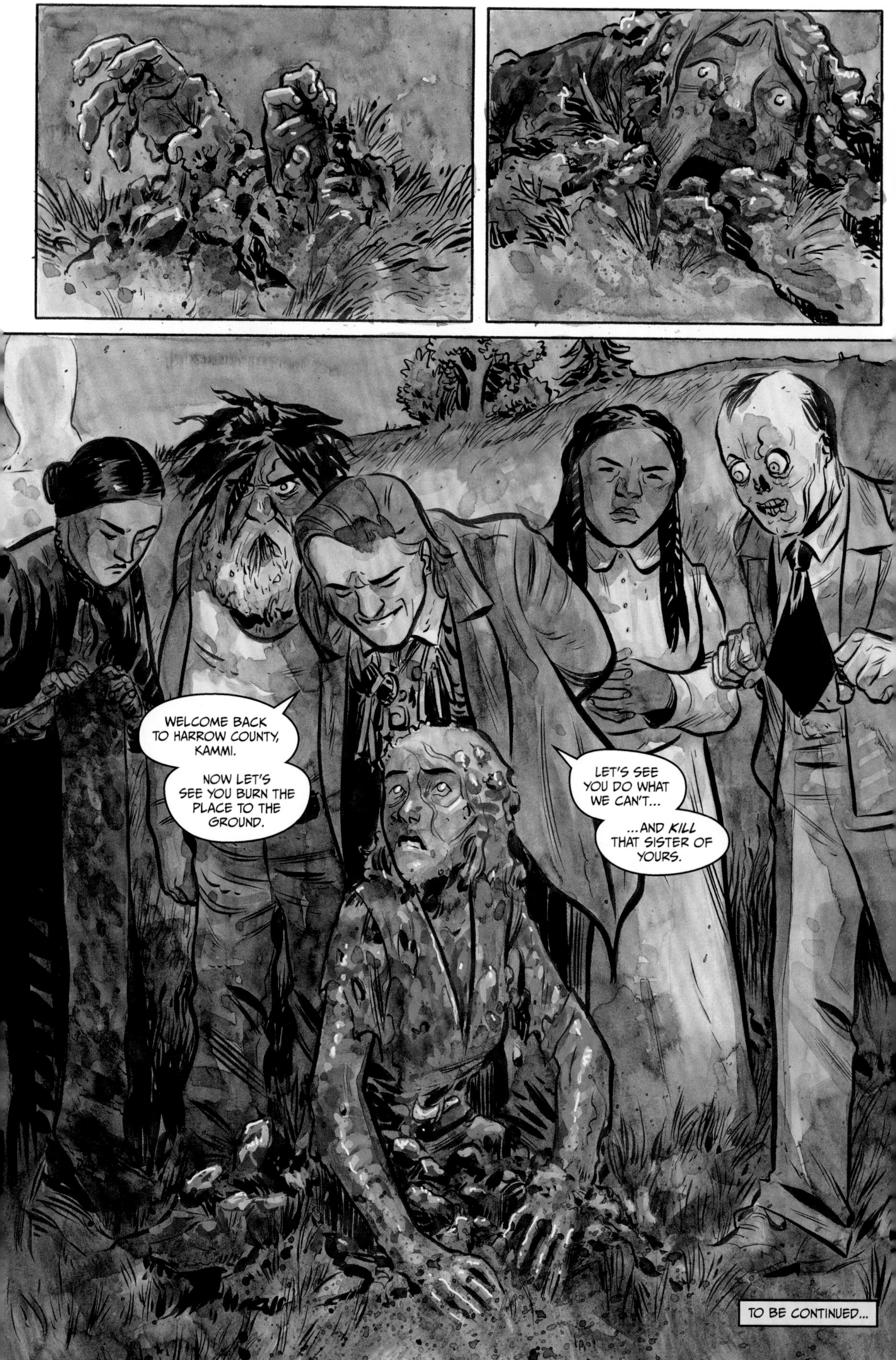
WELCOME BACK TO HARROW COUNTY, KAMMI.
NOW LET'S SEE YOU BURN THE PLACE TO THE GROUND.
LET'S SEE YOU DO WHAT WE CAN'T...
...AND KILL THAT SISTER OF YOURS.
TO BE CONTINUED...

HARROW
⟶ SKETCHBOOK ⟵
COUNTY

NOTES BY
TYLER CROOK

Ⓐ

Ⓑ

TC: These are some of the rejected sketches for the *Harrow County* #21 cover. Usually I try to find a couple of different moments to play around with, but I really liked the idea of Emmy interacting with a broken bottle. I liked how it set up the question of Emmy's relationship with Lovey. So I ended up just doing three different ideas of how to present the same event.

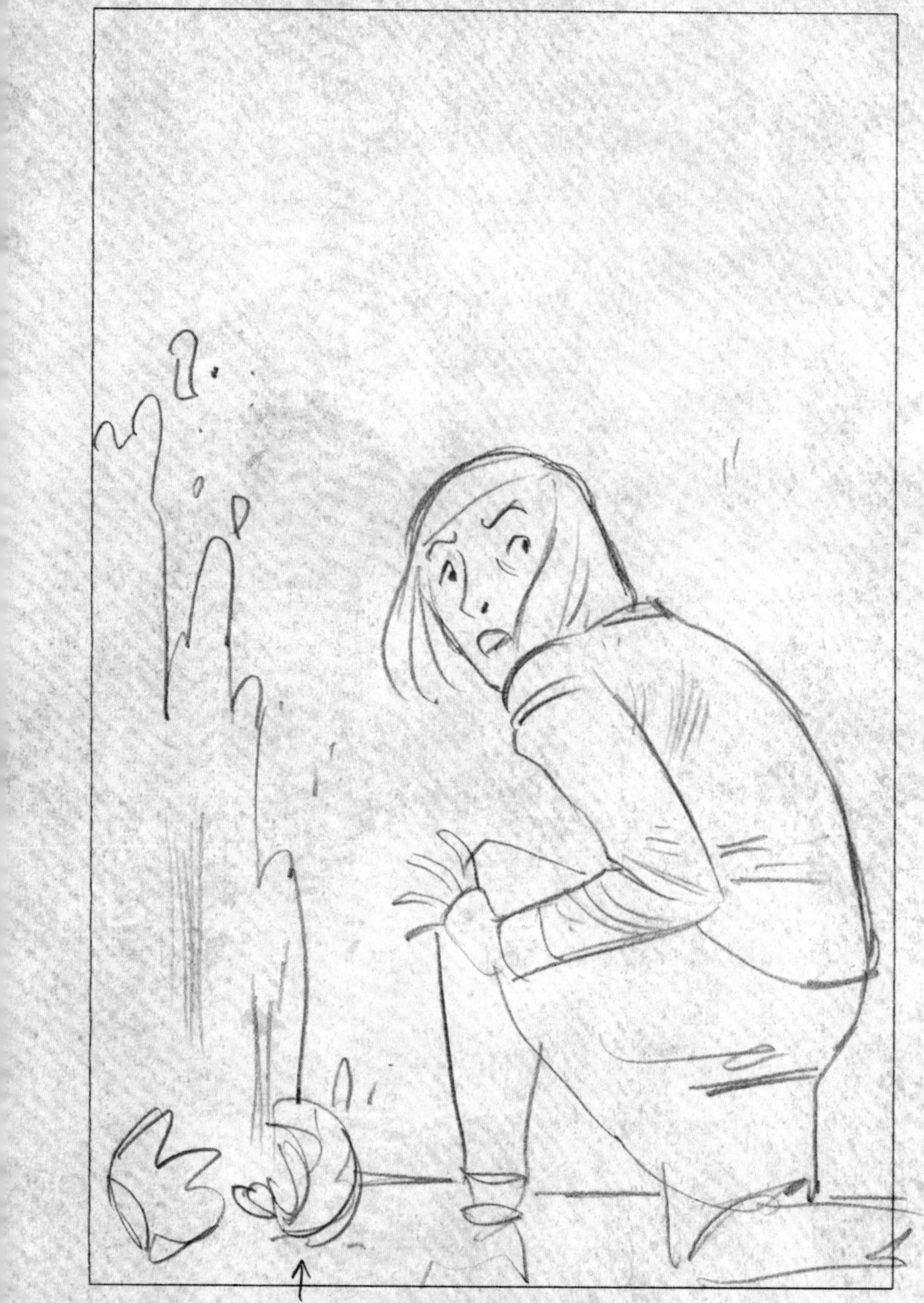

BROKEN
JAR

C

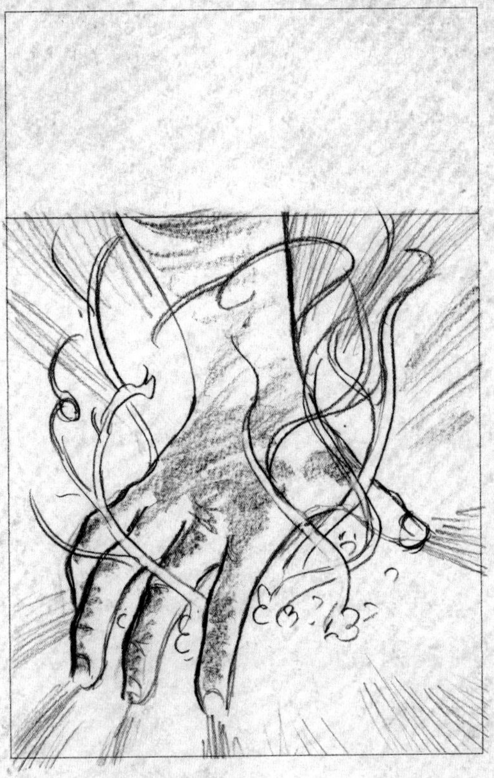

(A)

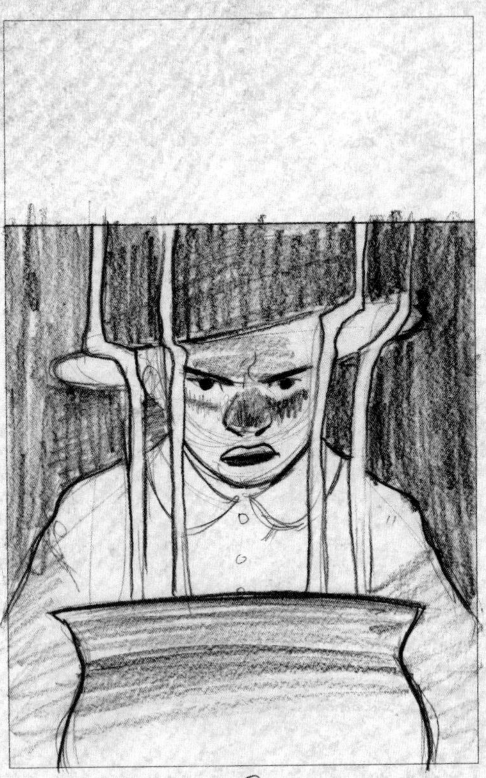

(B)

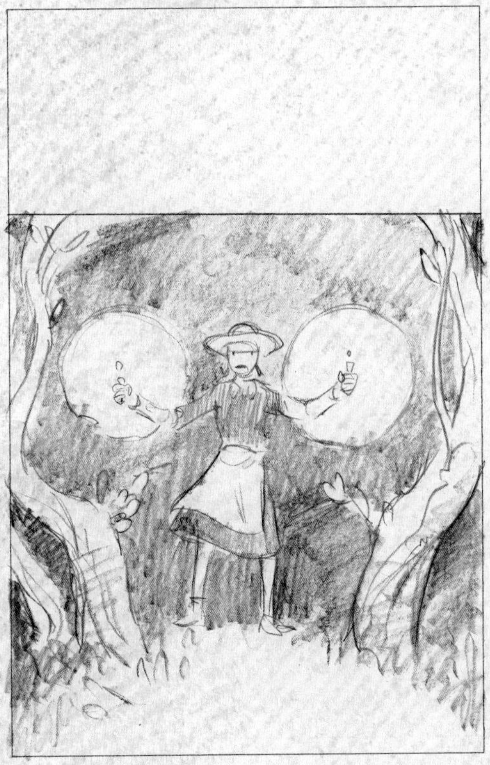

(C)

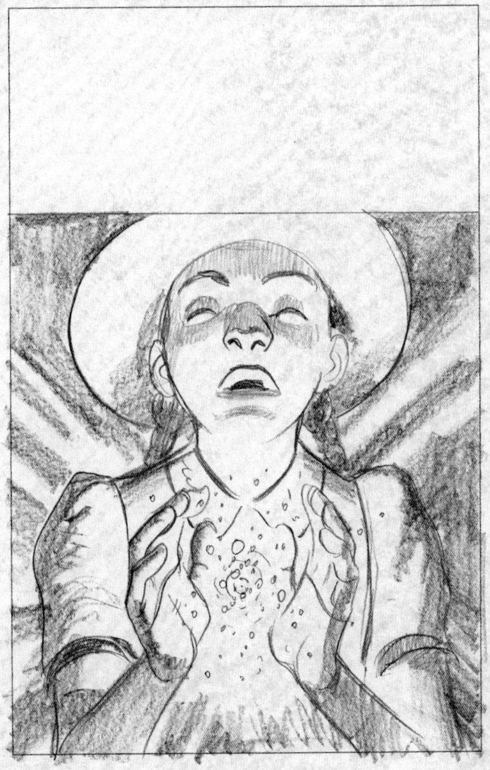

(D)

TC: Here I was playing with ideas about how to show Bernice growing into her own witch powers. I really liked the one where Bernice is holding candles and forming a skull, but we had already used that gag back for issue #5.

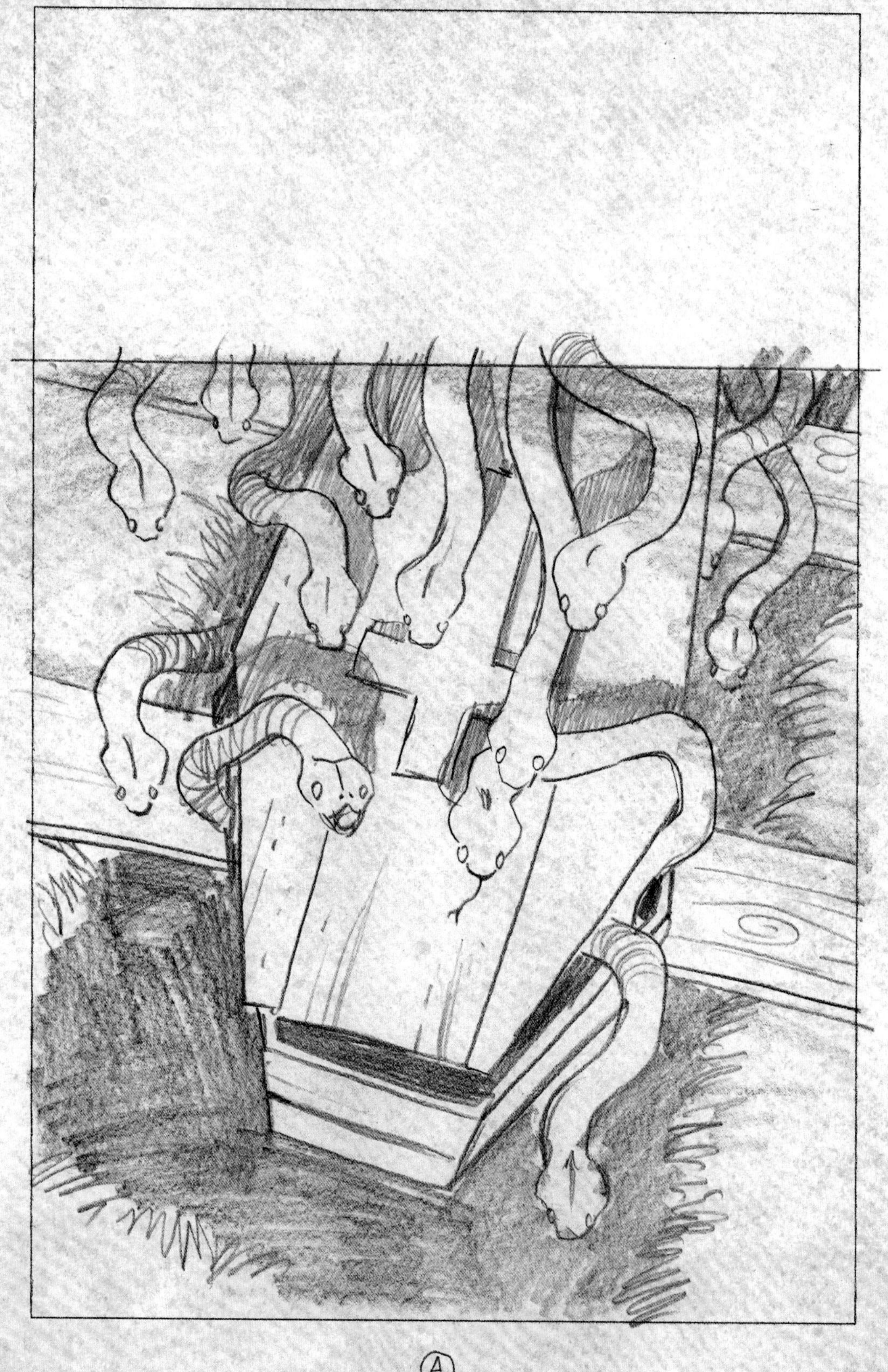

TC: This ended up being one of my favorite covers. I think the idea and the composition from the sketch made it all the way to the final art.

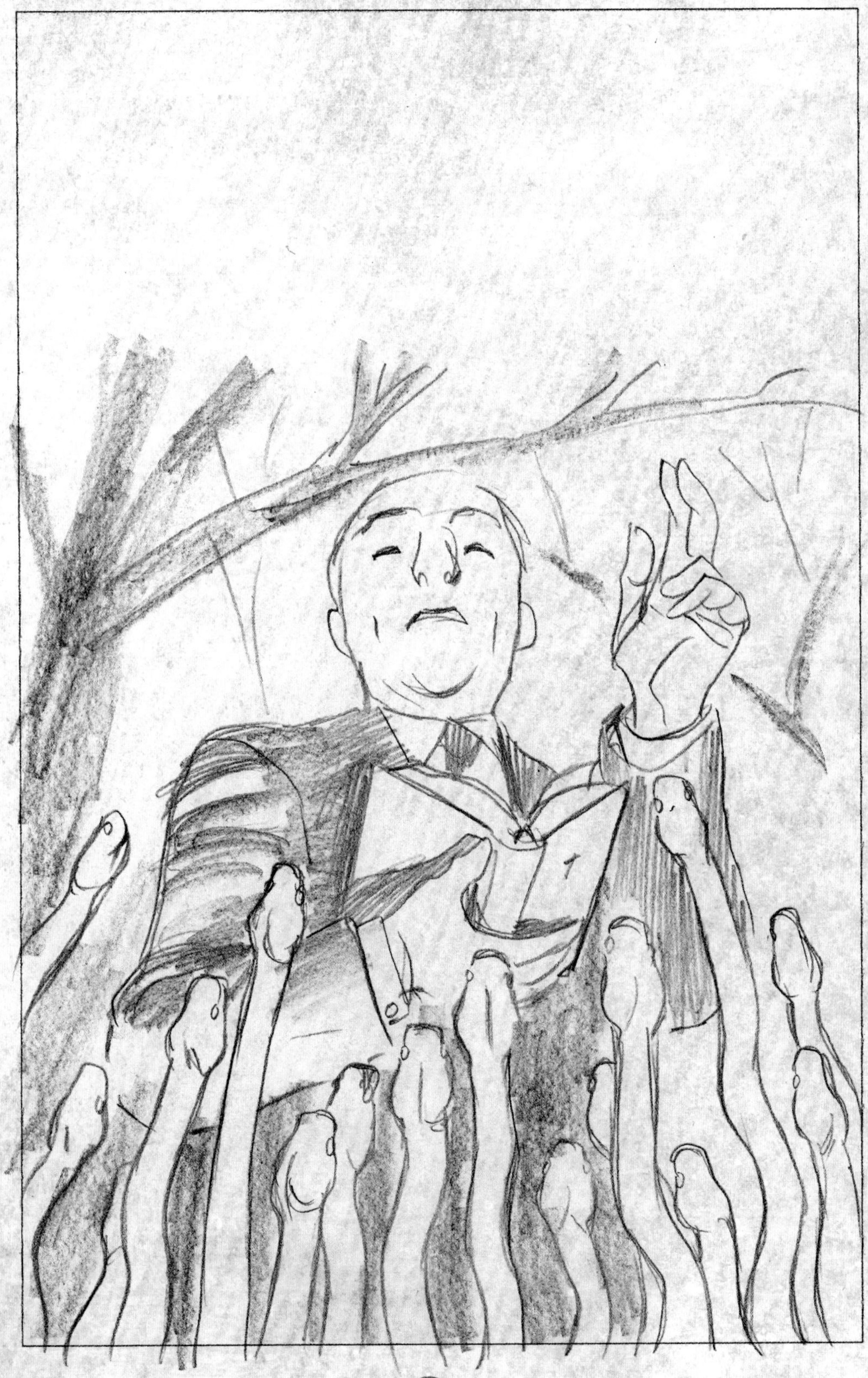

TC: We rejected this cover idea because it didn't make any sense for the preacher to be preaching to the snakes.

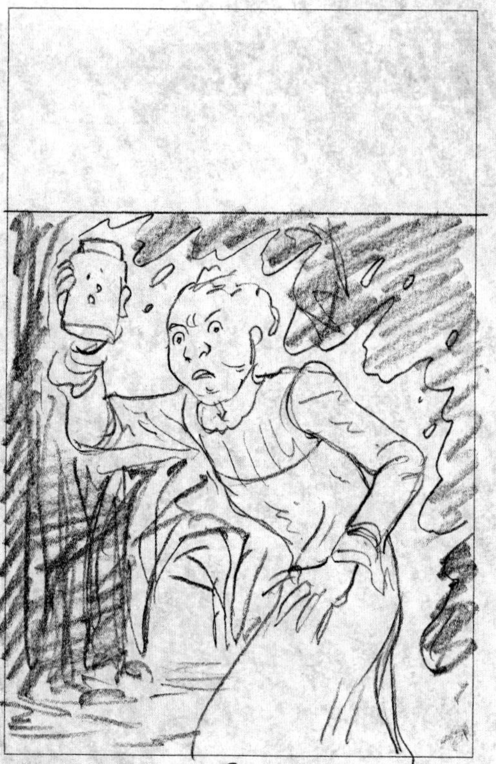

A

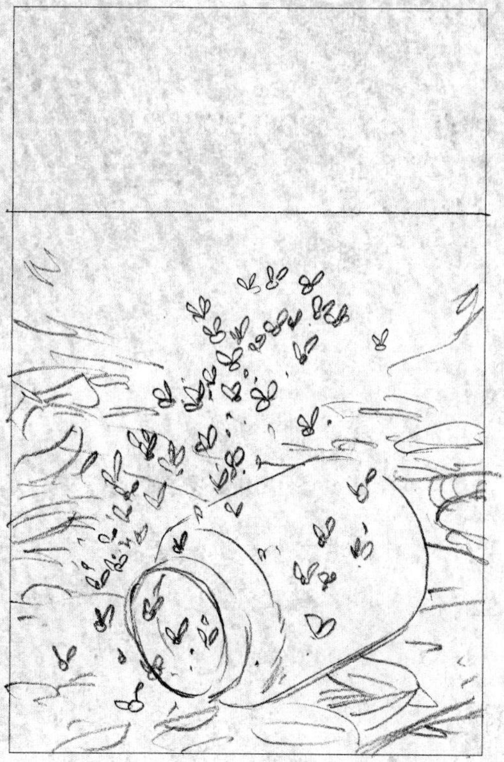

B

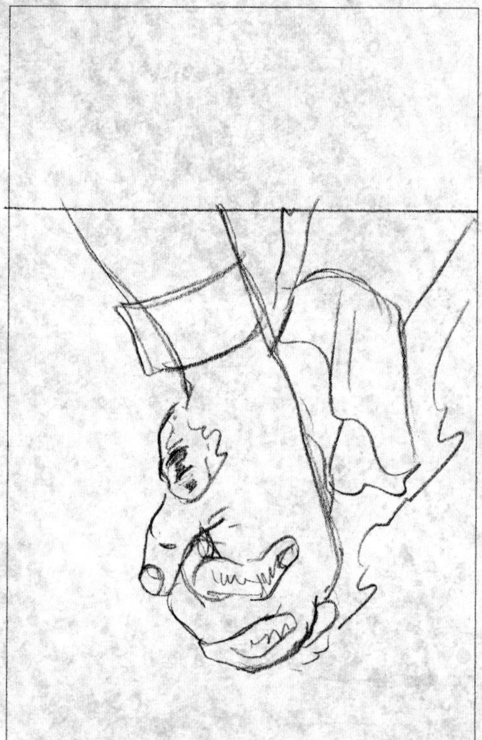

C

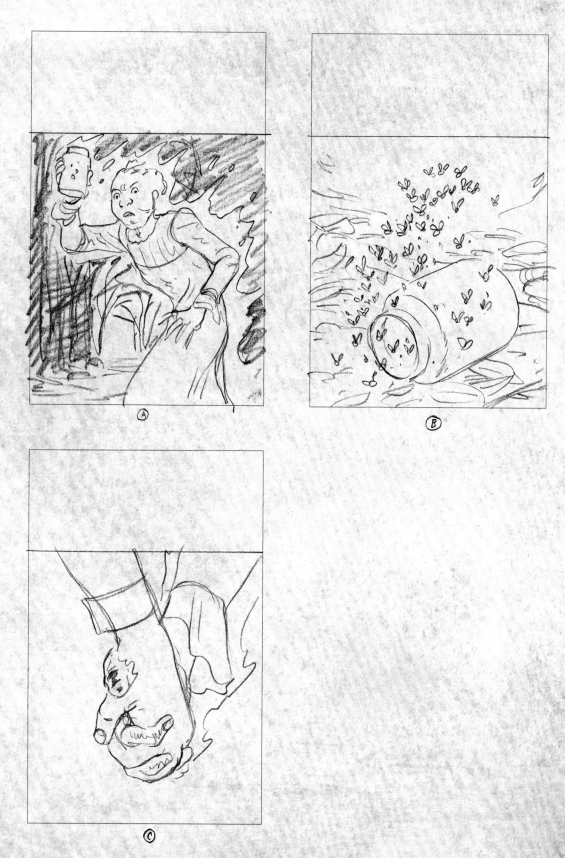

TC: **For issue #24 I was really into the idea of Bernice holding hands with a burning ghost that we later find out is Lovey. It's one of those cases I think where the idea isn't very well served by the sketch. I was really happy with the one we chose . . . but sometimes it's hard not to dream about the road not taken.**

HARROW
— BESTIARY —
COUNTY

THE SKINLESS BOY

Some say this creature had a name once, just like he had a skin, but both have been lost to him. Legend holds that he wandered too far from home one day, getting lost in the deepest part of the woods. Come nightfall, a pack of hungry wild dogs caught his scent and set about chasing him. Unable to shake the hounds, the boy plunged into a tangle of briar bushes. He pushed through as the thorns tore at his flesh, sweat running down into hundreds of stinging cuts and scrapes. By the time he reached the other side of the tangle, his skin hung in ribbons from his muscle and bone. And even then he wasn't safe. The dogs had circled around the briars, and they were waiting to fall upon him when he dragged himself out of the brush.

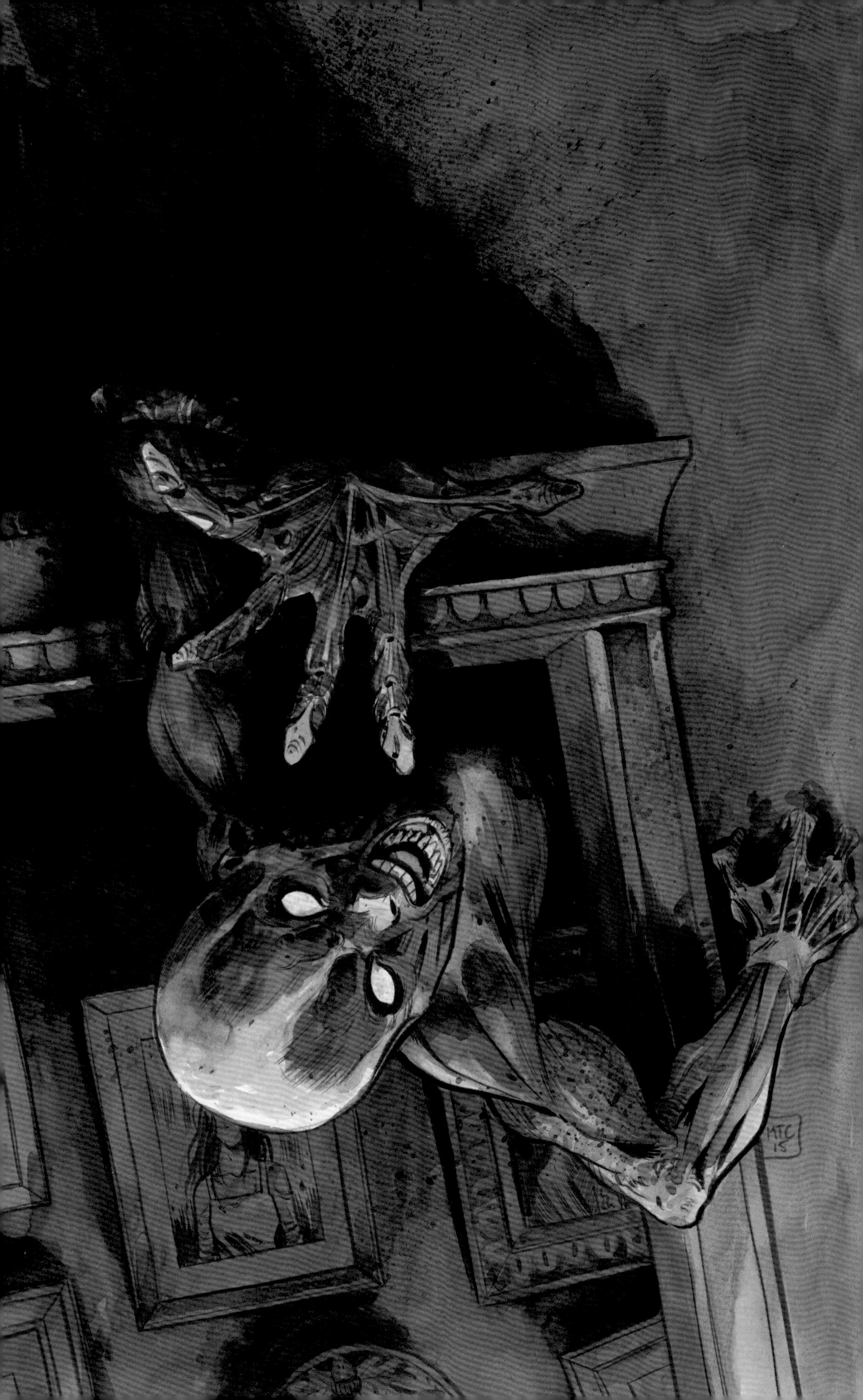
MTC
15

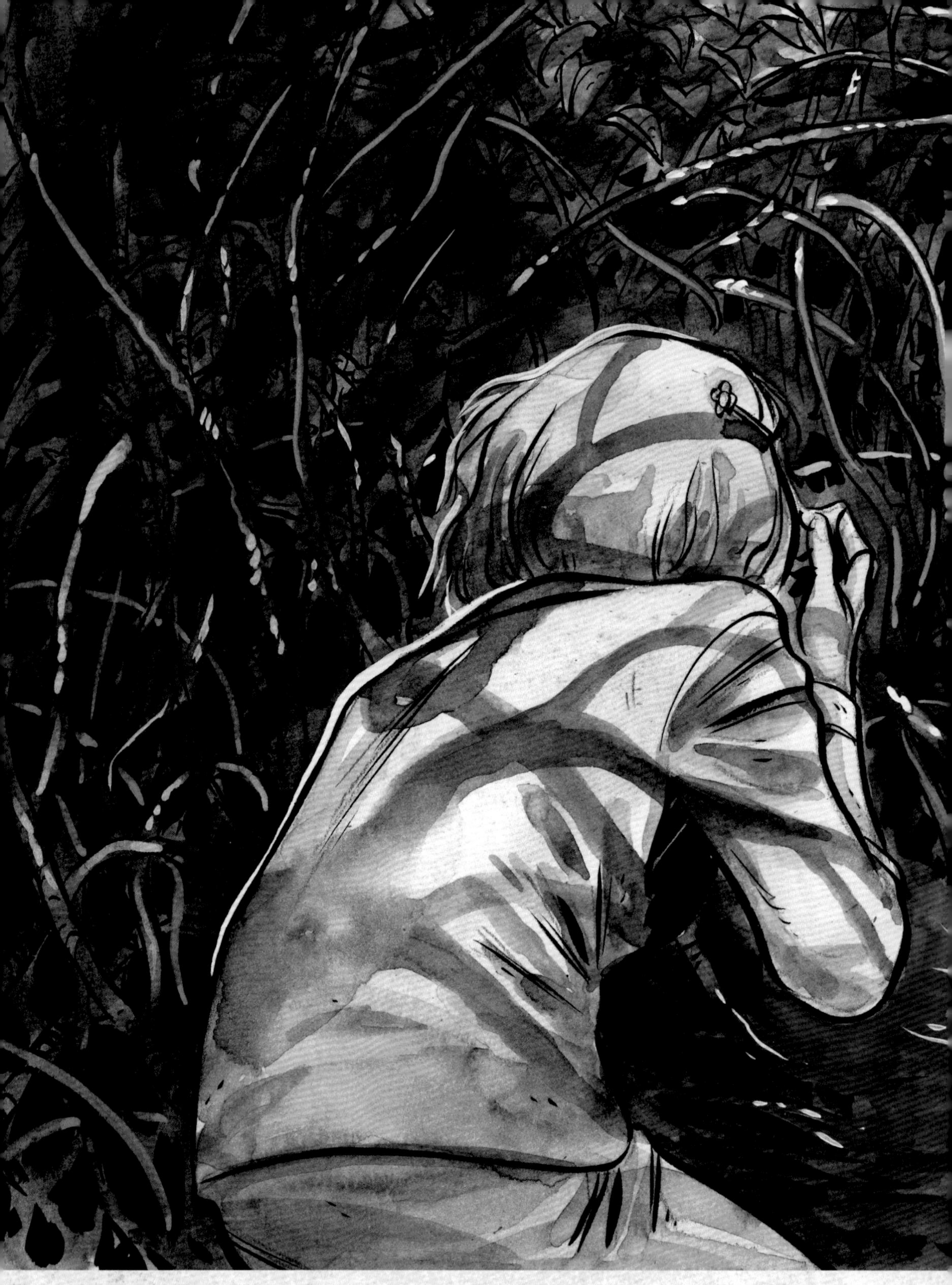

THE TATTERED SKIN

The Skinless Boy's flayed skin still twitches and squirms like a thing alive. While the Skinless Boy can't speak, the Skin hisses and whispers, revealing those things its wayward body sees on its wanderings.

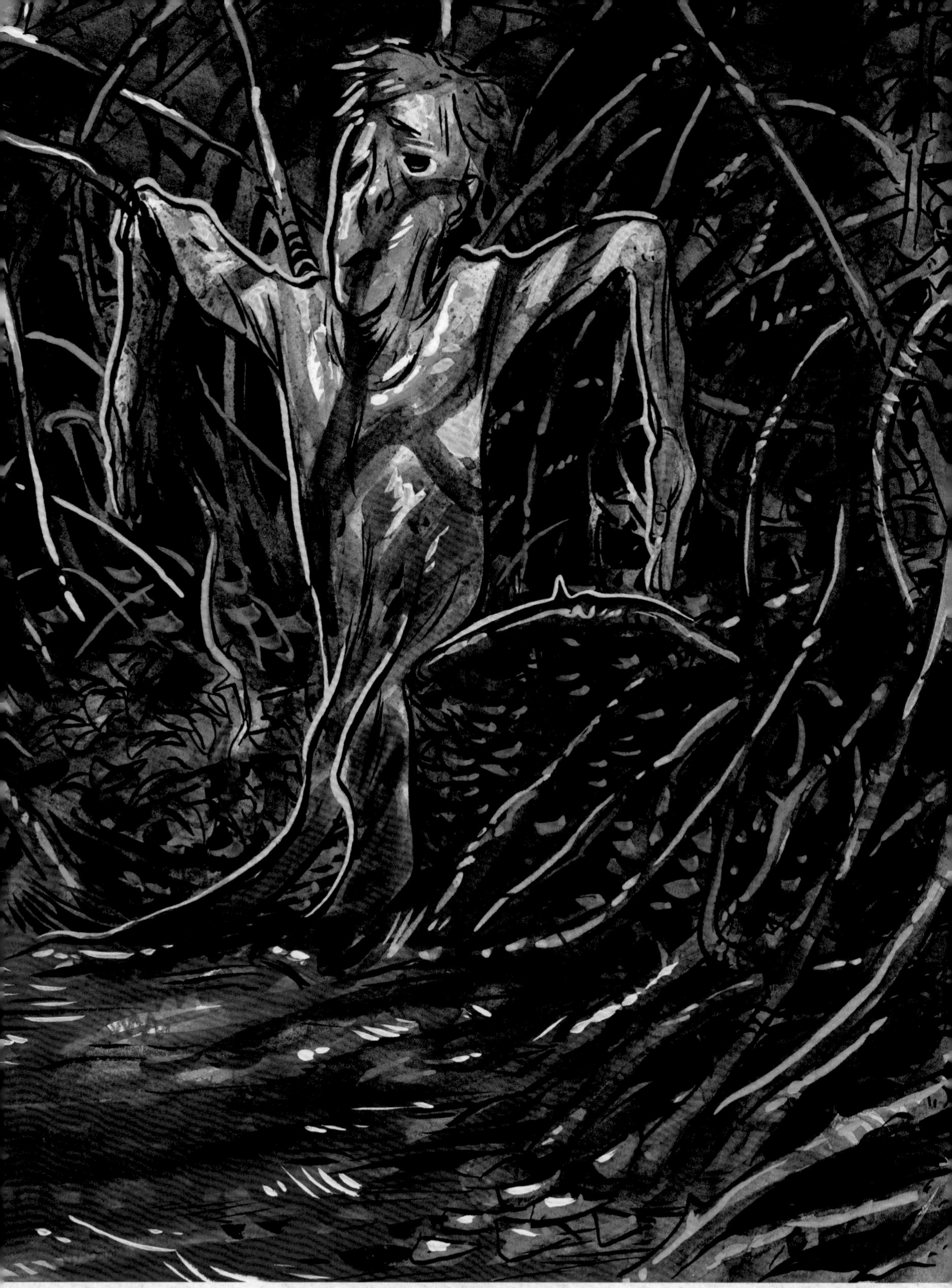

WOODLAND GHOSTS

If you're wandering through the woods around Harrow County, you might just stumble across an old cemetery. Tread carefully. If the gravestones are worn bare, make sure you're well on your way home before nightfall. Come dark, lost souls crawl out from the shadows and they light the night with eerie flames, hoping desperately that the glow they cast might illuminate the etchings on the headstones and remind them who they once were.

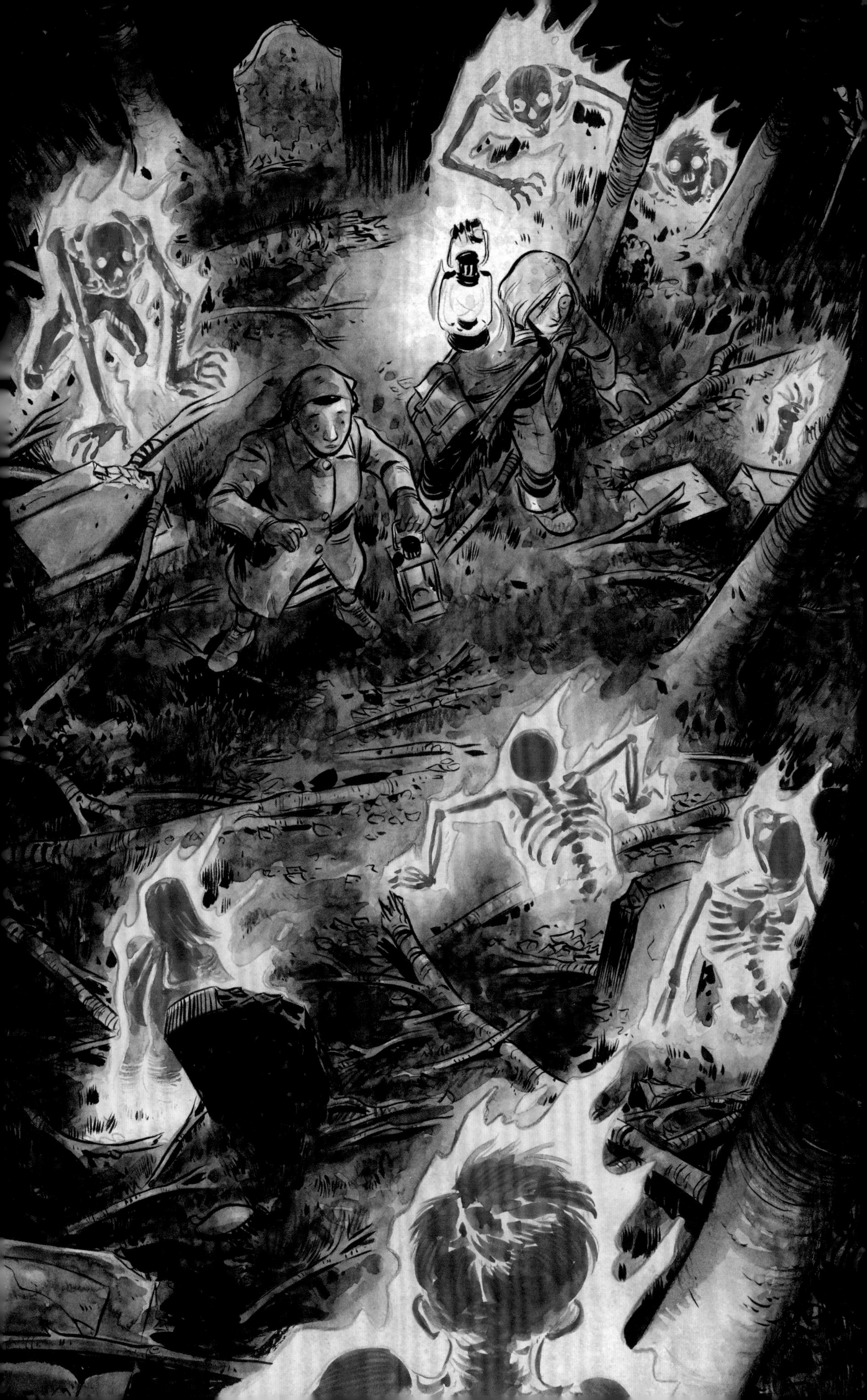

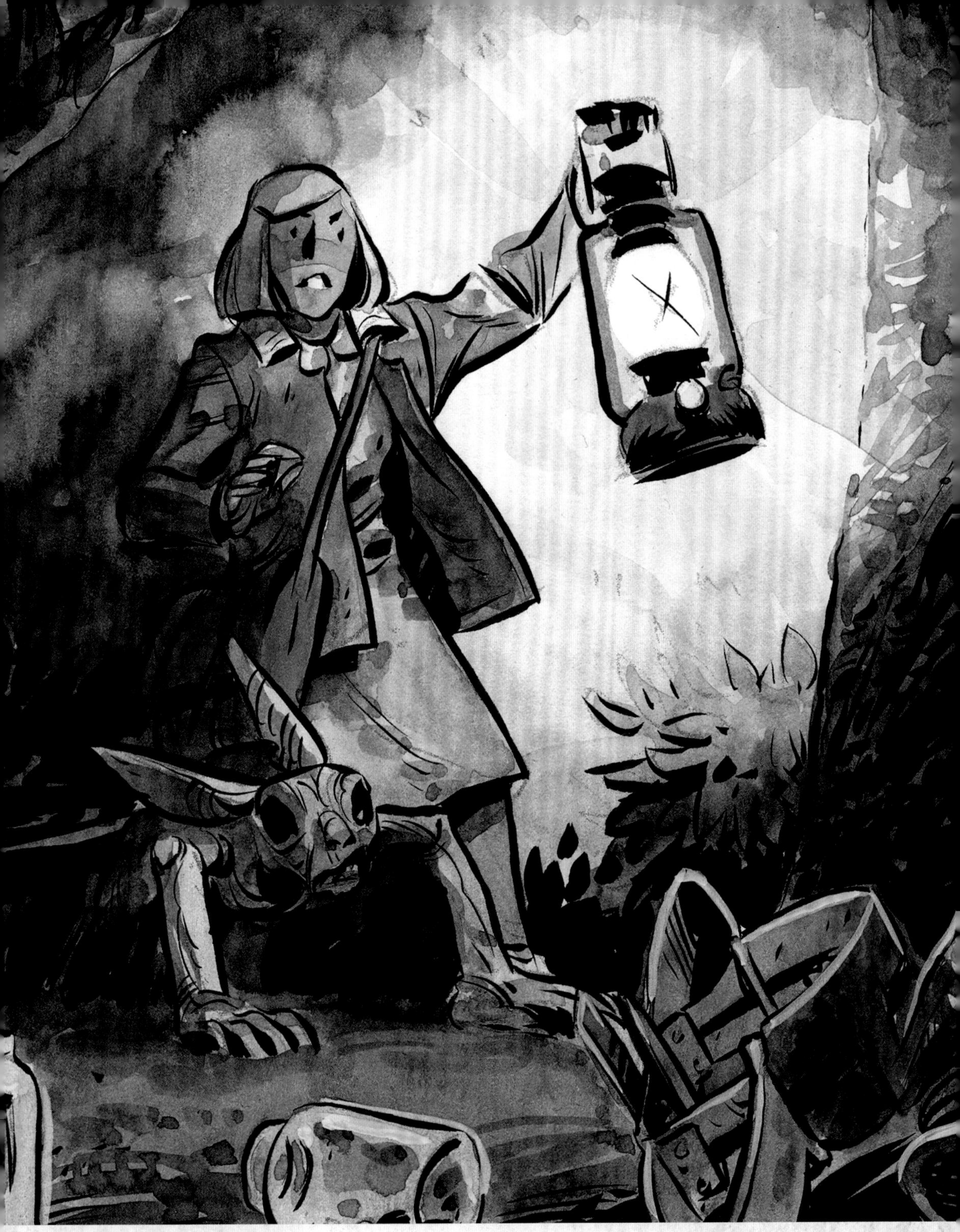

GOBLINS

Goblins and gremlins are real, my friends, but they aren't indigenous to Harrow. They were brought across the ocean as servants by those who dabbled in weird magic. As the old magicians died off, though, the goblins found they had no cause to continue with their chores. Their minds eventually turned to mischief-making. They were common in the Appalachian Mountains for a time, but they eventually made their way to Harrow County, where they found fertile ground for mayhem.

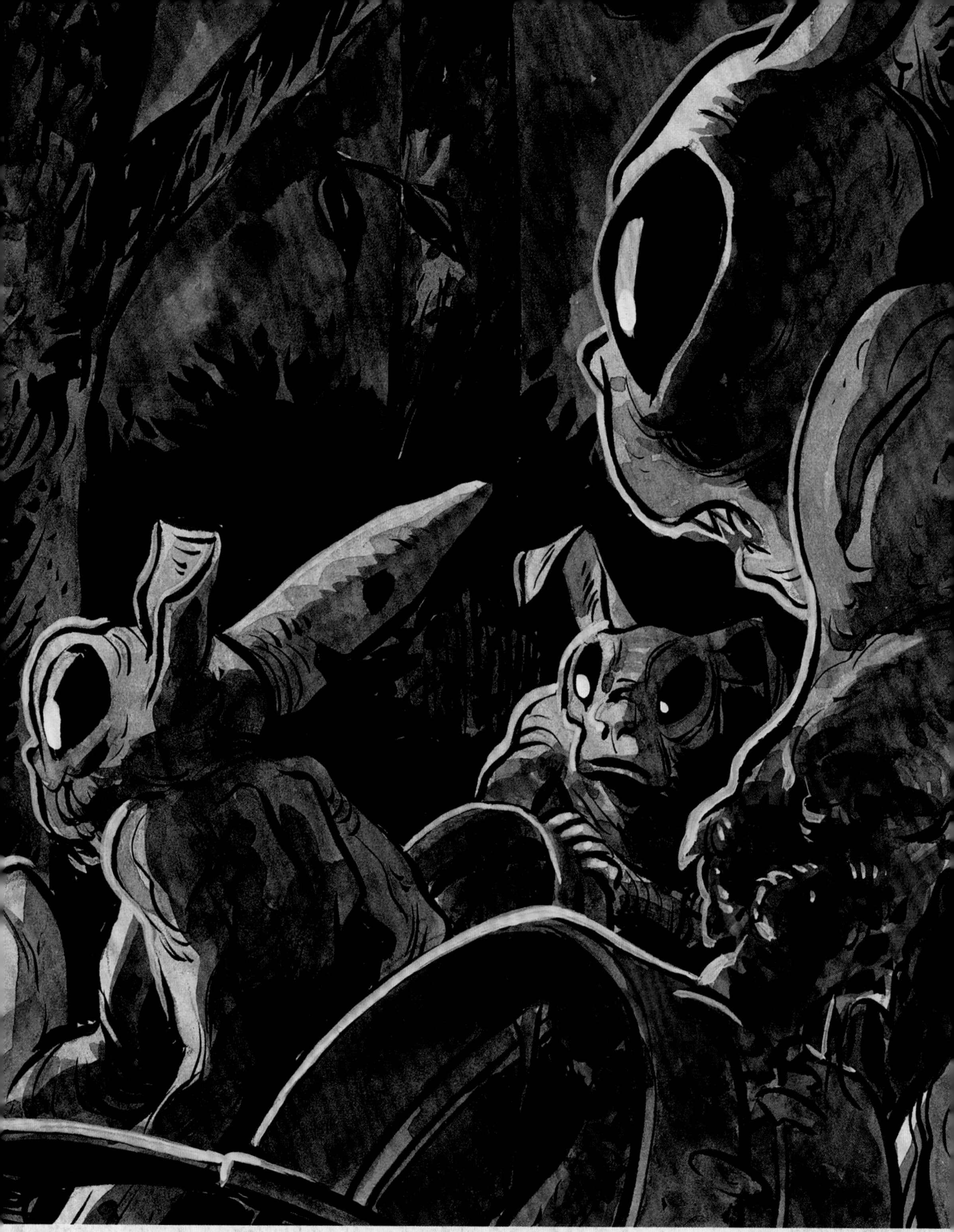

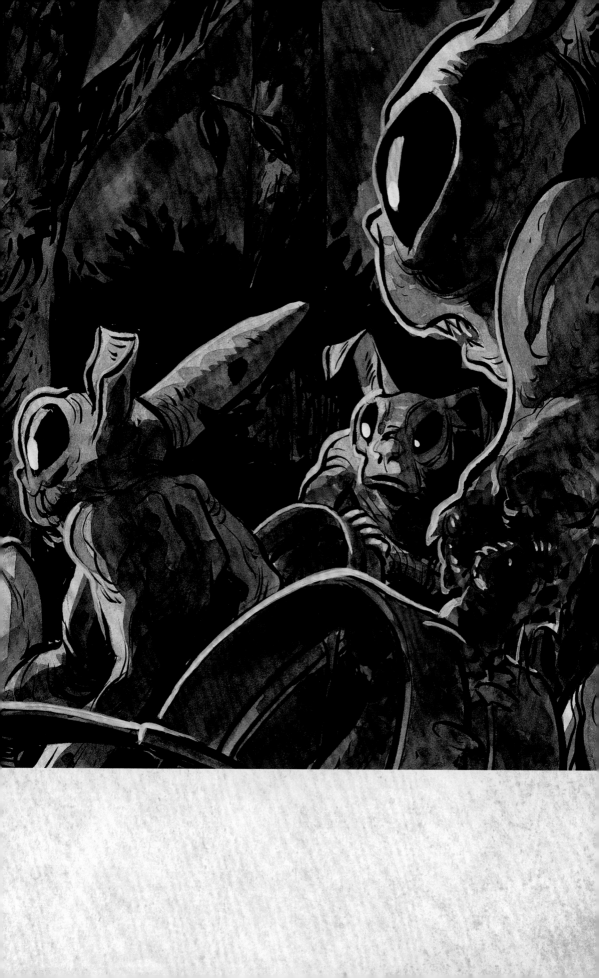

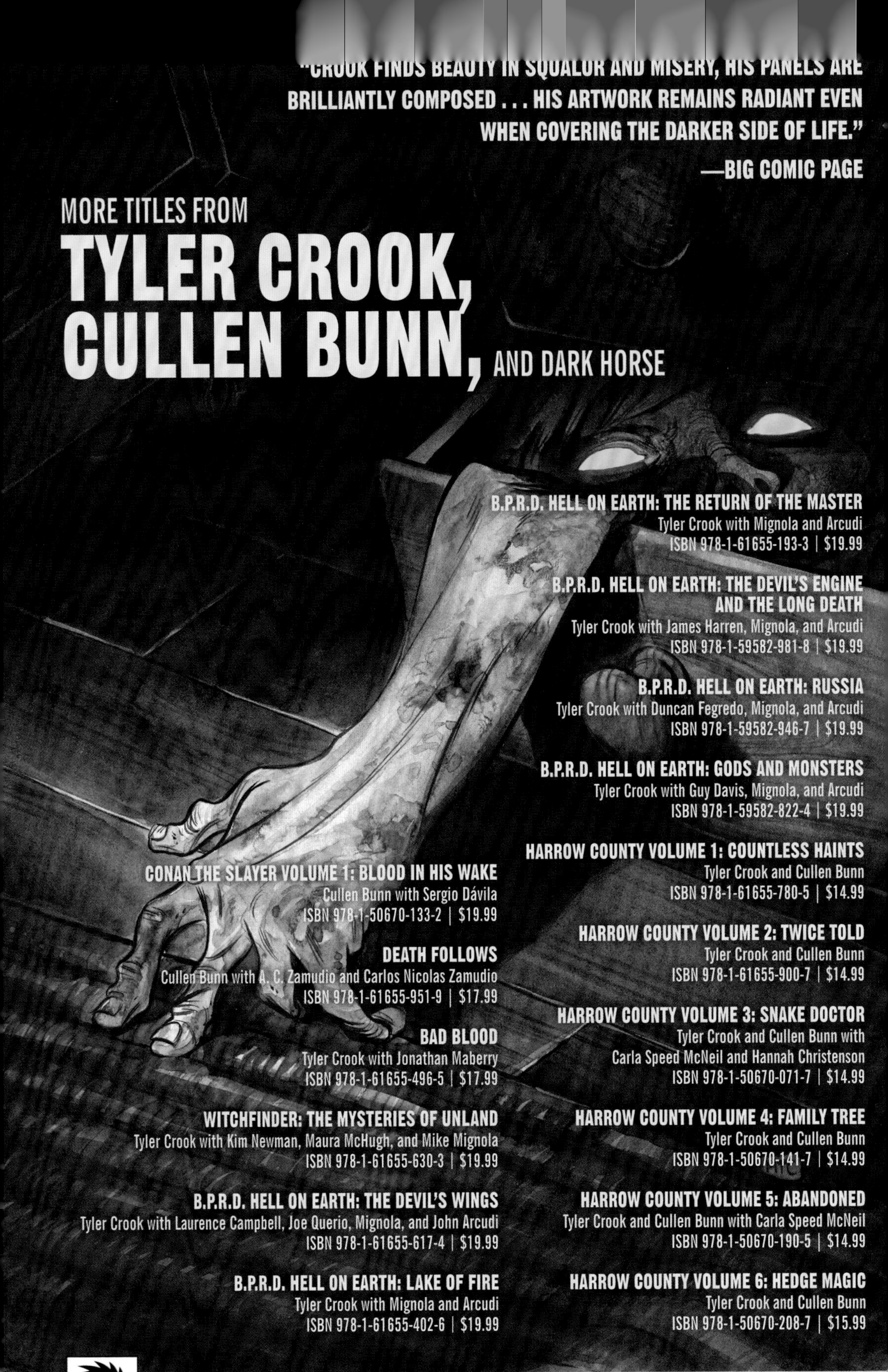

"CROOK FINDS BEAUTY IN SQUALOR AND MISERY. HIS PANELS ARE BRILLIANTLY COMPOSED . . . HIS ARTWORK REMAINS RADIANT EVEN WHEN COVERING THE DARKER SIDE OF LIFE."

—BIG COMIC PAGE

MORE TITLES FROM
TYLER CROOK, CULLEN BUNN, AND DARK HORSE

B.P.R.D. HELL ON EARTH: THE RETURN OF THE MASTER
Tyler Crook with Mignola and Arcudi
ISBN 978-1-61655-193-3 | $19.99

B.P.R.D. HELL ON EARTH: THE DEVIL'S ENGINE AND THE LONG DEATH
Tyler Crook with James Harren, Mignola, and Arcudi
ISBN 978-1-59582-981-8 | $19.99

B.P.R.D. HELL ON EARTH: RUSSIA
Tyler Crook with Duncan Fegredo, Mignola, and Arcudi
ISBN 978-1-59582-946-7 | $19.99

B.P.R.D. HELL ON EARTH: GODS AND MONSTERS
Tyler Crook with Guy Davis, Mignola, and Arcudi
ISBN 978-1-59582-822-4 | $19.99

CONAN THE SLAYER VOLUME 1: BLOOD IN HIS WAKE
Cullen Bunn with Sergio Dávila
ISBN 978-1-50670-133-2 | $19.99

DEATH FOLLOWS
Cullen Bunn with A. C. Zamudio and Carlos Nicolas Zamudio
ISBN 978-1-61655-951-9 | $17.99

BAD BLOOD
Tyler Crook with Jonathan Maberry
ISBN 978-1-61655-496-5 | $17.99

WITCHFINDER: THE MYSTERIES OF UNLAND
Tyler Crook with Kim Newman, Maura McHugh, and Mike Mignola
ISBN 978-1-61655-630-3 | $19.99

B.P.R.D. HELL ON EARTH: THE DEVIL'S WINGS
Tyler Crook with Laurence Campbell, Joe Querio, Mignola, and John Arcudi
ISBN 978-1-61655-617-4 | $19.99

B.P.R.D. HELL ON EARTH: LAKE OF FIRE
Tyler Crook with Mignola and Arcudi
ISBN 978-1-61655-402-6 | $19.99

HARROW COUNTY VOLUME 1: COUNTLESS HAINTS
Tyler Crook and Cullen Bunn
ISBN 978-1-61655-780-5 | $14.99

HARROW COUNTY VOLUME 2: TWICE TOLD
Tyler Crook and Cullen Bunn
ISBN 978-1-61655-900-7 | $14.99

HARROW COUNTY VOLUME 3: SNAKE DOCTOR
Tyler Crook and Cullen Bunn with
Carla Speed McNeil and Hannah Christenson
ISBN 978-1-50670-071-7 | $14.99

HARROW COUNTY VOLUME 4: FAMILY TREE
Tyler Crook and Cullen Bunn
ISBN 978-1-50670-141-7 | $14.99

HARROW COUNTY VOLUME 5: ABANDONED
Tyler Crook and Cullen Bunn with Carla Speed McNeil
ISBN 978-1-50670-190-5 | $14.99

HARROW COUNTY VOLUME 6: HEDGE MAGIC
Tyler Crook and Cullen Bunn
ISBN 978-1-50670-208-7 | $15.99

DARK HORSE BOOKS

AVAILABLE AT YOUR LOCAL COMICS SHOP OR BOOKSTORE! • To find a comics shop in your area, call 1-888-266-4226.
For more information or to order direct visit DarkHorse.com or call 1-800-862-0052 Mon.–Fri. 9 a.m. to 5 p.m. Pacific Time. Prices and availability subject to change without notice.

DARK HORSE HORROR

drawing on your nightmares

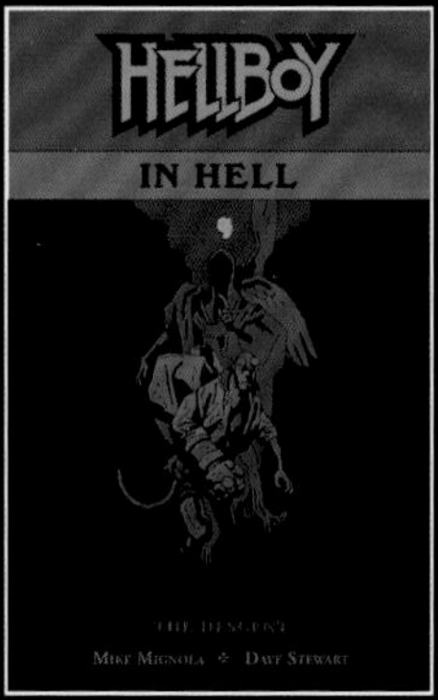

HELLBOY
IN HELL

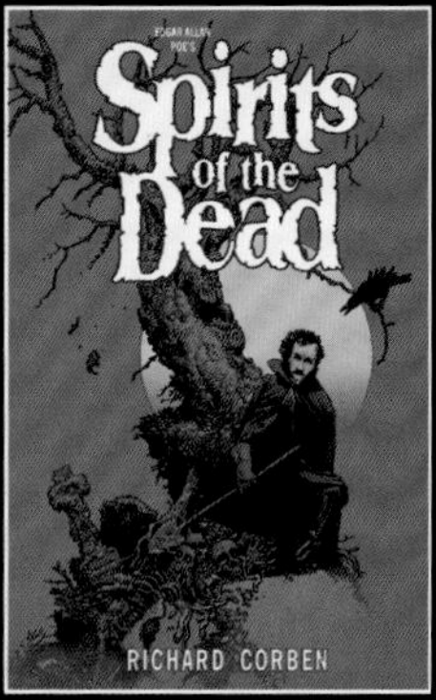

Spirits of the Dead
RICHARD CORBEN

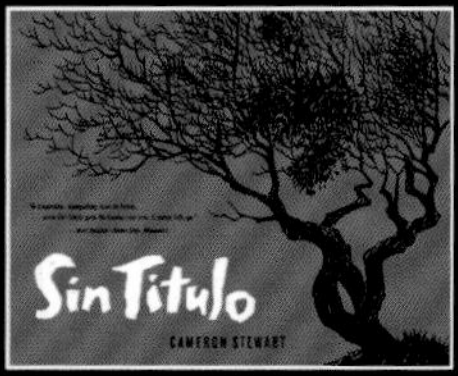

Sin Titulo
CAMERON STEWART

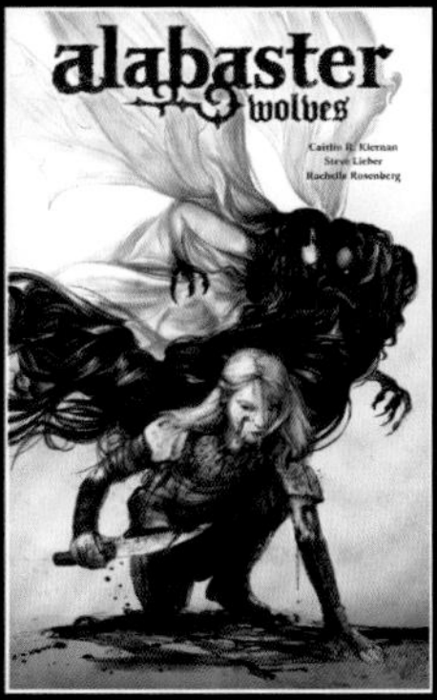

alabaster
wolves

HELLBOY IN HELL VOLUME 1: THE DESCENT
Mike Mignola
ISBN 978-1-61655-444-6 | $17.99

THE AUTHENTIC ACCOUNTS OF BILLY THE KID'S OLD TIMEY ODDITIES
Eric Powell, Kyle Hotz
ISBN 978-1-61655-470-5 | $24.99

EDGAR ALLAN POE'S SPIRITS OF THE DEAD
Richard Corben
ISBN 978-1-61655-356-2 | $24.99

COLDER VOLUME 1
Paul Tobin, Juan Ferreyra
ISBN 978-1-61655-136-0 | $17.99

SIN TITULO
Cameron Stewart
ISBN 978-1-61655-248-0 | $19.99

GRINDHOUSE: DOORS OPEN AT MIDNIGHT DOUBLE FEATURE VOLUME 1
Alex de Campi, Chris Peterson, Simon Fraser
ISBN 978-1-61655-377-7 | $17.99

GUILLERMO DEL TORO AND CHUCK HOGAN'S THE STRAIN VOLUME 1
David Lapham, Mike Huddleston
ISBN 978-1-61655-032-5 | $19.99

HARROW COUNTY VOLUME 1: COUNTLESS HAINTS
Tyler Crook and Cullen Bunn
ISBN 978-1-61655-780-5 | $14.99

ALABASTER: WOLVES
Caitlín R. Kiernan and Steve Lieber
ISBN 978-1-61655-025-7 | $19.99

DEATH FOLLOWS
Cullen Bunn, A. C. Zamudio, and Carlos Nicolas Zamudio
ISBN 978-1-61655-951-9 | $17.99

HOUSE OF PENANCE
Peter J. Tomasi and Ian Bertram
ISBN 978-1-50670-033-5 | $19.99

CREATIVE GIANTS!

GET YOUR FIX OF DARK HORSE BOOKS FROM THESE INSPIRED CREATORS!

MESMO DELIVERY SECOND EDITION

Rafael Grampá

Eisner Award–winning artist Rafael Grampá (*5*, *Hellblazer*) makes his full-length comics debut with the critically acclaimed graphic novel *Mesmo Delivery*—a kinetic, bloody romp starring Rufo, an ex-boxer; Sangrecco, an Elvis impersonator; and a ragtag crew of overly confident drunks who pick the wrong delivery men to mess with.

ISBN 978-1-61655-457-6 | $14.99

SIN TITULO

Cameron Stewart

Following the death of his grandfather, Alex Mackay discovers a mysterious photograph in the old man's belongings that sets him on an adventure like no other—where dreams and reality merge, family secrets are laid bare, and lives are irrevocably altered.

ISBN 978-1-61655-248-0 | $19.99

DE:TALES

Fábio Moon and Gabriel Bá

Brazilian twins Fábio Moon and Gabriel Bá's (*Daytripper*, *Pixu*) most personal work to date. Brimming with all the details of human life, their charming tales move from the urban reality of their home in São Paulo to the magical realism of their Latin American background.

ISBN 978-1-59582-557-5 | $19.99

THE TRUE LIVES OF THE FABULOUS KILLJOYS

Gerard Way, Shaun Simon, and Becky Cloonan

Years ago, the Killjoys fought against the tyrannical megacorporation Better Living Industries. Today, the followers of the original Killjoys languish in the desert and the fight for freedom fades. It's left to the Girl to take down BLI!

ISBN 978-1-59582-462-2 | $19.99

DEMO

Brian Wood and Becky Cloonan

It's hard enough being a teenager. Now try being a teenager with *powers*. A chronicle of the lives of young people on separate journeys to self-discovery in a world—just like our own—where being different is feared.

ISBN 978-1-61655-682-2 | $24.99

SABERTOOTH SWORDSMAN

Damon Gentry and Aaron Conley

When his village is enslaved and his wife kidnapped by the malevolent Mastodon Mathematician, a simple farmer must find his inner warrior—the Sabertooth Swordsman!

ISBN 978-1-61655-176-6 | $17.99

JAYBIRD

Jaakko and Lauri Ahonen

Disney meets Kafka in this beautiful, intense, original tale! A very small, very scared little bird lives an isolated life in a great big house with his infirm mother. He's never been outside the house, and he never will if his mother has anything to say about it.

ISBN 978-1-61655-469-9 | $19.99

MONSTERS! & OTHER STORIES

Gustavo Duarte

Newcomer Gustavo Duarte spins wordless tales inspired by Godzilla, King Kong, and Pixar, brimming with humor, charm, and delightfully twisted horror!

ISBN 978-1-61655-309-8 | $12.99

SACRIFICE

Sam Humphries and Dalton Rose

What happens when a troubled youth is plucked from modern society and thrust though time and space into the heart of the Aztec civilization—one of the most bloodthirsty times in human history?

ISBN 978-1-59582-985-6 | $19.99

AVAILABLE AT YOUR LOCAL COMICS SHOP OR BOOKSTORE
To find a comics shop in your area, call 1-888-266-4226. For more information or to order direct: ON THE WEB: DarkHorse.com
E-MAIL: mailorder@darkhorse.com / PHONE: 1-800-862-0052 Mon.–Fri. 9 a.m. to 5 p.m. Pacific Time.